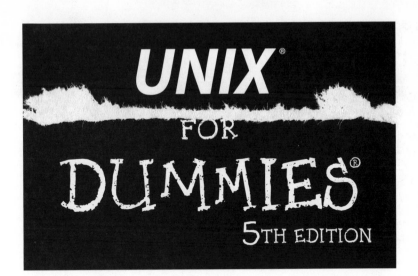

UNIX®
FOR
DUMMIES®
5TH EDITION

UNIX® FOR DUMMIES® 5TH EDITION

by John R. Levine and Margaret Levine Young

WILEY

Wiley Publishing, Inc.

UNIX® For Dummies®, 5th Edition

Published by
Wiley Publishing, Inc.
111 River Street
Hoboken, NJ 07030-5774

Copyright © 2004 by Wiley Publishing, Inc., Indianapolis, Indiana

Published by Wiley Publishing, Inc., Indianapolis, Indiana

Published simultaneously in Canada

For general information on our other products and services or to obtain technical support, please contact our Customer Care Department within the U.S. at 800-762-2974, outside the U.S. at 317-572-3993, or fax 317-572-4002.

Wiley also publishes its books in a variety of electronic formats. Some content that appears in print may not be available in electronic books.

Library of Congress Control Number available from publisher.

ISBN: 0-7645-4147-1

Manufactured in the United States of America

10 9 8 7 6 5 4 3

5O/QZ/QR/QU/IN

WILEY   is a trademark of Wiley Publishing, Inc.

About the Authors

John R. Levine was a member of a computer club in high school — before high school students, or even high schools, had computers — where he met Theodor H. Nelson, the author of *Computer Lib/Dream Machines* and the inventor of hypertext, who reminded us that computers should not be taken seriously and that everyone can and should understand and use computers.

John wrote his first program in 1967 on an IBM 1130 (a computer somewhat less powerful than your typical modern digital wristwatch, only more difficult to use). He became an official system administrator of a networked computer running UNIX at Yale in 1975. He began working part-time (for a computer company, of course) in 1977 and has been in and out of the computer and network biz ever since. He got his company on Usenet (the Internet's world-wide bulletin-board system) early enough that it appears in a 1982 *Byte* magazine article on a map of Usenet, which then was so small that the map fit on half a page.

Although John used to spend most of his time writing software, now he mostly writes books (including *UNIX For Dummies* and *Privacy For Dummies,* both published by Wiley Publishing, Inc.) because it's more fun and he can do so at home in the tiny village of Trumansburg, New York, where he is the sewer commissioner (Guided tours! Free samples!) and can play with his small daughter when he's supposed to be writing. John also does a fair amount of public speaking. (Go to `www.johnlevine.com` to see where he'll be.) He holds a BA and a PhD in computer science from Yale University, but please don't hold that against him.

In high school, **Margaret Levine Young** was in the same computer club as her big brother, John. She stayed in the field throughout college against her better judgment and despite John's presence as a graduate student in the computer science department. Margy graduated from Yale and went on to become one of the first PC managers in the early 1980s at Columbia Pictures, where she rode the elevator with big stars whose names she wouldn't dream of dropping here.

Since then, Margy has co-authored more than 25 computer books about the topics of the Internet, UNIX, WordPerfect, Microsoft Access, and (stab from the past) PC-File and Javelin, including *Dummies 101: The Internet For Windows 98*, *UNIX For Dummies*, and *WordPerfect For Linux For Dummies* (all published by Wiley Publishing, Inc.), and *Windows XP: The Complete Reference* and *Internet: The Complete Reference* (published by Osborne/McGraw-Hill). She met her future husband, Jordan, in the R.E.S.I.S.T.O.R.S. (that computer club we mentioned). Her other passion is her children, along with music, Unitarian Universalism (`www.uua.org`), reading, and anything to do with eating. She lives in Vermont (see `www.gurus.com/margy` for some scenery).

Dedication

John and Margy both dedicate this book to their dad, wherever he is. When last sighted, he was traveling somewhere in China finding out just how great the wall is, unless he was at the beach here in the U.S. — he's a man who knows how to live!

Authors' Acknowledgments

The authors thank Antonia Saxon, Jordan Young, Sarah Willow Levine Saxon, Meg Young, and Zac Young for putting up with us while we updated this book. Thanks also go to our Internet providers: Finger Lakes Technologies Group and the Trumansburg Home Telephone Company (Trumansburg, NY), the Shoreham Telephone Company (Shoreham, VT), and SoVerNet (Bellows Falls, VT).

We thank Peter Seebach for research and revisions (you can guess what that really means) on KDE and GNOME in Chapters 4 and 17, and Nancy McGough for helping make our comments on Linux bear at least some relation to reality.

Chris Morris patiently shepherded the text from our hazy scribblings (electronically speaking) to a printed book with a blend of patience and midnight wit. He got lots of help, of course, from all the folks listed on the other side of this page.

Publisher's Acknowledgments

We're proud of this book; please send us your comments through our online registration form located at www.dummies.com/register/.

Some of the people who helped bring this book to market include the following:

Acquisitions, Editorial, and Media Development

Project Editor: Christopher Morris

(Previous Edition: Rebecca Whitney)

Acquisitions Editor: Steven Hayes

Copy Editor: Rebecca Senninger

Technical Editor: James F. Kelly

Editorial Manager: Kevin Kirschner

Permissions Editor: Laura Moss

Media Development Specialist: Travis Silvers

Media Development Manager: Laura VanWinkle

Media Development Supervisor: Richard Graves

Editorial Assistant: Amanda Foxworth

Cartoons: Rich Tennant (www.the5thwave.com)

Production

Project Coordinator: Courtney MacIntyre

Layout and Graphics: Seth Conley, Andrea Dahl, Lauren Goddard, Stephanie D. Jumper, Barry Offringa, Heather Ryan, Mary Gillot Virgin, Melanie Wolven

Proofreaders: Laura Albert, Andy Hollandbeck, Kathy Simpson, TECHBOOKS Publishing Services

Indexer: TECHBOOKS Publishing Services

Publishing and Editorial for Technology Dummies

    Richard Swadley, Vice President and Executive Group Publisher

    Andy Cummings, Vice President and Publisher

    Mary C. Corder, Editorial Director

Publishing for Consumer Dummies

    Diane Graves Steele, Vice President and Publisher

    Joyce Pepple, Acquisitions Director

Composition Services

    Gerry Fahey, Vice President of Production Services

    Debbie Stailey, Director of Composition Services

Contents at a Glance

Table of Contents

Introduction

∙∙

*W*elcome to *UNIX For Dummies,* 5th Edition! Although lots of good books about UNIX are out there, most of them assume that you have a degree in computer science, would love to learn every strange and useless command UNIX has to offer (and there are plenty), and enjoy memorizing unpronounceable commands and options. This book is different.

Instead, this book describes what you really do with UNIX — how to get started, what commands you really need, and when to give up and go for help. And we describe it all in plain, ordinary English.

About This Book

We designed this book to be used when you can't figure out what to do next. We don't flatter ourselves that you are interested enough in UNIX to sit down and read the whole thing. When you run into a problem using UNIX ("I thought I typed a command that would copy a file, but it didn't respond with any message . . ."), just dip into the book long enough to solve your problem.

We have included sections about these kinds of things:

- Typing commands
- Copying, renaming, or deleting files
- Printing files
- Finding where your file went
- Using the Internet from UNIX
- Storing and updating a Web site on a UNIX computer
- Connecting and communicating with people on other computers

In this fifth edition, we updated the information about Linux (the popular free version of UNIX), beefed up the information about the new KDE and GNOME window systems, and added information about Internet applications and hosting an Internet site on your own (or someone else's) UNIX computer.

Conventions Used in This Book

Use this book as a reference. (Or use it as a decorative paperweight — whatever works for you.) Look up your topic or command in the table of contents or the index; they refer to the part of the book in which we describe what to do and perhaps define a few terms, if absolutely necessary.

When you have to type something, it appears in the book like this:

```
cryptic UNIX command to type
```

Type it just as it appears. Use the same capitalization we do — UNIX cares deeply about CAPITAL and small letters. Then press the Enter or Return key (we call it Enter throughout this book). The book tells you what happens when you give each command and what your options are. Sometimes part of the command is in *italics;* the italicized stuff is a sample name, and you have to substitute the actual name of the file, computer, or person affected.

Chapter 24 lists error messages you may run into, and Chapter 25 lists common user mistakes. You may want to peruse the latter to avoid these mistakes before they happen.

Foolish Assumptions

In writing this book, we have assumed these things about you:

- ✔ You have a UNIX computer or remote access to one.
- ✔ You want to get some work done on it.
- ✔ Someone has set it up so that, if you turn it on (in many cases, it's left on all the time) or connect, you are talking to UNIX.
- ✔ You are not interested in becoming the world's next great UNIX expert.

How This Book Is Organized

This book has six parts. The parts stand on their own — you can begin reading wherever you want. This section lists the parts of the book and what they contain.

Part 1: Before the Beginning

This part tells you how to get started with UNIX, including figuring out which kind of UNIX you're using. (You need to know this information later because commands can differ from one type of UNIX to another.) You find out how to log in, type UNIX commands, and ask for help. For Linux users, we include a short chapter on what's it's all about, why Linux is cool, and how to get more information about Linux.

Part 11: Some Basic Stuff

Like most computer systems, UNIX stores information in files. This part explains how to deal with files — creating, copying, and getting rid of them. It also talks about directories so that you can keep your files organized, finding files that have somehow gone astray, and printing files on paper.

Part 111: Getting Things Done

This part talks about getting some work done in UNIX. It gives step-by-step instructions for using the most common text editors to create and change text files, running several programs at the same time (to get confused several times as fast), and making your Linux system behave, and gives you directions for a bunch of other useful UNIX commands.

Part 1V: UNIX and the Net

Most UNIX systems are connected to networks, and many are connected to the biggest network of them all: the Internet. This part prepares you for the world of communications, including instructions for sending and receiving electronic mail, for transferring files over the network, for logging in to other computers over the Internet, and for surfing on the World Wide Web. For those of you with some intestinal fortitude, we include an updated chapter on how to have your Internet site run on your very own UNIX computer.

Part V: Help!

If disaster strikes, check this part of the book. It includes information about what to do if something bad happens, what to do about backups, and what to do when you see common UNIX error messages.

Part VI: The Part of Tens

This part is a random assortment of other tidbits about UNIX, including common mistakes and how to get online help — all organized into two convenient ten-item lists, sort of.

Icons Used in This Book

Some particularly nerdy, technoid information is coming up, which you can skip (although, of course, we think that it's all interesting).

A nifty little shortcut or time-saver is explained, or a piece of information you can't afford to be without.

Yarrghhh! Don't let this happen to you!

Information that applies only if your computer is on a network. If it is not, you can skip to the next section.

Something presented in an earlier section of the book or something you need to remember to do.

The friendly penguin alerts you to information specifically about Linux (see Chapter 3 to find out what Linux is).

Where to Go from Here

That's all you need to know to get started. Whenever you hit a snag in UNIX, just look up the problem in the table of contents or index of this book. You will have the problem solved in a flash — or you will know to find some expert help.

Because UNIX is not designed to be particularly easy to use, don't feel bad if you have to look up a number of topics before you feel comfortable using the computer. Most computer users, after all, never have to face anything as daunting as UNIX (point this out to your Windows and Macintosh user friends)!

If you have comments about this book and your computer can send electronic mail via the Internet, you can send them to our friendly mail robot, which will write back, at unix5@gurus.com. (We authors also read your messages and write back if time permits.) Also visit our Web site, with book info and updates, at http://net.gurus.com. For information about the *For Dummies* books in general, write to info@wiley.com or surf on by www.dummies.com.

Authors' Note

Because we practice what we preach, the manuscript for this book was updated and edited using the free OpenOffice.org word processor on FreeBSD UNIX. We also used NetBSD and SuSE Linux for the KDE and GNOME examples, and a Web application on the Apache Web server on BSD/OS to pass around edited chapters among the authors and our editors. The net.gurus.com and www.dummies.com Web sites both run on Apache servers on UNIX; our UNIX mail server handles the mail at gurus.com; and our publisher's three UNIX mail servers handle the mail at wiley.com. None of that expensive Pacific Northwest software for us, thanks.

Part I
Before the Beginning

The 5th Wave   By Rich Tennant

"It's called 'Linux Poker.' Everyone gets to see everyone else's cards, everything's wild, you can play off your opponents' hands, and everyone wins except Bill Gates, whose face appears on the Jokers."

In this part . . .

Yikes! You have to learn how to use UNIX! Does this mean that you're about to get inducted, kicking and screaming, into a fraternity of hard-bitten, humorless nerds with a religious dedication to a 30-year-old operating system from the phone company? Well, yes and no. We hope that we're not humorless.

If you're like most UNIX users, a zealot stopped at your desk, connected your terminal or workstation, gave you five minutes of incomprehensible advice, demonstrated a few bizarre games (like roaches that hide behind the work on your screen), and disappeared. Now you're on your own.

Don't worry. This part of the book explains the absolute minimum you need to know to get your UNIX system's attention, persuade it that you are allowed to use it, and maybe even accomplish something useful.

Chapter 1

Log Me In, UNIX!

....

In This Chapter

▶ Turning your computer on and getting its attention

▶ Persuading your computer to let you use it

▶ Using usernames, passwords, and all that

▶ Logging out when you finish

....

*I*f you read the exciting introduction to this book, you know that we make some Foolish Assumptions about you, the reader. Among other things, we foolishly assume that someone else has installed and set up UNIX for you so that all you have to do is turn your computer on and tell UNIX that you're there, or that a computer running UNIX is somewhere on the network that you have access to.

If you don't have UNIX already set up on a computer, the best thing you can do for yourself is find a local UNIX guru or system administrator who is willing to get you up and running. Unless you really know what you're doing, installing and setting up UNIX can be painful, frustrating, and time-consuming. We recommend that you find something more enjoyable to do, such as cleaning out the grease trap under your kitchen sink or performing urgent home surgery on yourself. (You can learn how to administer a UNIX system with some patience and perseverance, but explaining how is way beyond the scope of this book because each version of UNIX has its own procedures.)

Turning Your Computer On and Off

If you think that turning your computer on and off is easy, you may be wrong. Because UNIX runs on so many almost-but-not-quite-compatible computers — all of which work somewhat differently — you first must figure out which kind of UNIX computer you have before you can turn it on.

If a train stops at a train station, what happens at a workstation?

A *workstation* is a computer with a big screen, a mouse, and a keyboard. You may say, "I have a PC with a big screen, a mouse, and a keyboard. Is it really a workstation?" Although UNIX zealots get into long arguments over this question, for our purposes, we say that it is. Most current UNIX systems are workstations.

Turning on a workstation is easy enough: You reach around the back and turn on the switch. Cryptic things that appear on-screen tell you that UNIX is going through the long and not-at-all-interesting process of starting up. Starting up can take anywhere from ten seconds to ten minutes, depending

TECHNICAL STUFF

What you were hoping we wouldn't tell you: The difference between a PC and a workstation

First, you have to understand that this isn't a technical question — it's a theological question. Back in the olden days (about 1980), telling the difference was easy. A workstation had a large graphical screen — at least, large by the standards of those days — a megabyte of memory, a fast processor chip, a network connection, and it cost about $10,000. A PC had a lousy little screen, 64K of memory, a slow processor chip, a floppy or two, and it cost more like $4,000.

These days, your typical $800 PC has a nice screen (much nicer than what the workstation used to have), hundreds of megabytes of memory, a fast Pentium processor, a big disk, speakers, and a network connection. That's much better than what people used to call a workstation. Does that make a PC a workstation? Oh, no. Modern workstations have even better screens, buckets of memory, a turbocharged processor chip — you get the idea. What's the difference?

Maybe it's the software that people use: Most workstations are designed to run UNIX (or, in a few cases, proprietary systems similar in power to UNIX), whereas PCs run Windows or Macintosh software. Wait — some perfectly good versions of UNIX run on PC hardware, and Windows 2000/NT runs on many boxes that everyone agrees are workstations, and the latest version of Mac OS is UNIX underneath. Now what? You can get into esoteric arguments about the speed of the connection between the guts of the computer on one hand and the disks, screens, and networks on the other hand and argue that workstations have faster connections than PCs, but some examples don't fit there, either.

As far as we can tell, if a computer is *designed* to run Windows or the Mac OS, it's a PC. If it's *designed* to run UNIX, it's a workstation. If this distinction sounds feeble and arbitrary to you, you understand perfectly. Here at *UNIX For Dummies* Central, we have a couple of large PCs running UNIX (which makes them look, to our eyes, just like workstations) and a couple of other, smaller ones running Windows. Works fine for us.

on the version of UNIX, number of disks, phase of the moon, and so on. Sooner or later, UNIX demands that you log in. To find out how, skip to the section "Logging In: U(NIX) Can Call Me Al," later in this chapter.

Turning *off* a workstation is a more difficult problem. Workstations are jealous of their prerogatives and *do* punish you if you don't turn them off in exactly the right way. Their favorite punishment is to throw away all the files related to whatever you were just working on. The exact procedure varies from one model of workstation to another, so you have to ask a local guru for advice. Typically, you enter a command along these lines:

```
shutdown +3
```

This command tells the workstation to shut down (in three minutes, in this example). With some versions of UNIX, that command is too easy. The version we use most often uses this command:

```
halt
```

If you use Linux, type this command to shut down the system right away:

```
shutdown now
```

The workstation then takes awhile to put a program to bed or whatever else it does to make it feel important, because it knows that you're waiting there, tapping your feet. Eventually, the workstation tells you that it's finished. At that point, turn it off right away, before it gets any more smart ideas.

An approved method for avoiding the hassle of remembering how to turn off your workstation is never to shut off your computer (although you can turn off the *monitor*). That's what we do.

A dumb terminal

The traditional way to hook up to a UNIX system is with what's known (sneeringly) as a dumb terminal. Nobody makes dumb terminals any more, but Windows PCs have a natural ability to play dumb, so they're commonly pressed into duty as terminals. You run a terminal emulator program on a PC, and suddenly the mild-mannered PC turns into a super UNIX terminal. (Truthfully, it's more the other way around: You make a perfectly good PC that can run *Doom* and other business productivity-type applications act like a dumb terminal that can't do much of anything on its own.)

When you finish with UNIX, you leave the terminal emulator, usually by pressing Ctrl+X or some equally arcane combination of keys. (Consult your local guru: No standardization exists.) Like Cinderella at the stroke of midnight, the terminal-emulating PC turns back into a real PC. To turn it off, you wait for the PC's disks to stop running (carefully scrutinize the front panel until all the little red or green lights go out) and then reach around and turn off the big red switch. If you don't wait for the lights to go out, you're liable to lose some files.

If you have a network installed, which these days has become so cheap that nearly everyone does, your PC running Windows probably has a network connection to your UNIX system. Windows 95/98/Me/NT/2K/XP, and the Mac OS (the Macintosh operating system) have the network stuff built in.

If you do have a network connection, you can use programs called `telnet`, `ssh`, or `putty` (described in Chapter 16) to connect to your UNIX system. After one of them is running and connected to your UNIX system, within your program's window you get a faithful re-creation of a 1970s dumb terminal and you can proceed to log in.

After you connect, you use it to communicate with the computer that is running UNIX. If the terminal is wired directly to the computer, UNIX asks you to log in before you can do anything else (see the section "Hey, UNIX! I Want to Log In," later in this chapter). If not, you may have to perform some additional steps to call the computer or otherwise connect to it.

An *X terminal* is similar to an extremely stripped-down workstation that can run only one program — the one that makes X Windows work. (See Chapter 4 to find out what X Windows are — or don't. It's all the same to us.) Turning an X terminal on and off is pretty much like turning a regular dumb terminal on and off. Because the X terminal doesn't run programs, turning it off doesn't cause the horrible problems that turning off a workstation can cause. You can get X software for Windows to make a Windows PC act like an X terminal, too. If you have such a PC, ask the person who set it up how to start it and stop it.

Hey, UNIX! I Want to Log In

Whether you use a remote PC or a workstation, you have to get the attention of UNIX. You can tell when you have its attention because it demands that you identify yourself by logging in. If you use a workstation, whenever UNIX finishes loading itself, it is immediately ready for you to log in (skip ahead to the section "Logging In: U(NIX) Can Call Me Al"). You terminal users (X or otherwise), however, may not be so lucky.

Direct access

If you're lucky, your keyboard and screen are attached directly to the main computer, either because the main computer is the only one and you're sitting at it, or someone's rigged up a remote PC to log in directly. If so, it displays a friendly invitation to start working, something like this:

```
ttyS034 login:
```

Well, maybe the invitation isn't that friendly. By the way, the `ttyS034` is the name UNIX gives to your terminal. Why doesn't it use something easier to remember, like Fred or Muffy? Beats us!

This catchy phrase tells you that you have UNIX's attention and that it is all ears (metaphorically speaking) and waiting for you to log in. You can skip the next section and go directly to "Logging In: U(NIX) Can Call Me Al."

If your UNIX system displays a terminal name, make a note of it. You don't care what your terminal's name is, but, if something gets screwed up and you have to ask an expert for help, we can promise you that the first thing the guru will ask is, "What's your terminal name?" If you don't know, the guru may make a variety of nerd-type disparaging comments. But, if you can say, "A-OK, Roger. That's terminal `tty125`," your guru will assume that you are a with-it kind of user and may even try to help you. (Even if her name isn't Roger.)

Yo, UNIX! — not-so-direct access

If you're connecting over the Internet or another network, either find a local network expert to tell you how to connect, or see Chapter 16 for some suggestions.

If you're using a PC with a modem, you probably have to tell the modem to call the UNIX system. Although all terminal emulators have a way to make the call with two or three keystrokes, all these ways are different, of course. (Are you surprised?) You have to ask your local guru for info.

After your terminal is attached to the computer, turned on, and otherwise completely ready to do some work, UNIX, as often as not, doesn't admit that you're there. It says nothing and seems to ignore you. In this way, UNIX resembles a recalcitrant child — firm but kind discipline is needed here.

The most common ways to get UNIX's attention are

✔ Press the Return or Enter key. (We call it the Enter key in this book, if you don't mind.) Try it two or three times if it doesn't work the first time. If you're feeling grouchy, try it 20 or 30 times and use a catchy cha-cha or conga rhythm. It doesn't hurt anything and is an excellent way to relieve stress.

✔ Try other attention-getting keystrokes. Ctrl+C (hold down the Ctrl key, sometimes labeled Control, and press C) is a good one. So is Ctrl+Z. Repeat to taste.

✔ If you're attached to UNIX through a modem, you may have to do some speed matching (described in a minute): Press the Break key a few times. If you're using a terminal emulator, the Break key may be disguised as Alt+B or some other hard-to-find combination. Ask your guru.

Two modems can talk to each other in about 17,000 different ways, and they have easy-to-remember names, such as B212, V.32, and V.32bis. (*Bis* is French for "and a half." Really.) After you call the UNIX system's modem with your modem, the two modems know perfectly well which way they're communicating, although UNIX sometimes doesn't know. Every modem made since about 1983 announces the method it's using when it makes the connection. Because the corresponding piece of UNIX code dates from about 1975, though, UNIX ignores the modem's announcement and guesses, probably incorrectly, at what's being used.

If you see something like ~xxx~~r.!" on-screen, you need to try *speed matching*. Every time you press Break (or the terminal emulator's version of Break), UNIX makes a different guess at the way its modem is working. If UNIX guesses correctly, you see the login prompt; if UNIX guesses incorrectly, you see another bunch of ~xxx~~~@(r)!" or you see nothing. If UNIX guesses incorrectly, press Break again. If you overshoot and keep Breaking past your matched speed, keep going, and it'll come around again.

After awhile, you learn exactly how many Returns, Enters, Breaks, and what-nots your terminal needs in order to get UNIX's attention. It becomes second nature to type them, and you don't even notice what a nerd you look like while you do it. You have no way around that last part, unfortunately.

Logging In: U (NIX) Can Call Me Al

Every UNIX user has a username and password. Your system administrator assigns you a username and a password. Although you can and should change your password from time to time, you're stuck with your username.

Before you can start work, you must prove your bona fides by logging in; that is, by typing your username and password. How hard can typing two words be? Really, now. The problem is this: Because of a peculiarity of human brain wiring, you will find that you can't enter your username and password without making a typing mistake. It doesn't matter whether your username is a1 — you will type A1, 1a, a;L, and every other possible combination.

UNIX always considers upper- and lowercase letters to be different: If your username (sometimes also called your *login name*) is egbert, you must type it exactly that way. Don't type Egbert, EGBERT, or anything else. Yes, we know that your name is Egbert and not egbert, but your computer doesn't know that. UNIX usernames almost always are written entirely in lowercase. Pretend that you're a disciple of e. e. cummings.

When you type your username and password and make a mistake, you may be tempted to press Backspace to clear your mistake. If only life were that easy. Guess how you clear typing errors when you type your username and password? You press the # key, of course! (We're sure that it made sense in 1975.) Some — but not all — versions of UNIX have changed so that you can use Backspace or Delete; you may have to experiment. If you want UNIX to ignore everything you typed, press @, unless your version of UNIX has changed the command key to Ctrl+U (for *untype,* presumably — doubleplusungood). So, Egbert (as you typed your username), you may have typed something like this:

```
ttyS034 login: Eg##egberq#t
```

Finish entering your username by pressing Enter or Return.

After you type your username, UNIX asks you to enter your password, which you type the same way and end by pressing Enter (or Return, but we call it Enter). Because your password is secret, it doesn't appear on-screen as you type it. How can you tell whether you typed it correctly? You can't! If UNIX agrees that you typed your username and password acceptably, it displays a variety of uninteresting legal notices and a message from your system administrator (usually delete some files, the disk is full) and passes you on to the shell, which you find out about in Chapter 2.

If UNIX did not like either your username or your password, UNIX says Login incorrect and tells you to start over with your username.

In the interest of security, UNIX asks you for a password even if you type your username wrong. This arrangement confuses the bad guys — but not nearly as much as it confuses regular users. So, if UNIX rejects your password even though you're sure that you typed it correctly, maybe you typed your username incorrectly.

Password Smarts

Like every UNIX user, you should have a password. You can get along without a password only under these circumstances:

- ✔ You keep the computer in a locked, windowless room to which you have the only key, and it's not connected to any network.

- ✔ You don't mind whether unruly 14-year-olds borrow your account and randomly insert dirty knock-knock jokes in the report you're supposed to give to your boss tomorrow.

The choice of your password deserves some thought. You want something easy for you to remember but difficult for other people to guess. Here are some bad choices for passwords: single letters or digits, your name, the name of your spouse or significant other, your kid's name, your cat's name, or anything fewer than eight characters. (Bad guys can try every possible seven-letter password in less than a day.)

Good choices include such things as your college roommate's name misspelled and backward. Throw in a digit or two or some punctuation, and capitalize a few letters to add confusion, so that you end up with something like yeLLas12. Another good idea is to use a pair of words, like fat;Head.

You can change your password whenever you're logged in, by using the passwd program. It asks you to enter your old password to prove that you're still who you are when you logged in (computers are notoriously skeptical). Then the passwd program asks you to enter your new password twice, to make sure that you type it, if not correctly, at least consistently. None of the three passwords you type appears on-screen, of course. We show you how to run the passwd program in Chapter 2.

Some system administrators do something called *password aging;* this strategy makes you change your password every once in awhile. Some administrators put rules in the passwd program that try to enforce which passwords are permissible, and some even assign passwords chosen randomly. The latter idea is terrible because the only way you can remember a password you didn't choose is to write it on a sticky note and stick it on your terminal, which defeats the purpose of having passwords.

In any event, be sure that no one other than you knows your password. Change your password whenever you think that someone else may know it. Because UNIX stores passwords in a scrambled form, even the system administrator can't find out what yours is. If you forget your password, the administrator can give you a new one, but she can't tell you what your old one was.

If you really want to be paranoid about passwords, don't use one that appears in any dictionary. Some system breakers may decide to use the UNIX password-encryption program to encrypt every last word in a dictionary and then compare each of the encrypted words to your password. It's another thing to keep you awake at night.

Ciao, UNIX!

Logging out is easy — at least compared to logging in. You usually can type **logout**. Depending on which shell you're using (a wart we worry about in Chapter 2), you may have to type **exit** instead. In many cases, you can press Ctrl+D to log out.

You know that you have logged out successfully because UNIX either invites the next sucker to log in, hangs up the phone, or, if you're connected by `telnet` or `ssh`, disconnects from your program.

Chapter 2

What Is UNIX, Anyway?

In This Chapter

▶ Why you care: A little boring UNIX history

▶ Finding out which version of UNIX you have

▶ Using the UNIX shell

▶ Avoiding shell traps and pitfalls

This entire chapter tells you how to figure out which kind of UNIX system you have gotten involved with. If you *really* don't think that you care, skip this chapter. As you read the rest of this book and run into places where you need to know which kind of UNIX or shell you are using, you can always come back here.

Why Do We Ask Such Dumb Questions?

"What is UNIX?" UNIX is UNIX, right? Not entirely. UNIX has been evolving feverishly for close to 30 years, sort of like bacteria in a cesspool — only not as attractive. As a result, many different varieties of UNIX have existed along the way. Although they all share numerous characteristics, they differ (we bet this doesn't surprise you) just enough that even experienced users are tripped up by the differences between versions.

May a thousand UNIXes flower

Indulge us while we tell a historical parable. Imagine that UNIX is a kind of automobile rather than a computer system. In the early days, every UNIX system was distributed with a complete set of source code and development tools. If UNIX had been a car, this distribution method would have been the same as every car's being supplied with a complete set of blueprints, wrenches, arc-welders, and other car-building tools. Now imagine that nearly all these cars were sold to engineering schools. You may expect that the students would get to work on their cars and that soon no two cars would be the same. That's pretty much what happened to UNIX.

Bell Labs released the earliest editions of UNIX only to colleges and universities. (Because Bell Labs was The Phone Company at that time, it wasn't supposed to be in the software business.) From that seed, a variety of more-or- less scruffy mutants sprang up, and different people modified and extended different versions of UNIX.

Although about 75 percent of the important stuff is the same on all UNIX systems, knowing which kind of UNIX you're using helps, for two reasons. First, you can tell which of several alternatives applies to you. Second, you can impress your friends by saying things like "HP-UX is a pretty good implementation of BSD, although it's not as feature-full as Solaris." It doesn't matter whether you know what it means — your friends will be amazed and speechless.

Throughout this book, we note when we discuss a command or feature that differs among the major versions of UNIX. And when we talk about the popular Linux system, you see our cute Linux icon in the margin. We don't waste your time with a family tree of UNIX systems. The following sections describe the most common kinds.

The two main versions of UNIX are BSD UNIX and System V. Although they differ in lots of little ways, the easiest way to tell which one you're using is to see how you print something. If the printing command is lp, you have System V; if it's lpr, you have BSD. (If the command is print, you cannot be using UNIX; nothing in UNIX is that easy.)

Here are the major types of UNIX you're likely to run into:

✔ **Berkeley UNIX:** One of the schools that received an early copy of UNIX was the University of California at Berkeley. Because no student's career was complete without adding a small feature to Berkeley UNIX, you can still see on every part of BSD UNIX the greasy fingerprints of a generation of students, particularly a guy named Bill, about whom you hear more later.

The Berkeley people made official Berkeley Software Distributions of their code (named BSD UNIX) and gave numbers to its versions. The final and most widely used version of BSD UNIX is Version 4.4. Berkeley graduates fanned out across the country, working for and even starting new companies that sell descendants of BSD UNIX, including Sun Microsystems (which markets Solaris), Hewlett-Packard (HP-UX), and IBM (AIX). Most workstations run some version of BSD UNIX.

✔ **Post-Berkeley BSDs:** Shortly before 4.4BSD came out, the folks at Berkeley realized that they had made so many changes to BSD over the years that practically none of the original Bell Labs code was left. Several groups quickly rewrote the missing 1 percent, adapted the BSD code for 386 and newer PC-compatible machines, and made all the code available over the Internet. Three projects (called FreeBSD, OpenBSD, and NetBSD) continued to improve and update the freely available BSD, and a company called Berkeley Software Design, now part of Wind River Systems, offers a commercially supported version of BSD/OS.

✔ **System V:** Meanwhile, back at The Phone Company, legions of programmers were making different changes to UNIX. They gave their versions of UNIX Roman numerals — which are classier than plain ol' digits. Their current version of UNIX is known as System V. The many subversions of System V are known as System V Release 1 (SVR1) and SVR2, SVR3, and SVR4. Most non-workstation versions of UNIX are based on System V or, occasionally, its predecessor, System III. (What happened to System IV? Not ready for prime time, we guess.)

Sun Microsystems, from the BSD camp, and AT&T, of the System V camp, decided to bury the hatchet and combine all the features of BSD and System V into the final incarnation of System V, SVR4. SVR4 has so many goodies that it's only slightly smaller than a blimp. If your system runs SVR4 or its descendants, you have to pay attention to our hints about both BSD *and* System V. The last version of SVR4 was SVR4.4. (Where *do* they get these numbers?) System V was eventually sold to Novell (the NetWare people), which retitled it UNIXWare. Novell eventually sold it to a Microsoft affiliate called the Santa Cruz Operation (better known as SCO), which retitled it UnixWare (don't ask).

Helpful advice to Sun users: Although Sun changed the name of its software from SunOS to Solaris, it didn't change the way the software worked. If you use Solaris 1.0, follow the instructions for BSD UNIX. Because Solaris 2.0 is based on SVR4, however, you have to worry about both BSD and System V. Is this stuff clear? We're still confused about it.

✔ **OSF/1:** When System V and BSD UNIX merged to form SVR4, many UNIX vendors were concerned that, with only one version of UNIX, the market confusion would be insufficient. They started the Open Software Foundation, which makes yet another kind of UNIX: OSF/1. Although OSF/1 is mostly BSD, it is also a goulash of some System V and many other miscellaneous eyes of newts and toes of frogs.

OSF/1 has largely disappeared; if you use OSF/1, however, pay attention to the BSD advice in this book, and you will be okay.

✔ **Linux:** Without a doubt, the most surprising UNIX development in recent years has been the appearance — seemingly from nowhere (but actually from Finland) — of Linux, a rather nice, freely available version of UNIX. Linux is such a big deal that we devote an entire chapter to it (the next one, in fact). Chapter 14 also has stuff about Linux for those brave souls who run their own Linux systems.

Linux resembles SVR4 as much as it resembles any other version of UNIX.

Why you should fight rather than switch

The question, "Which is better: UNIX or Windows 2000 or XP?" has sparked a religious war between UNIX crusaders and the high priests of marketing at Microsoft Corporation. Microsoft would have you believe that Windows 2000 and XP, its industrial-strength versions of Windows, are a snazzy new alternative to UNIX, a tired old system that wore out its welcome in the last days of disco. According to Microsoft, UNIX is expensive and impossible to use without a degree in computer science. Windows 2000 and XP are cheaper and easier to use, and, because it's a Microsoft product, it's just plain better. So you should junk your UNIX computers and replace them with Windows servers and workstations *right now, before it's too late!* (If we were cynical, we would point out that Microsoft has no UNIX version of its own to sell. But we're not cynical. Are we?)

In spite of rather extravagant Microsoft claims of Windows superiority, the evidence is decidedly mixed. Although many businesses seem to have made the switch from UNIX to Windows successfully, they're usually on the small- to medium-size end of the spectrum. If you have to support a large company that depends on an extensive network to handle high volumes of traffic and to serve critical applications and information, you're much better off sticking with UNIX.

In case your system administrator is considering making an ill-advised switch from UNIX servers to Windows servers, here are a few points you should try to work in during your next conversation at the company water cooler.

Windows servers tend to *go down* — stop working properly for one reason or another — fairly regularly. UNIX servers, on the other hand, tend to work perfectly for months on end. Running your company's phone sales department on a Windows server means running the risk of cutting off all your callers until you can get your server to *reboot,* or recover from one of its little episodes.

According to various independent reports, Windows chronically has more security *bugs* (problems with the way the system behaves) than UNIX. Windows simply doesn't have the built-in security and permissions features that UNIX has always had.

As far as processing power goes, Windows can't hold a candle to UNIX. Windows servers now have a four-processor limit, although UNIX machines can handle many, many more. UNIX can handle larger files, and its architecture provides as much as 4 *billion* times more data space than Windows (yup, we said *billion*). In practice, this statement means that you have to replace each of your UNIX machines with multiple Windows machines to maintain the same amount of computing power.

Which brings us to the question of cost. Although individual Windows servers may be cheaper than individual UNIX servers (although that's less true now that the hardware they run on is the same), the apparent price advantages quickly evaporate when you consider the number of servers you need and the cost of administering and maintaining them, not to mention hidden costs from server downtime and data loss.

We could go on (and if you want to meet us over a couple of beers, we certainly will). Suffice it to say that the Microsoft rumors about the imminent death of UNIX have been greatly exaggerated.

Oh, and by the way, UNIX still leads the way when it comes to serving Web sites. The Apache server, which we discuss in Chapter 20, is still the most widely used Web server in the world today. And it doesn't cost much. In fact, it's free.

What's GNU?

No tour of UNIX versions is complete without a visit to the Free Software Foundation, in Cambridge, Massachusetts (not to be confused with the OSF, Open Software Foundation, which is about six blocks down the street). The FSF was founded by a brilliant but quirky programmer named Richard Stallman, who came from MIT, where people wrote lots and lots of software and gave it all away. He firmly (some would say fanatically) believes that all software should be free, and he set up the FSF to produce lots of high-quality free software, culminating in a complete, free version of UNIX. Despite quite a bit of initial skepticism, the FSF has raised enough money and been given and lent enough equipment to do just that. The FSF's project GNU (for *GNU's Not UNIX*) has so far produced versions of most of the UNIX user-level software. The best-known and most widely used pieces are the text editor GNU Emacs (which we discuss in Chapter 10), most of the other basic UNIX utilities, and the GNU C compiler (GCC), which is now used on all the free versions of UNIX, including Linux, as well as on a few commercial ones.

The GNU crowd continues to work on new stuff, including its *pièce de résistance,* the GNU Hurd, a complete working version of the guts of the UNIX system. Early on, fans of free software awaited the GNU Hurd with great eagerness; now that Linux and the freely available BSD versions have arrived, however, their eagerness has abated somewhat. Hurd or no Hurd, GNU Emacs, GCC, and the GNU utilities are here to stay. The FSF says you should call Linux GNU/Linux, because so much GNU software is in Linux, but almost nobody does. (There's probably more BSD than GNU software in Linux, actually.)

What the FSF means by "free" software is a little different from what you may expect: It means freely available, not necessarily available for free. It means that if you can find someone willing to pay you a million bucks for some GNU software, that's perfectly okay. That person, and anyone else to whom you give or sell GNU software, however, must be free to give or sell it, in turn, to other people without restriction. The intention is that people can make money by supporting and customizing software, not by hoarding it. Although opinions vary about the long-term practicality of this plan, for now the FSF surely has written some popular software, and at least one company, named Cygnus Support, makes a good business supporting it.

How Can You Tell?

When you log in to your UNIX system, a variety of copyright notices usually flash by, with an identification of the type of UNIX you are accessing. Carefully scrutinize the information on-screen, and you may be able to tell which version you have.

Another approach is to type the command **uname** and press Enter. Sometimes this command displays the name of your computer (such as `aardvark` or `acctg3`). Sometimes, however, the command displays the version of UNIX you are running. On Linux systems, it says `Linux`.

If you can't tell which UNIX version you have, break down, grovel, and ask your local UNIX expert. When you figure out which type of UNIX you are running, write it down on the Cheat Sheet in the front of this book. You never know when you may need to know this stuff.

If you're connected to your UNIX system over a network from a PC or an X terminal, the type of UNIX you're using depends on the maker of the main computer you're attached to — not on the maker of the PC or terminal. You generally see the identification of the main computer in a message it sends to the terminal just before or just after you log in.

Cracking the Shell

Now that you have figured out which general variety of UNIX you have, you must figure out one other vital consideration: which shell you're using. You may say, "I don't want to use *any* shell; I just want to get some work done," but the shell is the only way to get to where you want to be.

The guts of UNIX are buried deep in the bowels of the computer. The guts don't deign to deal with such insignificant details as determining what users may want to do. That nasty business is delegated to a category of programs known as shells. A *shell* is a program that waits for you to type a command and then executes it. From the UNIX point of view, a shell is nothing special, other than the first program UNIX runs after you log in. Because you can designate any old program to run when you log in, any fool can write a shell — indeed, many have done so. About a dozen UNIX shells are floating around, all slightly incompatible with each other (you probably guessed that).

Fortunately, all the popular shells fall into two groups: the Bourne (or Korn or BASH) shell and the C shell. If you can figure out which of the two categories your shell is in, you can get some work done. (You're getting close!)

You can easily tell which kind of shell you're using. If UNIX displays a $ after you log in, you have a Bourne-style shell; if UNIX displays a %, you're using the C shell. Traditionally, System V systems use the Bourne shell, and BSD systems use the C shell. These days, however, because all versions of UNIX come with both shells, you get whichever one your system administrator likes better. Preferences in command languages are similar to preferences in underwear: People like what they like, so you get what you get, although these days most of the people we know like BASH, a souped-up Bourne-style shell.

You can disregard this discussion about the true nature of shells

What UNIX calls a shell, many other people — especially DOS users — call a *command processor.* What DOS users call a shell is a fancy graphical program that is supposed to make the computer easier to use by displaying cute little icons for programs and files and other such user-friendly goodies.

Because the people who wrote UNIX didn't go for all this wimpy, frou-frou, hand-holding stuff, their idea of a shell was a program in which you

could type zq to run a program called zq. (These guys were notoriously lazy typists.) Although user-friendly shells are available for UNIX, they're not widely used, and we don't mention them again in this book.

If a Windows or Macintosh fanatic says rude things about the UNIX shell, you can respond that, although UNIX may be somewhat challenging to use, as a UNIX user, at least you're not a wimp.

Linux systems usually come with the BASH shell, a Bourne-style shell.

After you determine whether you have a Bourne-style shell ($) or a C shell (%), note this fact on your Cheat Sheet in the front of this book.

If you use a GUI (see Chapter 4), you see windows and icons, not a boring little UNIX prompt, after you log in. You still need to use a UNIX shell from time to time, however, usually to perform housekeeping tasks.

The Bourne and Bourne Again shells

The most widely used UNIX shell is the Bourne shell, named after Steve Bourne, who originally wrote it. The Bourne shell is on all UNIX systems. It prompts you with $, after which you type a command and press Enter. Like all UNIX programs, the Bourne shell itself is a program, and its program name is sh. Clever, eh?

A few alternative versions of the original Bourne shell exist, most notably the Bourne Again shell (or BASH, whose program name is bash) from the GNU crowd. This version of the Bourne shell is used in many places because of its price — it's free. Some people claim that it's still overpriced, but we don't get into that. BASH is enough like the original Bourne shell that anything we say about the Bourne shell applies also to BASH. The most notable advantage of BASH is that it has *command editing,* a fancy way of saying that you can press the arrow keys on your keyboard to correct your commands as you're typing them, just as you can with DOS (oops, better not say that when any UNIX fans are listening).

The Korn-on-the-cob shell

After the Bourne shell was in common use for a couple of years, many people thought that the shell was so simple and coherent that a single person could understand all its features and use them all effectively. Fortunately, a guy named Dave Korn remedied this shameful situation, who added about a thousand new features to the Bourne shell and ended up with the Korn shell (called ksh). Because most of the new features are of interest only to people who write *shell scripts* (sequences of shell commands saved in a file), you can consider the Korn shell the same as the Bourne shell. Most versions of the Korn shell also have command editing.

She sells C shells

No, the C shell wasn't written by someone named C. It was written by Bill, the guy we mentioned earlier. (He sells C shells by the C shore? Probably.) We would discuss our opinion of the C shell at length, except that Bill is 6'4", in excellent physical shape, and knows where we live. The C shell's program name is csh.

The most notable difference between the C shell and the other leading shell brands is that the C shell has many more magic characters (characters that do something special when you type them). Fortunately, unless you use a number of commands with names like ed!3x, these characters aren't a problem.

Who says the C shell isn't user-friendly?

If you use the C shell, be aware that some punctuation characters do special and fairly useful things.

An exclamation point (!) tells the C shell to do a command again. Two of them (!!) means to repeat the last command you typed. One of them followed by the first few characters of a command means to repeat the last command that started with those characters. For example, to repeat the last cp command you gave, type

```
!cp
```

This command is great for lazy typists.

You can also use carets (^) to tell the C shell to repeat a command with some change. If you type this line:

```
^old^new
```

the C shell repeats the last command, substituting "new" for "old" wherever it appears in what you typed. You can use slashes (/) in a similar way, although carets are easier to use. The C shell also uses colons (:) to perform truly confusing editing of previous commands, which we don't get into.

In Chapter 7, we tell you more about reissuing shell commands.

Many versions of the C shell exist; most of them differ in which bugs are fixed and which are still there. You may run into programs called zsh and tcsh, two slightly extended C shells with command editing.

Are Any Good Programs On?

You may be wondering why we refer sometimes to commands and sometimes to programs. What's the difference?

A *command* is something you type that tells UNIX (or actually the shell) what to do. A *program* is a file that contains executable code. The confusion comes because in UNIX, to run a program, you just type its name. (In old-fashioned operating systems, you usually typed something like RUN BUDGET_ANALYSIS to run a program called BUDGET_ANALYSIS.)

When you type a command, such as ls or cp or emacs (a text editor we talk about in Chapter 10), the shell looks at it carefully. The shell knows how to do a few commands all by itself, including cd and exit. If the command isn't one that the shell can do by itself, the shell looks around for a program stored in a file by the same name.

Old DOS users may recognize the way this process works — commands DOS can do itself are called *internal commands,* and commands that require running another program are called *external commands.* Internal commands are also called *built-in commands.*

Finally! You're Ready to Work

We wrap up this chapter with a little advice about hand-to-hand combat with the shell. You can give many commands to your shell. Every shell has about a dozen built-in commands, most of which aren't very useful on a day-to-day basis. All the other commands are the names of other programs. The fact that every UNIX system has hundreds of programs lying around translates into hundreds of possible shell commands.

One nice thing about UNIX shells is that, within a given shell, the way you type commands is completely consistent. If you want to edit a file called my-calendar, for example, and use an editor called e, you type this line:

```
$ e my-calendar
```

Ending command lines without hard feelings

Remember to end every command line by pressing Enter. UNIX is pretty dumb; in most cases, your pressing Enter is the only way UNIX can tell that you have finished doing something.

With a few programs, notably the text editors vi, pico, and emacs, you don't need to press Enter anywhere; we point out those exceptions. Everywhere else, remember to press the Enter key at the end of every line.

Now you know which kind of UNIX you are using, which shell you are using, and why you care. In the following sections, we show you a few UNIX (or shell) commands you can use to begin getting something done.

As always, press Enter at the end of the line to tell the shell you have finished. The shell runs the e editor, which does whatever it does. When you finish, you return to the shell, where you can issue another command.

Whenever you see a UNIX prompt (either $ or %), a shell is running, waiting to do your bidding. Throughout this book, we usually refer to the entire package — UNIX plus shell — as UNIX. We say, "Use the ls command to get UNIX to display a list of files" rather than "Use the ls command to get the shell to get UNIX to display a list of files." Okay?

We could tell you the password, but then we'd have to kill you

When you logged in, you probably hated your password because someone else picked it. Hating your password is a good reason to change it. Another reason you may want to change it is that, to get this far, you enlisted the aid of some sort of expert and had to reveal your password. This section shows how to change your password: Use the passwd command.

This stuff is easy. Just type this line:

```
passwd
```

As always, press Enter after typing the command. The passwd command asks you to type your current password to make sure that you are really you. (If it didn't check, whenever you wandered off to get some more coffee, someone could sneak over to your desk and change your password. Not good.) Type your current password and press Enter. The password doesn't appear on-screen as you type, in case someone is looking over your shoulder.

Then `passwd` asks for your new password. (Chapter 1 has lots of sage advice about how to choose a password.) You have to type the new password twice so that `passwd` is sure that you typed it correctly. Assuming that you type the new password twice in the same way, `passwd` changes your password. The next time you log in, you are expected to know it.

If you forget your password, you have no way to retrieve it; not even your system administrator can tell you what it is. The administrator can assign you a new one, though, and you can change it again, preferably to something more memorable than the one you forgot.

What's my file?

This section discusses a command you use frequently: the `ls` command, which lists your files. Chapters 5 and 6 talk more about files, directories, and other stuff `ls` helps you with; for now, here's `ls` Lesson 1. Type the following line (we're not telling you to press Enter anymore because we know that you have the hang of it):

```
ls
```

The `ls` command lists the names of the files in the current directory. (Chapter 6 talks about directories.)

Oops!

If you are a world-class typist, you can skip this section. If you make thousands of typos a day, as we do, pay close attention. If you type something wrong, you can probably press the Backspace key to back up and retype it. If that doesn't work, though, all is not lost. Try the Delete key, the # key (Shift-3), or Ctrl+H. One of these combinations should work to back you up.

To give up and start the entire line over again (not usually necessary with nice, short commands, such as `ls`), press Ctrl+U. If that doesn't work, press the @ key (Shift+2).

Don't turn off the computer if you make a typo!

To repeat something we have hinted at: If you make a mistake and all is not going well, do *not* turn off the computer, unplug it, or otherwise get unnecessarily rough. Although PC users get used to just turning the darned thing off if things aren't going well, UNIX computers don't respond well to this approach.

Instead, suggest politely to UNIX that it stop doing whatever it is you don't like. To stop a command, press Ctrl+C, or, on some systems, the Break key or the Delete key.

If the situation is out of control, UNIX is running a program you don't want, and you can't get it to stop, you can use some Advanced and Obscure Techniques to wrestle extremely recalcitrant programs into line. See Chapter 24 if you're desperate.

Play it again, Sam

Sometimes, you may want to issue the same command again (because it was so much fun the first time). If you use the C shell, type this line:

```
!!
```

If you use the BASH shell, press the up-arrow key to see the last command you typed and then press Enter.

In the Korn shell, you can type this line to reissue a command:

```
r
```

If you use the Bourne shell, you're out of luck and must type your command again.

Everything you want to know about typing commands — but are afraid to ask

This list shows a wrap-up of what to do when UNIX displays a prompt (either $ or %) and you want to type a command:

- ✔ As you type, the cursor moves along to indicate where you are. The cursor looks like an underline or a box.

- ✔ If you make a typing mistake, press Backspace (or try Delete, #, or Ctrl+H).

✔ To cancel the entire command before you press Enter, press Ctrl+U (or try @).

✔ When you finish typing a command, press Enter. (If you don't, UNIX — and you — wait forever.)

✔ If you issue a command that UNIX (actually, the shell) doesn't know, you see a message like this:

```
blurfle: Command not found.
```

This message means that you typed the command wrong, you typed a command that UNIX doesn't know (maybe a DOS command crept in), or someone hasn't told UNIX the right places to look for programs.

✔ Don't stick extra spaces in the middle of commands, as in **pass wd**. Type the command exactly as we show it. On the other hand, *do* type a space after the name of the command but before any additional information you have to type on the line (read more about that subject in Chapter 5). Also, do not capitalize except where you know that the command has a capital letter.

✔ You know that a command resembles a sentence, but you don't end it with a period. UNIX doesn't like the period, and UNIX is extremely unforgiving.

TIP

The UNIX cast of special characters

One of the more exciting aspects of typing shell commands is that many characters are special. They have special meanings to UNIX; the next few chapters discuss some of them. Special characters include the ones in this list:

```
<  >  '  "  *
{  }  ^  !  \
[  ]  #  |  &
(  )  $  ?  ~
```

Spaces also are considered special because they separate words in a command. If you want to put special characters in a command, you must quote them. You *quote* something by putting quotation marks around it. Suppose that you have a file called c* (not a great idea, but sometimes you get these things by mistake). You can edit it by typing

```
e "c*"
```

You can use either single or double quotation marks, as long as you're consistent. You can even quote single quotation marks with double quotation marks and quote double quotation marks with single quotation marks. Is that clear? Never mind.

Chapter 3

A Few Lines on Linux

. . . .

. . . .

*L*inux is the hottest thing to arrive in UNIX-land in years: a wildly popular, completely free version of UNIX. It is (quite deliberately) similar to other versions of UNIX; for the most part, then, everything in this book that applies to other versions of UNIX also applies to Linux.

Many ISPs use Linux on their servers because it's fast, flexible, and free. Even if you don't use Linux locally, if you have a Web site hosted at your ISP, you may well find that a Linux box is serving up your Web pages.

Out of the Frozen North

In 1992, a guy in Finland named Linus Torvalds took a then-popular, small, educational version of UNIX called Minix, decided it wasn't quite what he wanted, and proceeded to rewrite and extend it so that it was more to his taste. Lots of enthusiastic programmers have started projects like that, but to everyone's astonishment, Linus *actually finished* his. By mid-1993, his system had long since left its Minix roots and was becoming a genuinely usable version of UNIX. Linus's system was picked up with great enthusiasm by programmers, and later by users, all over the Internet. It spread like crazy, to become the fastest-growing part of UNIX-dom.

Linux is popular for three reasons:

▶ It works well, even on a small, cheap PC. A 386 PC with 4MB of random-access memory (RAM) and a 40MB hard drive can run Linux — barely. (You can find computers like that for $5 at the thrift store these days.) On a top-of-the-line Pentium PC, its performance approaches that of a full-blown traditional UNIX workstation.

✔ Lots of enthusiastic people are working on Linux, with wonderful new features and additions available every day. Many of them even work.

✔ It's free!

The many developers of Linux proudly describe it as a "hacker's system," one written by and for enthusiastic programmers. (This classic meaning of *hacker* should not be confused with the other, media-debased "computer vandal" definition.) These programmers keep up the development of Linux at a brisk pace, and a new "development" version is made available on the Internet every few days. Every once in a while, the developers decide that they have gotten enough bugs out of their recent developments, and they release a "stable" version, which stays constant for months rather than days. Most normal people use the stable version rather than a development version. Using a development version of Linux is sort of like living in a house inhabited by a large family of carpenters and architects: Every morning when you wake up, the house is a little different. Maybe you have a new turret, or some walls have moved. Or perhaps someone has temporarily removed the floor under your bed. (Oops — sorry about that.)

Linux started life as the operating system of choice for students and other cheapskates . . . er . . . users who wanted a UNIX system of their own but couldn't afford a traditional UNIX workstation. As Linux has matured into a stable, reliable UNIX system, this base has expanded to include companies and institutions that *could* afford traditional UNIX workstations, but found that Linux enabled them to add PC-based workstations at a fraction of the cost. In fact, Linux is now conservatively estimated to have more than 18 million users, making it the second or third most popular operating system in the world, behind Windows and about even with the Macintosh operating system.

What's Old, What's New

The original guts of Linux were written from scratch by Linus Torvalds and have since been greatly changed and extended by other people. He based Linux more or less on System V (on *descriptions* of System V; there's no code from System V). Most programs that people actually use (the shells and other commands) come either from 4.4BSD or from the GNU project, which modeled most of them after the Berkeley UNIX versions, so most of the commands are BSD-ish. Because the networking programs are adapted from the Berkeley ones, they also are all BSD-ish.

Technically speaking, Linux refers only to the operating system "kernel." When most people refer to a Linux system, though, they usually mean the whole package: operating system plus the GNU programs that come with it. Like all UNIX systems, Linux systems can run various shells, editors, and other software. Most versions of Linux use BASH as the default shell because it's also new and snazzy.

How free is free?

Linux is *free software*. In the UNIX software biz, "free" has a concrete meaning that is different from public domain and different from shareware.

Linux is made available under the GNU General Public License (GPL), Version 2, the same license the Free Software Foundation uses for most of its programs. The license has seven pages of legalese, much of which is about where copyright notices have to appear and stuff like that, but the basic plan is simple. In short, it says:

✔ You can copy and distribute Linux and other GPL software, and you can charge for it.

✔ *But,* anyone to whom you distribute it has the right to give copies away for free.

✔ *And* you must include the source code (or make it available for no more than a reproduction fee) in the distribution.

The idea is that people are permitted, even encouraged, to distribute copies of GPL software and to sell maintenance service, as long as the software itself remains freely available.

Don't confuse free software with *shareware,* which is software for which you are supposed to pay the original author if you use it, or with *public domain* software, with which you can do anything you want.

Although the GPL was subject to considerable debate and a fair amount of ridicule when it first came out in about 1990, it has worked pretty much the way its authors intended — GPL software (including Linux) is widely available, and people do indeed constantly work on and improve it.

Keep in mind that because Linux is a moving target, with frequent improvements to the programs, the version of Linux you use is probably not exactly the same as the version described in any book, including this one. At the time we wrote this edition of this book, the latest stable version of Linux was 2.5.75, but even if you have a more recent version, the basic structure is the same.

A look at the various Web sites and Usenet newsgroups dedicated to Linux shows a veritable flurry of Linux-related activity. New programs, extensions, and enhancements for Linux appear daily, it seems. Red Hat Linux, for example, now offers a range of snazzy new products, including a secure Web server, several Microsoft Office-like suites of desktop tools including ApplixWare and OpenOffice.org, and fully graphical integrated desktops (see Chapter 4 for details about UNIX desktops).

Several organizations have set up computer clusters — hundreds of computers acting like one enormous supercomputer — built out of ordinary Linux systems connected by fast Ethernets. You can get the source code, operating system, and management tools to set up such a cluster off the Internet for free (at www.beowulf.org). Or if you want all your computing in one place, you can buy a multi-million dollar IBM mainframe computer and run Linux on it, too.

You say to-may-to, I say tomahto

A frequent concern of newcomers to Linux is how to pronounce it correctly, in order not to sound uninformed. It's simple: However you pronounce it is wrong — or right, depending on your audience. Among English speakers in the United States, at least, opinions seem to be divided about evenly between "Line-ucks" and "Linn-ucks."

The name Linux is derived from the first name of its creator, Linus Torvalds. The "Line-ucks" group holds that the pronunciation is based on the usual English pronunciation of Linus. Linus Torvalds himself, though, a Swedish-speaking Finn, has helpfully provided an audio file on the Internet in which he provides the definitive answer in both English and Swedish. In the file, he says, "Hello, this is Lee-noos Torvalds, and I pronounce Lee-nooks as Lee-nooks." It's up to you whether you want to say "Linux" with a Swedish accent, but to our ears his reading sounds much closer to the Anglicized "Linn-ucks," so that's what we use.

In Chapter 14, we talk about the latest releases of the most popular versions of Linux. In Chapter 26, we describe a number of ways you can get additional information about Linux, including reading one of a number of Usenet newsgroups about Linux or subscribing to a Linux magazine.

Where's Linux?

Linux development happens mostly on the Internet, and if you have an Internet connection, you can download the entire system at no charge. You *do* need either a fast connection or great patience because the system takes up several CD-ROMs full of data. A typical 56 Kbps dialup connection takes about a day and a half to download a version of Linux. Quite a few bulletin-board systems around the world make Linux code available. A more practical approach is to buy or borrow a CD-ROM version of Linux, which you can install in an hour or so.

Sounds great, doesn't it? You can install a version of UNIX on your very own computer! Keep in mind one tiny little snag, however: That makes *you* the system administrator. You have to learn how to create user accounts, deal with disks that fill up, and install and configure software. It's not impossible (far from it — John has done it for years), but you have much to learn.

The details of installing and setting up Linux are way beyond the scope of this book. In Chapter 14, we barely touch on a few basics of administering a Linux system. For more details, take a look at *Linux For Dummies,* 5th Edition, by Dee-Ann LeBlanc (published by Wiley Publishing, Inc.); and *Running Linux,* by Welsh and Kaufman (O'Reilly & Associates).

A Whole Lotta Kinds of Linux

The main Linux project develops the Linux *kernel,* the heart of the system that runs programs, handles files, networks, virtual memory, and lots of other crucial details. But to have a usable system, you also need text editors and file copiers, and all of the other programs that we take most of this book to describe. Because the Linux kernel is free software, and a huge variety of editors, file copiers, and so forth are available, anyone who cares to do so can collect his or her favorites into what's known as a Linux *distribution.* Some of the best-known distributions include Red Hat, Debian, Gentoo, Mandrake, Slackware, and SuSe, but a whole lot more is out there. (The list at `www.linux.org` has close to 200.)

Which Linux distribution should you choose? We were afraid you'd ask. Some of the distributions are for special purposes, such as Knoppix, which runs off a CD without needing to be installed on your hard drive (a good choice if you want to try Linux quickly), or FlightLinux, intended for controlling experiments in outer space. But the mainstream versions, including the ones we mention in this chapter, all work fine, so we suggest that you use whatever your friends use, so you have people you can commiserate with to solve problems.

Part II
Some Basic Stuff

Arthur inadvertently replaces his mouse pad with a Ouija board. For the rest of the day, he receives messages from the spectral world.

YOU WILL FORGET YOUR PASSWORD. YOUR HARD DISK WILL CRASH AAAHAHAHAHA

In this part . . .

*U*NIX, like other computer systems, keeps your information in things called *files*. When you work with UNIX, you frequently need to make new files, rename files, make copies of particularly interesting files, get rid of files that have outlived their usefulness, find a file you temporarily mislaid, or print what's in a file.

This part of the book also talks about *graphical user interfaces* (GUIs), with sort of clever names like KDE and GNOME, which let you use a mouse to point at things on-screen. Most people find GUIs a big improvement over typing commands, but you have to know what to point at and click. You're about to find out!

Chapter 4

Opening Windows on UNIX

. . . .

. . . .

*T*o answer your first question, GUI stands for *graphical user interface* and really *is* pronounced "gooey." We prefer the term WIMP, which stands for *windows, icons,* and *mouse pointing,* but for some reason the term never caught on. Fast-track executives would rather be gooey than wimps, we suppose.

A *GUI* is a combination of a graphics screen (one that can show pictures in addition to text), a mouse (or something like it), and a system that divides the screen into several windows that can show different things at the same time. All GUIs work in more or less the same way because they're all based on the same original work done at Xerox about 20 years ago. The details differ enough, though, to make you want to tear your hair out.

UNIX Gets All GUI

The earliest UNIX systems didn't have fancy, screen-oriented windowing systems. They didn't have screens at all, in fact — they used loud, rattling terminals that printed on actual paper. (The historically minded can find these types of terminals in the Computer Museum in Boston and the Smithsonian Institution in Washington, D.C. Yes, really.) As the years went by, UNIX appeared on computers that did have screens (most notably Sun workstations), and various windowing systems appeared.

Under the hood in Mac OS X

Apple programmers wrote the first nine versions of the Macintosh operating system all by themselves. But in OS X, they wised up and jumped on the free UNIX bandwagon. Underneath all of the Mac-fullness, OS X is based on a version of FreeBSD. If you look in the Utilities folder in the Applications folder, you find the Terminal program, which gives you the classic UNIX shell.

Although the Mac Finder looks a lot like some X desktops, or maybe the other way around, the OS X window system (known as Aqua) isn't X; it's the old Mac window system rewritten for UNIX. But if you want X, Apple is happy to give it to you. Visit www.apple.com/macosx/x11 where you can download a version of X for OS X, integrated with Aqua so you can run Mac OS programs and X programs together, and even cut and paste between them. The X programs may look a little strange on the Mac desktop, because they still look like UNIX programs, but that's how you know it's UNIX. Looks odd, but works great.

One thing about the UNIX community you've probably come to appreciate by now is that you can't get everyone to agree on anything, except of course that UNIX is better than every other kind of system and that anyone who thinks otherwise is silly. So, not surprisingly, a variety of incompatible windowing systems arose, each different from the other in various, not particularly interesting, ways. Nearly all the windowing systems were *proprietary* (they belonged to one system vendor or another), and, of course, no vendor would dream of admitting that someone else's window system was better than theirs.

X marks the window

Universities also had a bunch of window system projects. One of the more successful was the X Window project at MIT (alleged to be a successor to the W Window project at Stanford — as far as we know, no one created a V Window project). The X Window system had many virtues, not the least of which were that it worked adequately well and it was available for free to anyone who wanted it. So X became the window system everyone used.

Almost all UNIX systems that have any sort of GUI now use one based on the X Window system (frequently abbreviated to just *X Windows,* which has been known to drive UNIX purists crazy because it sounds too much like that *other* famous operating system from Redmond, Washington). Old Sun workstations used systems called SunView or NeWS; NeXT machines use NeXTStep (are tHoSE wOrDS cAPiTaLIzed corREctlY?); other than those exceptions, however, you almost certainly get X Windows.

X (which is an even shorter abbreviation for X Window system) has many advantages as a windowing system:

- ✔ It runs on all sorts of computers, not just those that run UNIX.

- ✔ It is *policy independent:* A program can make the screen look any way it wants; the screen is not constrained to a single style, as it is on the Macintosh or with Microsoft Windows. (As you may imagine, this capability is not an unmitigated blessing. Read more about this subject in "Just my look" later in this chapter.)

- ✔ It uses a networked client-server architecture (love those buzzwords). You can run X on one computer, and the programs that display stuff on-screen can be on entirely different computers connected by a network.

- ✔ MIT gives it away.

You can imagine which of these important advantages is the one that really made all the computer makers choose X. Even though MIT gives away the base version of X, unless you happen to be using the exact same kind of computer the guys at MIT use (or you feel like compiling and debugging a gazillion lines of C code), you don't get it for free. You must buy a version tailored for the particular kind of screen and adapter on your computer. An exception is XFree86, a free version of X used by most PC-based UNIX systems, such as Linux, which is described in Chapter 3.

How your screen looks depends on which GUI you use. The first part of this chapter talks about things that are the same for all GUIs. Later, we talk about how to tell which GUI you are using and how to do things that work differently for each GUI.

"I'm not just a server — I'm also a client!"

X was designed from the beginning to work with computer networks. It makes a clear distinction between the *server* program, which handles the screen, keyboard, and mouse, and the *client* program, which does the actual computing. Although the two programs are running more often than not on the same computer, they don't have to be. (Readers who saw John on *The Internet Show* on public TV a few years ago may recall one demonstration of an online subway map of Paris. That was an X application, with the X server running on a PC in the TV studio in Texas and the client program on a computer in France, connected by way of the Internet.)

The networkability (is that a word?) of X is most useful in two ways. One way is that you can be sitting at an X workstation attached to a local network and have windows attached to client programs running on computers all over the network, often on computers considerably more powerful than yours, particularly if you're running on an old PC. *X terminals,* stripped down PCs, used to run only one program, the X server, but these days PCs have gotten so cheap that they cost less than any plausible X terminal. Should you find yourself using an X terminal, it works just like a UNIX workstation except, of course, that all of the programs you run have to be on other computers.

A few cool X programs

Because MIT gives away X Windows, X quickly became the standard window system at hundreds of colleges and universities around the world. Students, who have a sincere dedication to doing something other than what they are supposed to be doing (not like the rest of us — no way), quickly wrote all sorts of silly programs — nominally to test either X or their understanding of it and generally to have fun. Assuming that these programs are installed on your computer, you only have to type their names in a window containing a UNIX shell to run them (read more about this subject in Chapter 7). A few of the better-known fun X programs are in this list:

✔ **xeyes:** Pops up a large pair of eyeballs that watch the mouse cursor as you move it around the screen. According to the manual, it checks up on you and reports back to the boss. Hmmm.

✔ **xsnow:** Puts a snowstorm on the screen background. Snowflakes fall down the screen and pile up on top of your windows. The -santa option makes an occasional reindeer-drawn sleigh fly across your screen. Ho, ho, ho.

✔ **xsol:** Plays a game of Klondike solitaire against you. You click the deck to turn over the next card and drag cards to move them around. It's as good a way as any to learn how to handle the mouse, or at least that's the excuse you can use when your boss comes by. Because the computer controls the card deck, you can't cheat, which means that winning in one trip through the deck is

practically impossible. We've won honestly once in about two years of play. The program enables you to turn over the deck and try again, which enables you to win nearly half the time, albeit without honor.

✔ **xphoon:** Displays in the background of your screen a detailed, full-screen picture of the moon as it appears today. In a classic display of dedicated geek programming, it correctly computes the relative angular positions of the earth, moon, and sun based on the current time and date and shows the moon's current phase (full, quarter, half, or whatever). It's useful for people who work in windowless offices and have forgotten what the sky looks like.

✔ **xmille:** Plays the Parker Brothers game Mille Bornes against you. It keeps a running score and plays a mean game. Click the deck with the left mouse button to draw a card, click a card in your hand to play it, and click a card with the middle button to discard it. During the past year or so, we have won 34 games and lost 42, with each game consisting of about five hands.

✔ **xroach:** Lots of yucky roaches scurry around the screen and hide under the windows, just like in real life. If you run the program with the -squish option, you can squish the roaches by clicking them, leaving an authentic smudge of roach guts on your screen. (UNIX geeks consider this program to be humor at its finest.)

We've got something in common

A few companies doing UNIX apparently decided that they had gone too far in the customizability department, so they got together with the Open Software Foundation to create something called the Common Open Software Environment, which describes how to build UNIX programs so that they all act and look something like each other (or at least like they come from the same planet). In 1995, this group came out with the Common Desktop Environment, or CDE, which is a UNIX windowing system that bears more than a passing resemblance to the Macintosh and (Microsoft) Windows desktops. Surprisingly, CDE began to catch on, especially among Microsoft Windows and Macintosh users who were new to UNIX or who needed to use *both* Windows or Mac OS alongside their UNIX workstations. CDE does much more than manage your UNIX windows. We talk about CDE in the section "CDE: A Desktop for All Seasons," later in this chapter.

The KDE environment, which we also discuss later in this chapter, looks a lot like CDE. Because CDE costs money and KDE is free, you're more likely to run into KDE these days.

Just my look

Most windowing systems on most kinds of computers make programs use a consistent style. All Macintosh programs, for example, look pretty much the same: They all use the same menu, the same little window when you want to select a file, and similar windows to turn options on and off. One Microsoft Windows program looks much like all the others: They all use similar sets of windows.

Do all X Windows programs have a consistent look? Of course not — that would be too easy. This situation is what the X crowd means by *policy independence:* X is utterly agnostic about what windows should look like on-screen, how keystrokes and mouse clicks should be interpreted, and pretty much anything else that affects a user. This lack of policy was part of the original appeal of X because no matter which window system you are used to, you can make X look just like that system. The good news is that X offers great flexibility. The bad news is that the word *inconsistent* barely scratches the surface of what you run into.

Makeup artists for your windows

One of the ways in which X avoids having any policy built in is that it foists much of the general window-management jobs onto a program called a *window manager.* (Catchy name, huh?) The window manager handles jobs such as creating borders around each application's main windows; controlling how you move, resize, switch among, and iconify windows; and most of the other tasks that aren't part of any particular application. It's possible to run X without any window manager, although it's rather unpleasant because, without one, you have no way to do some things, such as move a window.

A field guide to window managers

A bunch of competing window "looks" are on the UNIX market. To tell which one you're stuck with . . . er, have the pleasure to use, look at the border around the windows on your screen. If they have 3-D–style borders with sharp corners, as shown in Figure 4-1, you're using the Motif Window Manager (MWM); its free look-alike counterpart, FVWM; or DTWM, the Desktop Window Manager that comes with the Common Desktop Environment (CDE). If the borders have rounded corners, as shown in Figure 4-2, you're using OpenLook. If they have a thin border around the sides and bottom and top borders like those shown in Figure 4-3, you're probably using a program called TWM, which comes with the base version of X and is still sometimes used because it is simple and small.

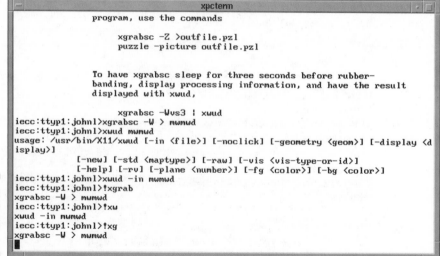

Figure 4-1:
A typical
Motif
window.

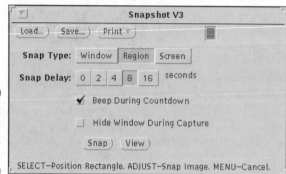

Figure 4-2:
A typical
OpenLook
window.

```
 xpcterm                                                                    
iecc:ttyp1:johnl>who -a
     .           system boot  Dec 12 12:32
     .           run-level 2  Dec 12 12:32    2      0    S
bcheckrc         .            Dec 12 12:33  0:20       5   id=bchk term=0   exit=77
brc              .            Dec 12 12:33  0:20      15   id= brc term=0   exit=0
brc              .            Dec 12 12:33  0:20      19   id=  mt term=0   exit=0
rc2              .            Dec 12 12:49  0:20      23   id=  r2 term=0   exit=0
root             console      Dec 29 20:16  0:01   17956
sleep            .            Dec 12 12:49  0:20     130   id=  wt term=0   exit=0
johnl            vt01         Dec 21 15:19  0:01    5938
LOGIN            vt02         Dec 29 20:16 20:48   17955
LOGIN            ttyd1        Dec 30 16:24  0:52    2827   492-3869
faxserve         .            Dec 26 11:45  0:20   24871   id=  F2
johnl            ttyp2        Dec 30 17:16    .     3053   id=  p2 term=112 exit=2
johnl            ttyp1        Dec 30 16:55    .     3054
johnl            ttyp0        Dec 30 16:55  0:15    3055
johnl            ttyp3        Dec 30 16:56  0:20    3086   id=  p3 term=112 exit=2
johnl            ttyp4        Dec 30 16:12  1:04   19342   id=  p4 term=112 exit=2
johnl            ttyp5        Dec 23 18:41   old   11186   id=  p5 term=112 exit=2
LOGIN            .            Dec 15 15:28  0:20   25517
LOGIN            .            Dec 15 15:30  0:20   25532
LOGIN            ttyd2        Dec 17 18:55   old    5561   id=  02 term=15  exit=0
iecc:ttyp1:john
iecc:ttyp1:johnl>xgrabsc -W > twmwd
```

Figure 4-3:
A typical
TWM
window.

The Open Software Foundation, the same people who provide the OSF/1 version of UNIX, created Motif, based on some work done by their members Hewlett-Packard and Digital Equipment. Motif is much more complete than its competition (it has a provision for handling languages other than English, for example), and because DEC made it cheap for software vendors to use, it became the primary X Windows manager until KDE and GNOME came along.

People using the Common Desktop Environment (CDE) get the Desktop Window Manager, or DTWM. CDE comes with all kinds of nifty and zoomy programs, although underneath the glitz it's just a version of Motif, so it looks pretty much the same.

Lots of other window managers exist, although the ones described in this section are the most common ones. After several years of window system warfare, Motif and its clone FVWM have emerged as the clear favorite window managers, so that's what we concentrate on here. Even if you use a different window manager, it probably works about the same way that Motif does.

Considerably more than you want to know about window managers, toolkits, and X

If you're dying to know more about how the X Window system works, strap on your safety belts because we're going to get a little technical. If you're dying to know how to *use* your window manager and couldn't care less about how it *works,* skip down to the section "Stupid Window Manager Tricks." If you're sticking with us, just don't say that we didn't warn you.

Déjà vu déjà vu

Readers familiar with Microsoft Windows 95 or NT may find the Motif window manager to be strangely familiar. Its windows don't look all that much like Windows windows, although the mouse and keyboard techniques are extremely similar. That turns out to be no coincidence. Because Hewlett-Packard has a super-duper application environment it sells for both Windows and X, it deliberately made its X package (from which much of Motif is derived) as similar to Windows as possible.

For users who switch back and forth between Windows and Motif (we authors, for example), this capability is a blessing because the mouse moves and keystrokes our fingers have memorized for one system work by and large in the same way in the other. This practically unprecedented level of compatibility exists between UNIX and something else, so we figure that, deep down, it must have been an oversight.

The X Window system divides the work of controlling what's on-screen among three separate kinds of programs:

- ✓ **X server:** Draws pictures on-screen and reads user input from the keyboard and mouse

- ✓ **Window manager:** Controls where windows appear on-screen, draws borders around windows, and handles basic window operations, such as moving windows, shrinking windows to an *icon* (a little box representing that window), and expanding icons to windows

- ✓ **Clients:** Programs that do some real work

For any particular screen, there's one X server, usually (but not always) one window manager, and a bunch of clients. Every client communicates with the server to tell it what to draw and to find out what you did; the server communicates with the window manager when the user asks for a window-management operation, such as changing the size of a window. Although the server, window manager, and clients usually run on the same computer, X Windows enables them to exist on separate machines connected by a network. It is not unusual to have a setup in which the server runs on an X terminal, the window manager runs on a nearby workstation, and the clients are on various machines scattered around the network.

The window manager is usually a regular UNIX program. You can stop one window manager and start another if you decide that you don't like the way your windows look. Client programs can ask the X server to ask the window manager to do some specialized operations. A terminal program, for example, can ask the window manager to enable a user to change the size of the window only to a size that is a whole number of lines of text. (This kind of communication starts to resemble that in the ancient Roman Empire, in which proconsuls could officially speak only to procurators, who could speak to senators, and so on. Computers are like that.) If no window manager exists, no window-management operations are available.

Writing an X program is a great deal of work. To make life easier for programmers, a programmer can build on *toolkits* of program code that are already written. MIT sends out X Toolkit (immediately called Xt by the usual lazy typists). This toolkit provides a set of basic window functions that most programs use. Starting with Xt, different people have produced libraries of *widgets,* or screen elements a program can use. A menu or a file-selection panel is a widget, for example. The Motif widget set is for programs that want to look like Motif. The Athena widgets from MIT's Project Athena aren't particularly attractive, but many programs use them because (where have we heard this before?) they're available for free. You can also find other toolkits for other window systems, including KDE and GNOME.

FVWM: The chameleon of window managers

Because Motif isn't free, it isn't included with most Linux and BSD systems. (Nothing prevents you from running Motif under Linux or BSD, but most people aren't prepared to pay more for a window manager than they paid for the whole operating system and its included software.) Instead, with Linux, you often find the window manager called FVWM.

The origins of the name FVWM are forever lost in the mists of history. The *VWM* part stands for *virtual window manager.* The *F* part is a mystery, though. *Fine* and *feeble* are two frequently offered possibilities.

The "virtual" part of this window manager is one of FVWM's best-loved features. Rather than having just a single desktop, you can have any number of virtual desktops, each with its own independent set of windows open. Because each desktop is the size of the screen, this feature enables you to think of your screen as a porthole looking at part of a much larger screen behind it.

FVWM usually displays a little map of all the virtual desktops at your disposal; Most systems have either four or nine, although theoretically you can have as many or as few as you want.

You move around among all your desktops by pressing the Ctrl key and then the arrow key for the direction of the next desktop according to the little map. Is your desktop getting too crowded with windows? No need to close some of them; just pop on over to another desktop. You can have dozens of programs open without getting too crowded; never has slowing your system to a crawl been easier!

FVWM is almost infinitely configurable. You can make it look like practically anything, although its default look is nearly identical to Motif. A version of FVWM known as FVWM95 looks remarkably similar to — you guessed it — Windows 95. (Whether this is A Good Thing is a favorite point of religious arguments among many Linux users.) Not only do its window borders mimic Windows 95, but it also even features a Start button with pull-up menus. FVWM95 is found by default on recent releases of Red Hat Linux (discussed in Chapter 14). Another popular mutation of FVWM is called AfterStep, which looks just like the NeXTStep window system.

FVWM has become enormously popular on free UNIX versions. You can even find it on some large commercial systems.

How do I start Motif, anyway?

You may think that this question is a simple one to answer, but, because UNIX is involved, it's not. The short answer is "Run mwm" (the Motif window manager), although that technique is not useful because you have to run mwm at the right time and place.

If you're lucky, your system manager sets up everything for you automatically. If you're on an X terminal or a workstation running xdm (the X display manager), X is already running when you sit down and waiting for you to enter your username and password, and Motif starts as soon as you log in.

The next best thing is that you're at a workstation that is set up to run X after you log in so that X and Motif start automatically when you log in.

Failing that, you have to start X and Motif yourself after you log in to UNIX. The two most common start-up commands are startx and xinit. If you're not sure which one to use, try them and see what happens. What happens is that your screen goes *kerflooie!* for a few seconds when it switches from old, dumb, terminal mode to new, cool, graphical X mode; a few windows appear, running xterm (the dumb terminal emulator that runs under X); and Motif starts and draws attractive borders around all the windows.

If none of those things works, we've run out of ideas, and you have to ask your local expert how to start X and Motif on your computer or X terminal.

What all this means is that any particular X client uses one of the widget sets to control what that client's window looks like. A program that uses the Motif toolkit, for example, is a Motif program. Because clients are separate from window managers, however, the Motif window manager (named mwm — the lazy typists strike again) can be running and draw a Motif border around the windows of clients using other toolkits.

Because of the constant danger that GUI systems could begin to make sense to users, UNIX people have learned to obfuscate things by using "Motif" to refer to both the Motif window manager and the Motif toolkit, which are, of course, completely separate entities. When people refer to "Motif," therefore, they may be referring to the window manager or maybe to the toolkit. Or both. Often it's difficult to tell. This confusion is all just part of the proud legacy of UNIX evolution.

One school of thought says that we all would be better off if X Windows had picked a window style and stuck with it so that we would have a single window manager and a single set of widgets — as every other window system does — although it's much too late now for that.

Stupid Window Manager Tricks

We now delve into the nitty-gritty details of how to get stuff done using whatever window manager you happen to have on your computer. Because Motif is the most common window manager, we spend a fair amount of time on it in this book. If something we say is specific to Motif, we tell you.

If you're lucky enough to have some version of the Common Desktop Environment (CDE), KDE, or GNOME, you can skip to the appropriate section later in this chapter. Because the Common Desktop Environment is built on Motif and KDE looks a lot like CDE, we recommend that you read this section anyway to find out the basics about windows, icons, mice, and the various and sundry widgets you encounter.

Opening a new window

When you run a new X program, generally speaking, it opens a new window. In some cases, you want to tell a program that's already running to open another window (another file for a word processor, for example), although the way you do that is specific to each program. You have to read the manual (gasp!) for the program.

You usually have at least one terminal window running. A *terminal window* isn't as sinister as it sounds: It's a window that acts like a terminal. The usual program is called xterm; it acts much like an antique DEC VT100 terminal. Most systems also have a modified terminal program that acts like the computer maker's favorite terminal. Hewlett-Packard systems have hpterm, for example, which acts like an HP terminal, and some PC UNIX systems have xpcterm, which acts like a PC console. For most purposes, all these terminal programs act the same. They start up running a UNIX shell, and you type commands just as we describe in this book.

You can use one of two ways to start a new program that opens a new window: the GUI-oriented, user-friendly way and the easy way.

Follow these steps for the GUI-oriented, user-friendly way:

1. **Move the cursor so that it's not in any of your current windows.**

2. **Click the Menu mouse button.**

   This button is the last one (the right-most button unless you have a left-handed mouse) in OpenLook and the first button otherwise.

About your mouse

Your mouse (or mouse-like thing) has some buttons on it. Take a moment to count the buttons. Finished counting? (How long could it have taken?) We hope that you found three buttons. If you found only two buttons, you have a problem because most X programs are written with three-button mice in mind and don't work well with two-button mice. Some X servers can be configured to enable you to get to all the X features by using only two buttons, although getting a three-button mouse is much easier. We've found some perfectly usable ones at our local computer store for $10 or less.

3. **Drag the mouse up and down the menu that pops up until you find the program you want.**

4. **Let go of the button.**

   Sometimes you have nested menus: When you pick an item from the first menu, a second menu pops up, and you must pick an item there, too.

The easy way to start a program has only one step:

1. **Go to a terminal window and type the name of the program you want to run.**

This approach is the same one you use to run any other program or to give a command. To display another terminal window, type **xterm** or the name of the terminal program you use.

Then you have the issue of where on-screen the new window appears. Some programs and window managers have strong opinions of their own, and the new window appears wherever the program or window manager thinks that it should. With other, less opinionated programs, you make the call: A ghostly window that appears floats near the middle of the screen. You move the ghost around with the mouse and click when the window is where you want it. At that point, the ghost materializes into the regular window. This latter scheme is usually more convenient because the locations the opinionated programs choose for window placement are rarely where you want them. Beware of one thing, though, while the ghost is on-screen: All other windows are frozen. If you leave the ghost on-screen for a long time (while you're at lunch or overnight), all the others can become rather constipated waiting for the screen to unfreeze so that they can update their windows. If you're using Motif, your local guru can switch your system between opinionated mode and floating-ghost mode.

Some systems have desktop manager programs (unrelated to window manager programs) that attempt to make handling programs and files easier. Desktop managers have sets of icons you click to start common programs. They enable you to click filenames to edit the file, for example — sort of like the Macintosh Desktop. Opinions vary on how useful these desktop managers are. We haven't been crazy about them, although trying them for a few minutes is worth your time because some people find them much easier to use than menus and shell commands.

A quick mouse refresher

You probably know all about how to use your mouse. In the unlikely event that you're a little rusty on the terminology, though, here are a few basic terms:

Which button is which: The first button is the one on the left (unless someone has configured your mouse to be left-handed, and then the first button is the one on the right). Either way, the second button is the one in the middle. The third button is the one that isn't the first or second button. (What? You already figured that out?)

Cursor: The cursor is the little doozit (a highly technical term) on-screen that shows where the mouse is pointing. The cursor often changes shape as you move it from one window to another to give you a hint of what's going on in a window. The most common cursor shapes are a black X (when you're not in any window), a little arrow (in windows with graphics), a little vertical hairline (in windows of text), and a little leftward-pointing finger (in windows with links, such as Help systems and Web browsers).

Click: To click something, move the cursor to the thing you want to click, and then press and release the mouse button. Unless otherwise directed, use the left-most mouse button. Clicking is also called *selecting* the screen item; it means that you want to do something with the item you just clicked.

Double-click: To click the same button twice quickly, usually with the first button.

Drag: To drag something, move the cursor to the drag-ee, press down the mouse button, move the mouse while holding down the button, and then let go of the button when you get to where you want the drag-ee to be. Most non-Motif programs use the left button to drag stuff, and Motif programs use the middle button.

You use dragging in two main ways. The first is for *pop-up menus.* When you press one of the mouse buttons, a menu appears, with a list of possible things to do. While you are holding down the button, drag the cursor to the item on the menu you want and then let the button go. If you change your mind and don't want to do any of the things on the menu, drag the cursor entirely off the menu before letting go of the button.

The second way to use the drag technique is to outline some part of a window. You move to one corner of an area you want to select, press a mouse button, drag to the opposite corner of the area, and let go; at this point, a box on-screen shows the area you outlined.

Icon do this with a picture

GUIs are crazy about pictures (they're graphical, after all), especially cute, little ones. The cutest, littlest ones you run into are called icons. An *icon* is a little picture in a little box on-screen that represents a window. When you tell X Windows to "iconify" a window, the window disappears and an icon remains. When you double-click (or single-click if you're not using Motif) the icon, the window comes back just as it was before. Being able to reduce windows to icons enables you to shove programs out of the way and not lose what you are doing — one of the best things about window systems. Figure 4-4 shows a pair of icons, one for an e-mail program and one for a terminal program. If new mail arrives, the little flag on the mail icon flips up, which is almost useful enough to make up for its X-treme cuteness.

Figure 4-4:
Icons are
windows in
a miniature
disguise.

Window wrangling à la Motif

Motif (or, more particularly, the Motif window manager) draws a border around every window on your screen, as shown in Figure 4-5. The border gives you considerable control over the window, enabling you to move it, hide it, change its size, and perform other tasks.

The borders of some windows are missing some or all of the buttons we discuss in this section. That's because not all windows allow all functions. If the button's not there, you can't do what it would have done anyway.

You frequently will find that you don't like the way the windows on your screen are arranged. You can do lots of things to alleviate this problem and simultaneously waste lots of time. We have found that, by giving your dedicated attention to window management, you can spend the entire day at the computer apparently working but not accomplishing anything. Because a little rearrangement is inevitable, the following sections are thumbnail sketches of what you can do and how to do it with Motif:

  ✔ **Change the layering.** Change which windows are in front of other windows, much like shuffling the papers in the pile on your desk. Unless you're a masochist, you want the active window (the window you're using) to be the one in front.

✔ **Move windows around the screen.** This process is even more similar to shuffling the papers on your desk.

✔ **Turn windows into icons and vice versa.**

✔ **Change the size of windows.** Create larger areas for long files you're editing, for example.

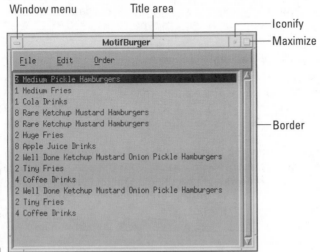

Figure 4-5:
A typical
Motif
window.

Switching and layering your windows

Suppose that you have two or three windows on-screen. How do you tell UNIX which window you want to use? The answer is (wait, no — how did you know that this answer was coming?) *it depends.* In line with the standard X rule of never making up its mind about anything, you can switch windows in two different ways:

✔ **Click-to-type, or explicit focus:** Move the mouse cursor to the window you want to use, and click the mouse in it somewhere. The window moves to the front (any overlapping windows drop behind it so that you can see the entire window).

✔ **Move-to-type, or pointer focus:** Move the mouse cursor into the window you want to use. Even though the window may be partially obscured by other windows, it becomes active. You can tell when a window is *active* because the border around it changes color. Click the window's title bar if you want to move it to the front. Motif also enables you to move a window up front like this: Move the cursor into the window, hold down the Alt or Meta key, and press F1.

If you have to "click to type" and hate it — or don't and really want to — a guru skilled in the ways of X (naturally called an X-pert) can change some parameters and turn "click to type" on or off. We recommend that you live with whatever you have. So many changeable parameters are available that, after you begin fiddling with them, it can become X-asperating to figure out X-actly how your X-pert left them, and you will utter an X-cess of X-pletives.

You can tell which is the active window because the Motif window manager changes the color of its border to a distinctive darker color. The Motif standard window-switching rule is click-to-type.

"Where, oh, where has my window gone?"

In Motif, you put the cursor in the title bar, press the first mouse button, and drag the window to where you want it (that is, you move the window as you hold down the mouse button). This action also brings the window to the front because you use the same button to do that.

You can move windows so that they are partially off the edge of the screen, sort of like pushing papers to the side of your desk so that they hang over the edge (except that windows are less likely to fall on the floor). This capability is sometimes useful if the interesting stuff in the window is all at the top or all on one side.

Stashing your windows

The title bar of the window has little buttons you can click. Near the right end of the title bar is a little box that contains a small dot; when you click it, you *iconify* the window; that is, the window turns into an icon.

To get the window back, double-click the icon with the first mouse button.

Icons normally appear in the lower-left corner of the screen, although you can move them around by dragging the icon around with the mouse. After you move an icon, if you restore the window and then re-iconify it, the icon reappears where you left it. You can lay out the icons to your taste by iconifying every window on-screen, moving the icons to tasteful positions, and then restoring the ones you want to use.

Curiouser and curiouser: Changing window sizes

The last little bit of window magic involves changing window sizes. Motif has gone to a great deal of trouble to let you change the size of your windows, which tells us that they gave up trying to make them the right size in the first place. Oh, well. Little "grab bars" are in each corner of most windows. (The few windows you can't resize don't have grab bars.) You move the cursor to one of the grab bars, click the first mouse button, drag the corner to where you want it (make the window larger or smaller), and release the button.

Then do it again two or three times because you never get it right on the first try. Motif also has grab bars (thin, gray borders) on the top, bottom, and sides of every window, which enable you to change the height of a window without changing the width or vice versa.

Some programs have strong feelings about how big their windows should be. In some cases, they don't let you shrink the window to less than a minimum size. In other cases, you can't change the size. For these programs, attempts to resize just don't work. You can click and drag the borders all you want, but nothing moves.

Motif has a shortcut to enable you to expand a window to fill the entire screen. Click the little box-in-a-box at the right end of the title bar. If you do the same thing again, the window shrinks back to normal size.

In practice, we rarely blow up windows to full-screen size because few UNIX programs take advantage of the entire screen. The full-screen option was much more important when screens were smaller.

Getting rid of windows

Your screen often becomes cluttered with windows you no longer need. You already know how to turn them into icons to get most of the screen space back, but sometimes you just want to make the program go away.

If 57 different programs are running, even if most of them are snoozing behind their icons, it can put enough of a load on your computer to slow down the ones you want to use.

Most programs have a natural way to exit. In terminal windows, you log out from the shell by typing **exit** or **logout** in the terminal window. Real windows-oriented programs usually have menus of their own with a Quit or Exit option that cleans up and makes the program stop. Because some programs just won't die, however, you have to take drastic measures.

In Motif, click the little bar in the box at the left end of the title bar; a menu of window operations pops up, as shown in Figure 4-6. The Restore, Move, Size, Minimize, and Maximize choices are equivalent to the border-clicking techniques we discussed in the preceding section. (Minimize is Motif-ese for *iconify*.) The two remaining options can be useful, though. The Lower option pushes the window behind all the rest so that it doesn't obscure any other windows. That option is useful when you want to work on something else for a while. Close closes the window and usually also ends the program that started it. This option can be handy for programs that get stuck or don't have any normal way to exit.

Figure 4-6:
The Motif
window
menu.

Motif offers a set of keyboard equivalents for mouse-haters. To display the window menu, press Shift+Esc or Alt+spacebar. Then either press the cursor keys and Enter to choose one of the entries, or press the underlined letter in the entry you want. To move or resize windows, you press the cursor keys to move or resize the window and then press Enter when you finish.

You can also press the Alt+key equivalents on the menu, such as Alt+F9 for to minimize a window. If your keyboard has two Alt keys (as most PC keyboards do), you may find that the two Alt keys work differently. Individual programs recognize the left Alt key on our system, and the Motif window manager recognizes the right Alt key.

Motif uses confusing and inconsistent names in the window-operations menu. Close destroys the window and the program, and Minimize turns the window into an icon.

Ta-ta for now

The last little detail is how to tell X Windows that you're finished with it. The way you do that (we're getting tired of saying this) varies from one system to another. You have to stop the start-up program, which is usually a terminal window named `login` or the window manager itself. If you see a window named `login`, go to the login window and type **exit** or **logout** to exit that shell.

If your start-up program is the window manager, you must persuade the window manager to exit. You can't kill it the way you kill other programs, because the window manager doesn't have a particular window. In Motif, you move the cursor outside any window, press the first mouse button, and select the Quit item from the menu that pops up. Motif pops up another box, incredulous that you claim that you want to leave a program as wonderful as itself, so you have to click OK to assure it that you are indeed such an ingrate.

TIP

How do I leave Motif, anyway?

This question is only slightly less complicated than the one about starting Motif. As usual, you are the victim of a blizzard of options. Here are some likely possibilities:

✔ **Log out by leaving the Motif window manager.** In this case, move the mouse cursor outside any windows, click and hold the right mouse button to display the Motif root menu, slide the cursor down to Quit, and release the button. Motif displays an incredulous little box asking whether you really want to leave mwm. Click OK.

✔ **Log out by closing the main** xterm **window.** The trick is to figure out which window is the main one. If one of them is labeled Login or Console, that's it. Switch to that window by moving the mouse to that window and clicking the left mouse button. Then type exit to the shell in that window.

When X and Motif exit, the screen usually *ker-flooies!* again when it goes back to dumb terminal mode. (If your system uses the X display manager, your system may immediately go back to the login screen, in which case you're finished.) If you end up back at a shell prompt in dumb terminal mode, you then have to exit from that as well by typing exit to that shell.

CDE: A Desktop for All Seasons

If you ever use a Macintosh or one of those *other* Windows computers, then you know what a *desktop* is. When you start up a computer with the Macintosh or Windows OS installed on it, slick-looking graphics and mouse-clickable icons and menus take over your entire computer screen, giving you a common workspace for all your programs and windows. That's the desktop.

The desktop gives you a slew of ways to keep track of your files and get your work done efficiently and painlessly. You can open multiple windows and switch between them with the click of a mouse button. You can do spiffy stuff such as dragging and dropping to share files and information among your programs. Graphical tools that come with the desktop give you views into the operating system, your files, and your network (if you're on one). Additional graphical tools let you do neat stuff, such as send and receive mail, manage print jobs, and change the way your desktop looks.

Although window managers (such as Motif) have been around for quite some time, real integrated desktops like the ones built into Windows and the Mac OS are just beginning to catch on in the UNIX world. Now you can choose from a whole crop of UNIX desktops. The first widely used UNIX desktop was the Common Desktop Environment, or CDE. CDE is the result of an unprecedented outbreak of cooperation among a number of UNIX vendors — including Hewlett-Packard, IBM, Novell, and SunSoft — and the Open Software Foundation (the same people who brought you Motif, remember?).

CDE desktops are not quite as simple, of course, as their Windows and Mac OS counterparts. The Mac and Windows desktops are developed and sold only by Apple and Microsoft, respectively. Each company that sells CDE along with UNIX, on the other hand, offers a slightly different version of CDE developed exclusively for its own version of UNIX. Unlike the Mac and Windows desktops, which are built in to the operating system and appear whenever you start up your computer (like it or not), CDE desktops are optional. You don't have to use CDE to use UNIX, and you (or, more likely, your system administrator) can decide whether to have CDE start up when you log in.

To enhance the confusion to acceptable UNIX-like levels, CDE is infinitely customizable by system administrators and UNIX hackers. You can make far-reaching changes to CDE by switching the CDE default window manager from DTWM to FVWM, for example. You can tell CDE to launch various programs automatically when you log in. You can change the way the keyboard behaves — and so on and so on, ad nauseum.

The good news is that the similarities among versions of CDE far outnumber the differences; after all, it's supposed to be a *common* desktop environment. In practice, and discounting any bizarre modifications that an overzealous UNIX system administrator may have made, using one version of CDE is very much like using another.

The following sections give you some idea of how to use the Common Desktop Environment. In the interest of keeping things as simple as possible, we don't worry about which version of CDE you're using, and we figure that you'll make whatever adjustments are necessary to account for the idiosyncrasies of your configuration.

Desktop, here we come!

Bringing up the desktop is much like starting Motif, a subject we cover in the sidebar "How do I start Motif, anyway?" earlier in this chapter. If you're lucky, your system administrator has set up your computer so that the CDE comes up when you turn on your computer or log in. If not, you have to refer to your local UNIX guru or system documentation to find out which command to run in which directory.

No matter what the start-up details are, the desktop heralds its imminent appearance by making your computer screen flicker like Dr. Frankenstein's laboratory on a stormy night and then replacing whatever your screen was displaying before with a drab gray background, on top of which appear various tools, toolbars, icons, and programs, depending on how your desktop is configured. You usually see a version of the FrontPanel across the bottom of your computer screen.

Front and center

The FrontPanel is similar to the control center for the desktop. Actually, it's more like the dashboard of a fancy car, which puts all the car's doohickeys and thingums within easy reach of the driver. As with all the elements of the desktop, you can customize the FrontPanel. Figure 4-7 shows a typical set of FrontPanel icons, buttons, and other clickable thingies.

Figure 4-7:
The
FrontPanel
puts the
desktop
front and
center.

At the center of the FrontPanel are four buttons, named One, Two, Three, and Four. These buttons let you manage as many as four *workspaces.* The idea is that the desktop is in reality four times as large as your computer screen; in other words, your computer screen shows only one-quarter of your desktop at a time. Each quarter is a workspace. You can have different icons, program windows, and whatnot set up in each workspace, all of which stay put and reappear just as you left them every time you return to the workspace. For example, you may dedicate one workspace to managing your UNIX environment, one workspace to dealing with all your communications (e-mail, FTP, networking), one workspace to your favorite games, and one workspace to doing work (such as writing the definitive guide to peas and how to eat them). Rename the workspace buttons Looks, Comms, Games, and Peas so that you can remember which workspace is which, and then switch among your workspaces by clicking the buttons. (We recommend switching from Games to Peas whenever your boss comes around the corner.)

Tools you can use

The icons to the left and right of the workspace buttons give you mouse-click access to a typical set of CDE tools. Reading from left to right in Figure 4-8, you see icons for Clock, Group Calendar Manager, File Manager, Terminal Emulator, Mail Tool, Print Manager, Style Manager, Applications Manager, Help Viewer, and Trash.

You can open each tool or tool set by double-clicking its icon in the FrontPanel. If the icon has a little upward-pointing triangle above it, you can click the triangle to pop up a menu of choices (the menu slides out from behind the FrontPanel like a window shade being drawn upward). Drag to the choice you want, and then release the mouse button to select it. You can close a pop-up (or slide-up) menu by clicking the square in the upper-left corner of the menu and choosing Close or by clicking the triangle again (it turned into a downward-pointing triangle while you weren't looking). The menu demurely slides down behind the FrontPanel until it disappears. Figure 4-8 shows the menu that appears when you click the triangle above the Applications Manager icon.

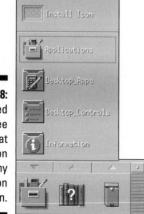

Figure 4-8:
Just popped
in to see
what
condition
my
condition
was in.

All the standard UNIX utilities and programs described in Part III of this book (such as `find`, `diff`, `ed`, `vi`, and `emacs`) get zoomy new graphical versions in the CDE, many of which are easier to use than their command-line equivalents (easier, that is, if you're used to using a mouse to do your computing). In fact, CDE desktops come with so many tools and utilities that an entire book is needed just to describe them all.

Filing without tears

The File Manager looks like the window shown in Figure 4-9, which appears when you double-click the File Manager icon on the FrontPanel.

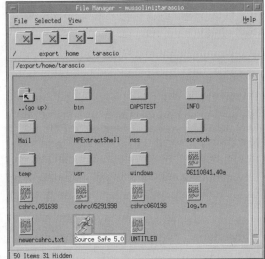

Figure 4-9:
Show
me some
files, man!

The CDE File Manager is much like the Mac OS Finder or Windows Explorer. You can use the CDE File Manager to browse through your files, launch programs, and, as its name implies, manage your files (open, copy, move, or delete them or have them over for dinner). The File Manager shows some kind of icon for each directory and file on your computer. Directory icons look like file folders; file icons look different depending on which type of file it is. Figure 4-9 shows icons for seven text files, which look like pieces of paper with writing on them (clever, no?). The icon with the runner on it launches a program (in this case, a program named Source Safe 5.0).

The "..(go up)" icon lets you travel up the directory tree toward the root directory. The series of folder icons at the top of the window shows your current location (and hence the directory that contains all the stuff you now see in the File Manager) relative to the root directory. You can jump to any directory in the branch of the tree you're on by clicking one of these folders. Pictograms (little pictures) on the folders tell you something about the directory's permissions; for example, a folder showing a pencil with a line through it means that you don't have write permission in that directory.

Not just another pretty face

We don't want to give the impression that the CDE brings only cosmetic enhancements to your UNIX system. The CDE does some heavy lifting, too. Among other features too numerous to mention, the CDE gives you easy and consistent network access, a standard way of printing from any application, session management, advanced collaboration tools such as e-mail clients and group scheduling utilities, GUI toolkits, and all kinds of full-fledged application development tools.

You can move files and directories from one location to another by dragging and dropping their icons. Being able to drag and drop in the File Manager means that you can do all kinds of cool and unexpected things. For example, you can drag a text file to the icon for the emacs editor to automatically launch emacs and open the text file you dragged. You can add icons to the FrontPanel by dragging them from the File Manager and dropping them on the FrontPanel's icon areas.

What's up, doc?

One of the most convenient, friendly, and ultimately un-UNIX-like features of the CDE is its Help Viewer. The Viewer, as shown in Figure 4-10, is a graphical help- and documentation-viewing program with full-fledged searching and printing capabilities. You can view all the man pages (online documentation, described in detail in Chapter 26) for your version of UNIX in a pleasant, readable format (a giant leap for UNIX-kind, as you know if you ever tried to make extensive use of traditional UNIX man pages) and journey hither and yon by means of an expandable and collapsible outline. The Viewer can even handle context-sensitive help (in other words, make a game attempt to guess exactly what information you need at any given moment so that you don't have to go hunting for it).

Having it your way

Customize, customize, customize! One of the joys of using the CDE is your ability to change the way your desktop looks and behaves by using the Style Manager (as shown in Figure 4-11). Use up all that pesky extra time by changing the colors of various window elements and text; choosing pretty backdrops to replace your desktop's monotonous gray background; adding pizzazz and generally making your desktop unusable by choosing decorative fonts, reconfiguring your keyboard, changing what the various buttons on your mouse do; and making a thousand other cunning modifications to your computing environment. Go ahead — indulge yourself. You haven't lived until you spend an entire afternoon designing a desktop scheme that expresses your innermost desires (especially when you should be doing something else).

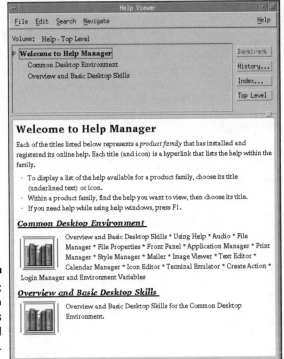

Figure 4-10:
The Help
Viewer tells
you all
about itself.

Figure 4-11:
The Style
Manager:
Where the
fashionable
desktop
goes for a
thorough
makeover.

Talkin' trash

The Trash tool is a great boon to UNIX users susceptible to blowing away important files with unforgiving UNIX commands such as rm. When you issue the rm command or one of its brethren, the files you delete are gone, plain and simple. When you're using the File Manager on the desktop, on the other hand, files you delete get put in a virtual trash barrel, where they hang around until you tell UNIX to get rid of them. If you delete a file by mistake, you can bring the file back to life by following these steps:

1. **Double-click the Trash tool icon.**

2. **Root around in the trash until you find the file.**

3. **Drag the file from the trash and drop it back into an appropriate location in the File Manager.**

Remember to empty the trash every now and again, or else you eventually run out of disk space.

Desktop, there we go!

The easiest way to get yourself out of the desktop is to click the Exit thingum near the workspace buttons on the FrontPanel, which drops you unceremoniously into good old traditional UNIX character mode. You can also lock the desktop (so that only someone who knows your username and password can get to it) by clicking the padlock icon in the center of the FrontPanel.

What's the "K" Stand For?

You could ask about the interface. You could ask about the history of the project. But the chances are, the first thing you want to know about the K Desktop Environment is what the K stands for. We can't tell you. Some Internet wags claim that, early in 1996, the project was going to be called the "Kool Desktop Environment," but being sure is impossible. Now, it doesn't stand for anything; it's just the letter K.

KDE is a full desktop environment, much like CDE — the similarity in names is probably not a coincidence — and provides a bewildering variety of choices and options. You can move the window widgets around. You can change what they look like. In the UNIX world, finding that your computer looks like — and can be used like — someone else's is very embarrassing. It's like showing up to a party in the same dress as someone else. KDE provides a good layer of insulation; even if you and your friend both use KDE, your computers won't look a bit alike.

If your system doesn't use a graphical login program, or start KDE automatically, the command you're looking for to start it is `startkde`. Not sure that's the right command? Look at Figure 4-12, which is one sample of what KDE might look like.

You can, of course, change what it looks like, using themes.

Themes

KDE has a broad variety of themes. Many of them are intended to look a great deal like other systems you might be familiar with — but be careful! The buttons won't always do what you expect them to do, and the mouse buttons and shortcut keys may be different. We recommend you pick a style that's different enough that you won't get tricked. Pick something bold, one that makes a statement about you. The statement might be "I set this up one afternoon, and forgot how to change it again, please won't somebody help me." That's okay. It's still a statement.

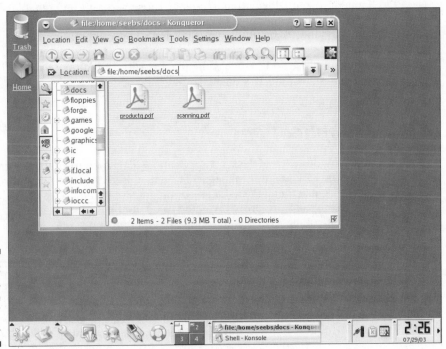

Figure 4-12:
KDE,
using the
"Keramic"
theme.

Shut up already!

Some installations of KDE come preconfigured to make a joyous noise unto the user. You get clicks, whistles, bongs, and whooshing effects. Thrilling for 30 seconds, neat for a minute, maddening after half an hour. Follow these steps to turn the sounds off.

1. **Start up** kcontrol.

2. **Open the Sound and Multimedia panel.**

3. **Select the System Notifications heading.**

4. **In the pop-up menu to the right, select the KDE Window Manager.**

5. **Press the More Options button.**

6. **Find the Quick Controls panel.**

7. **Select Sounds from the pop-up menu next to the Turn Off All button.**

8. **Click the Turn Off All button.**

Blissful silence.

Don't like it? That's what the Turn On All button is for. If cacophony is your thing, go wild.

If you find yourself wanting to change those settings, one reliable way to get to the settings program is to run the kcontrol program. You can run a command line in KDE by holding down the Alt key and pressing the F2 key. (Then let go of the Alt key. It's probably getting tired.) Type the command and press Enter. You'll spend the most time playing with the Appearance & Themes section at first. Try not to overdo it.

K applications

KDE provides a lot of desktop applications designed to share the look and feel of the KDE window manager. Their names generally start with a *K*, to help you recognize them. We list a few of the most common ones in Table 4-1. These programs are probably going to be on the toolbar at the bottom of the screen, if you haven't gotten around to customizing it yet.

Table 4-1	K Applications
Application	*What It Does*
Konqueror	File management and Web browsing — it's both a floor wax and a dessert topping!
KMail	Standard e-mail program

Application	What It Does
KOffice	An office suite — what did you expect?
KWrite	Word processor — part of KOffice
KSpread	Spreadsheet — part of KOffice
KBear	Graphical FTP client
KBiff	E-mail notifier

The best part about these applications — and you hear this a lot about software for X — is that they're free. They aren't 100 percent compatible with some of the big-name office software you might see, but they're pretty good, and you can't beat the price. Konqueror is a combination file manager and Web browser, which works a little like a program called Explorer you might see elsewhere.

Of course, you don't have to use these programs. You can use whatever you want under KDE. These programs are just the ones that fit in the best with the rest of KDE, using the same kinds of buttons and other window controls. Give them a try, though. A lot of people find that these programs do their jobs just fine. Konqueror is particularly impressive; a remarkably good Web browser, which is why Apple used it as the basis for its new Safari browser for the Macintosh. See Chapter 17 for details about Kmail, the KDE e-mail program.

Don't want to be productive? KDE comes with a lot of games. Every distribution has a different set of games, but there are enough of them to keep you entertained for a long time. If you try KPatience, don't forget to look in the Game Type submenu of the Settings menu — it plays more than one game, and you may like the others better.

Why biff?

According to the Jargon File, *biff* is a verb:

"To notify someone of incoming mail. From the BSD utility biff(1), which was in turn named after a friendly dog that used to chase frisbees in the halls at UCB while 4.2BSD was in development. There was a legend that it had a habit of barking whenever the mailman came, but the author of biff says this is not true."

We don't care whether Biff actually barked at the mailman; programs that alert you to incoming mail are still called biff.

Getting around

Getting around in KDE is pretty straightforward, except that the potential to change themes all the time makes giving much advice hard. If a button has an X, it probably closes a window. You can generally move windows by dragging the title bar, and resize them by dragging their corners. A right-click generally gives you a menu. Right-clicking the desktop itself gives you a top-level menu. Right-clicking a title bar gives you a selection of window options.

The file manager (which is actually our old friend Konqueror) is almost entirely predictable. It does have one little surprise for you, though. By default, it activates everything with a single click! So, if you're used to double-clicking, you may well launch things twice. This makes more sense on Web pages than for file management. If you want to select a file (without opening it), you must use Control-click or Shift-click. Shift-clicking two files also selects all the files between them; Control-clicking multiple files just selects the files you clicked.

KDE, like CDE, offers multiple workspaces. This is a good feature, and surprisingly hard to live without once you get used to it. However, in KDE, they're called *desktops*. It's still a great feature, and we really recommend you play around with it a bit. Having one desktop with nothing on it but a maximized browser window can be awfully convenient.

If you want to know more, try the online help. Right-click the desktop, and look at the Help submenu. Lots and lots of goodies are in here! KDE is way too large for us to cover it completely here, so we entrust you to the capable writers who have done the KDE documentation.

Say goodnight, Gracie!

You ran KDE, but now you're done? Look for the Logout option on the main KDE menu. You can also lock the screen, which means that no one else can do anything but watch the screen saver unless someone guesses your password. If you're going to be gone for a while, logging out is more polite. KDE may also offer you the chance to turn your computer off entirely when you ask to log out. If you're on some kind of shared system, don't do that, just log out.

A moving target

The descriptions of KDE and GNOME in this book are based mostly on KDE version 3.1 and GNOME version 2.2. Unlike CDE, KDE and GNOME are being actively developed, changed, updated, and revised. You might get a few surprises using newer or older versions, or even just versions that are configured differently by whoever compiled them. Any major release of these environments should work fine, though, so don't worry too much.

You Mean the Little Guys with the Hats?

Another desktop environment you might see is GNOME. It's supposed to be pronounced with a hard "g" — "guh-NOME." GNOME is started by running a program called `gnome-session`. GNOME comes with a large variety of themes and styles. In fact, you can configure GNOME to look enough like KDE to really annoy people who are expecting it to behave exactly the same, too.

GNOME is yet another complete desktop environment — icons, little pointy-clicky things, menus, the whole nine yards. If your system comes with GNOME, but not with CDE, that's fine. GNOME does all the same kinds of things. It's just a matter of personal preference, or what happens to be installed.

In Figure 4-13, you see a reasonably typical GNOME desktop. The bar at the bottom of the screen holds buttons for common activities, some of which bring up menus. The button that looks like a little computer monitor with a >_ in it opens a terminal window, which is handy if you want to take a break from the stressful world of mice and graphics and just type a little. Click the foot icon at the lower-left to open the main menu. This menu is where you find a lot of cool toys, such as the GNOME Control Center.

Themes

Depending on your configuration, GNOME can look confusingly similar to certain other desktop environments. It won't be the same, but it may be comforting, or it may be confusing. You can customize it a great deal. How? Start the GNOME Control Center application, and double-click the Theme icon. Play around. The most fun is to be had playing around with the Details button, which lets you mix and match parts of different themes. You can also, of course, come up with something totally unlike any other environment, and that may be the most fun you can have.

If you're from a Mac environment, and you miss the menu bar at the top of the screen, you can have it back, sort of. If you right-click the bar at the bottom of the screen, click the New Panel item on the pop-up menu and choose the Menu Panel item. It's not the same as the Mac's menu bar — for instance, programs won't put their menus up there, which makes it sort of silly. But it looks a bit similar, and you can put common menus up there. At least it has rounded corners!

Telling lawn gnomes from GNOME

A little unsure of how to tell a lawn gnome from the GNOME desktop environment? Here's a quick checklist.

Lawn gnome	The GNOME desktop environment
Wears pointy red hat	Runs on Red Hat

Traditional garb	Consistent look and feel
Has a beard	Has an e-mail client
Made of ceramic	Written in C++
Hand-painted	Custom themes
Silent 'G'	Hard 'G'

GNOME applications

Like KDE, GNOME provides a handful of applications that share its look and feel settings. The names aren't as standardized as the KDE ones — you can't just tack a K on the front of a word and expect it to do something — but it sounds cooler that way. Table 4-2 lists some of the more common GNOME applications.

Table 4-2	Common GNOME Applications
Application	*What It Does*
Evolution	E-mail client
Nautilus	File manager
Galeon	Web browser

GNOME, like KDE, comes with a broad selection of games to play. Tired of Solitaire? There are a dozen more games where that came from. The exact set of games installed varies from one system to another, but you can count on finding something more fun than working.

Evolution

Okay, we lied. Calling Evolution an e-mail client is like calling an aircraft carrier a biggish boat. Evolution does everything: contact management, scheduling, synchronizing with a Palm Pilot, you name it. But it also does e-mail. It's a lot like Outlook Express, only it won't send e-mail to your entire address book saying you love them. See Chapter 17 for details about the e-mail parts of Evolution.

Getting around

GNOME offers multiple workspaces, which are all the rage in UNIX window managers, and has the same basic approach to interfaces that KDE does. Right-clicking is almost always a good bet if you want options. For instance, if you want to move a window from one workspace to another, just right-click the title bar, and select one of the Move options.

If you're looking for help, try pressing F1 whenever you're lost or confused. Most of the time, GNOME brings up some online help for you.

A few buttons are generally on the panel at the bottom of the screen, next to the GNOME menu. If you right-click any of the buttons, you can remove or change it. If you right-click an empty part of the bar, you can add a new button, or one of the mini-apps designed to run there, such as a clock. Right-click the bar, select the Add to Panel option from the pop-up menu, and look at all the options you get. Note that it matters where you click. A new item is placed near where you clicked; it won't be shoved over by the other items on the panel.

Sooner or later, you'll want to quit. When that time comes, just select the Log Out option from the main GNOME menu. Now you can mutter "I can quit any time I want" under your breath, and make people nervous.

Terminal Happenings

Even though X Windows enables you to run all the coolest, awesomest, newest, most graphicalest programs, guess which program people use the most? It's called `xterm`, and all it does is act like the kind of VT100 dumb terminal that window systems are supposed to save us from. Such are the ways of progress.

The `xterm` program is one of the oldest programs that runs under X, and it has the greasy fingerprints of a dozen generations of programmers. As the README file in its source code notes, "This is undoubtedly the most ugly program in the distribution." Although `xterm` has more than 70 exciting options on its command line alone, we don't tell you about them.

Click, click

One place where `xterm` acts a little better than the dumb terminal it purports to emulate is in mouse handling. You can select text with the mouse and then paste the selected text into either the same or a different `xterm` window.

To select some text, move the mouse to the beginning of the text, press down the first (left) mouse button, and move the mouse to the end of the text. As you move the mouse, the selected text changes color. When you select it all, let go of the mouse button. Normally, `xterm` selects text character-by-character; if you double-click rather than just press the mouse button, however, it selects by word, and if you triple-click, it selects by line. Users who don't believe in walking and chewing gum at the same time have an alternative way to select text: Move to the beginning of the selection, click the left button, and then move to the end of the selection and click the right button.

Either way, after you select the text, move the mouse to the window where you want to paste it and click the middle button. If, after you select the text, a program erases the window, you can't see the selection anymore, although it's still there and you can still paste it.

Because most other programs that have text type-in areas use the same mouse conventions xterm does, you can select text from an xterm and paste it into other programs and vice versa.

Coming in for a save

The other thing that makes xterm occasionally useful is that you can save in a *log file* a transcript of what goes on in the window. To turn on logging, move the cursor into the xterm window, hold down the Ctrl key with your nonmouse hand, and then press and hold down the left mouse button to get a little menu like the one shown in Figure 4-14. Next, move the mouse down to Log to File, and let go of the mouse button. (This sequence isn't quite as hard as it sounds, fortunately.) A bunch of other options are on that menu, none of which we recommend other than the self-explanatory Redraw Window and Quit.

Main Options
Secure Keyboard
Allow SendEvents
Log to File
Redraw Window
Send STOP Signal
Send CONT Signal
Send INT Signal
Send HUP Signal
Send TERM Signal
Send KILL Signal
Quit

Figure 4-14: A few xterm menu options.

After that, everything you type in that window — including all the backspaces and other correction characters to remind you of what a rotten typist you are and everything UNIX types back — is written to a file. Which file? The answer varies, although it's usually a file in your home directory called XtermLog.12345, where the last five digits are made up to be unique. Type **ls Xterm***, and you'll probably find it. When you finish, to turn off the log, do the same Ctrl-and-mouse dance and choose Log to File again (it's checked to remind you that logging is turned on).

Logging is an optional feature of xterm, and some systems have logging turned off permanently. In that case, if you try to turn on logging, the terminal just beeps.

One last stupid xterm trick

If the text in your xterm window is insufficiently or excessively legible, you can make the type larger or smaller. Hold down the Ctrl key and press the right mouse button to display the xterm VT Fonts menu, from which you can select font sizes ranging from Unreadable to Huge. We recommend the Unreadable font, which scrunches your typical 80x40 character text window to a one-inch square that is indeed unreadable. When you tire of that option, choose the Default font to return things to normal.

Chapter 5

Files for Fun and Profit

. . . .

. . . .

A *file* is a bunch of information stored together, such as a letter to your mom or a database of customer invoices. Every file has a name. You end up with tons of them.

This chapter explains how to work with files, including getting rid of the ones you no longer want.

As a reminder, you must log in (as described in Chapter 1) before you can do any of the nifty things we talk about in this chapter. When you see the UNIX prompt (% or $), you're ready to rock and roll.

What Files Do You Have?

To see a list of your files (actually, a list of the files in the working directory, which Chapter 6 covers), type **ls** and press Enter. (This is positively the last time we nag you to press Enter.)

This command stands for **list**, but could the lazy typists who wrote UNIX have used the other two letters? No-o-o-o. This command lists all the files in your working directory. (Chapter 6 discusses directories and how to make lots of them.) The ls command just shows the names of the files in alphabetical order, like this:

```
bin/     budget-02   budget-03   budget-04   daveg draft
jordan   Mail/       meg         news.junk   zac
```

In some Linux systems, if the directory contains subdirectories, the subdirectory names appear in a different color (if your screen handles colors), which is very handy. In BSD UNIX, subdirectory names also have a slash after them. (Chapter 6 talks about subdirectories, if you're wondering what we are talking about.)

Let's see the nitty-gritty details

For more information about your files, use the -l option (*long form listing*):

```
ls -l
```

That's a small letter *l*, by the way, not a number *one*. This option tells ls to display tons of information about your files. Each line looks like this:

```
-rw-r--r--   1 john1     users      250 Apr  6 09:57 junk3
```

Later in this chapter, in the section "Who can do what?" we explain all the information in this listing. For now, just notice that the right-hand part of the line shows the size of the file (250 characters, in this example), the date and time the file was last modified, and the filename.

For shell-less Web site owners

A lot of people use UNIX only because they happen to have a Web site that's physically located on a UNIX machine. If you're one of these reluctant UNIX just-barely-users, you probably don't have access to a UNIX shell, but instead only use an FTP program to move files to and from your Web server (see Chapters 19 and 20).

Perhaps surprisingly, most of what's in this chapter still applies to you. All the same rules about filenames and permissions still apply, and

most FTP programs have an ls command that works about the same as the shell version.

When you're choosing names for your files, remember that upper- and lowercase are different, so you probably should make them all lowercase. Web servers use the filename to determine the type of material in a file, so HTML Web pages end with .html, GIF icons with .gif, JPEG pictures with .jpeg, and so forth. (Unlike some other systems, UNIX systems do not encourage you to abbreviate all the file types to three letters if the name is longer.)

To switch or not to switch?

Lots of UNIX commands have *options*. (They are also called *switches* because you switch the options on and off by typing or not typing them when you type the command. True geeks call them *flags*.) Options make commands both more versatile and more confusing. Probably the most widely used option is the -1 option for the 1s command, which tells 1s to display lots of information about each file. When you type a command with one or more options, keep this list of rules handy:

✔ Leave a space after the command name (the command 1s, for example) and before the option (the -1 part).

✔ Type a hyphen as the first character of the option (**-l**, for example).

✔ Type a space after the option if you want to type more information on the command line after the option.

✔ If you want to include more than one option, type another space, another hyphen, and the next option. You can usually string multiple options together after one hyphen; for example, -a1 means that you want option a and option 1.

Making files come out of hiding

You may have more files in your directory than you think. UNIX enables you to make things called *hidden files,* which are just like regular files except that they don't appear in normal 1s listings. Making a hidden file is easy — just start its filename with a period.

You can see your hidden files by typing

```
1s -a
```

To see all the information about your hidden files, type

```
1s -al
```

This command combines the -a and -1 options together so that you see the long version of the complete listing of files. You can get the same thing by typing

```
1s -a -1
```

but that requires typing an extra character and an extra space, an anathema to lazy UNIX typists.

Making a long listing stop and start when you're ready

If you have a large number of files, the 1s listing may fly right off the top of your screen. If you have this problem, type this line:

    1s | more

The vertical bar is called a *pipe* (we talk more about the pipe in Chapter 7). The | more option

after the basic 1s command tells UNIX to stop listing information to the screen just before the first file disappears from view. Press the space-bar to see the next screen of filenames.

Roger, 1 Copy

You can make an exact duplicate of a file. To do it, you must know the name of the file you want to copy, and you must create a new name to give to the copy. If a file contains your January budget (called budget.jan, for example) and you want to make a copy of it to use for the February budget (to be called budget.feb, for example), type this line:

    cp budget.jan budget.feb

The lazy typists strike again. Be sure to leave spaces after the cp command and between the existing and new filenames. This command doesn't change the existing file (budget.jan); it just creates a new file with a new name, and with the same contents.

A good way to lose some work

What if a file named budget.feb *already* exists? Tough cookies! UNIX blows it away and replaces it with a copy of budget.jan. It truly is an excellent idea to use the 1s command first to make sure that you don't already have a file with the new name you have chosen.

In most versions of UNIX, however, you can use the -i option to ask cp to inform you whether a file with the new name already exists. If it does, the -i option asks you whether to proceed. Type **cp -i** rather than just **cp** to use this nifty little feature.

If all goes well and cp works correctly, it doesn't show you any message. Blessed silence on the part of UNIX usually means that all is well. You should use the ls command to check that the new file really does exist, just in case.

What's in a name?

When you create a file, you give it a name. UNIX has rules about what makes a good filename:

- **Filenames can be pretty long; they're not limited to eight characters and a three-character extension.** In older versions of UNIX, the limit is 14 characters for a filename; newer versions have a huge limit — in the hundreds of characters — so you can call a file `Some_notes_I_plan_to_get_around_to_typing_up_eventually_if_I_live_that_long`.

- **Don't use weird characters that mean something special to UNIX or some shell you may encounter.** Stay away from these characters when you name files:

```
<  >  '  "  *
{  }  ^  !  \
[  ]  #  |  &
(  )  $  ?  ~
```

Stick mainly to letters and numbers.

- **Don't put spaces in a filename.** Although most programs let you put them in, spaces cause nothing but trouble because other programs simply cannot believe that a filename may contain a space, and because in shell commands, spaces separate filenames. Don't borrow trouble. Most UNIX people use periods to string together words to make filenames, such as `budget.jan.98` or `pumpkin.soup`. Underscores work, too.

- **UNIX considers uppercase and lowercase letters to be completely different.** `Budget`, `budget`, `BUDGET`, and `BuDgEt` are all different filenames.

Nuking Files Back to the Stone Age

You can also get rid of files by using the command the lazy typists call rm. To erase (delete, remove — it's all the same thing) a file, type

```
rm budget.feb
```

If all goes well, UNIX reports nothing, and you see another prompt. Use `ls` to see whether the `rm` command worked and the file is gone.

Watch out! Under most circumstances, you have *no way* to get a file back after you delete it.

To be safe, you can use the `-i` option to ask `rm` to ask you to confirm deletion of the file. This is a particularly good idea if you use wildcards to delete a group of files all at one time (see Chapter 7 for more info about wildcards). For example, if you type

```
rm -i last-years-budget
```

UNIX asks:

```
rm: remove `last-years-budget'
```

Press the y key to delete the file or the n key to leave it alone.

Big, big trouble

If you delete something really, really important and you will be called on to perform ritual seppuku if you can't get it back, don't give up hope. Your local UNIX guru should make things called *backups* on some regular basis. Backups contain copies of some or all of the files on the UNIX system. Your files may be among those on the backup. Go to the guru on bended knee and ask whether the file can be restored. If the file wasn't backed up recently, you may get an older version of it, but hey — it's better than the alternative.

Even before you get yourself into this kind of pickle, you may want to ask your UNIX expert to confirm that regular backups are made. Make sure that your important files are included in the backups. If no one is making regular backups, panic! This is not a safe situation. You had better talk to your system administrator about getting a backup system.

Good housekeeping

You should get rid of files you no longer use, for several reasons:

- Having all kinds of files lying around becomes confusing, and remembering which ones are important is difficult.

- Useless files take up disk space. Whoever is in charge of your UNIX system probably will bother you regularly to "take out the garbage," that is, to get rid of unnecessary files and free up some disk space.

On the other hand, making extra copies of files can be a good idea. If you have been working on a report for three weeks, making an extra copy every day or so isn't a bad idea. That way, if you make some revisions that, in hindsight, are stupid, you can always go back to a previous revision.

What's in a Name (Reprise)

Having given a file a name, you may want to change it later. Maybe you spelled it wrong in the first place. In any case, you can rename a file by using the `mv` (lazy typist-ese for *move*) command.

Suppose that you made a file called `bugdet.march`. Oops, dratted fingers. . . . Type the following line to correct the error in the filename:

```
mv bugdet.march budget.march
```

After `mv`, you type the current name of the file and then the name you want to change it to. Note that it can be harder to retype the same typo than to type the name correctly!

Because you can't have two files with the same name in the same directory, if a file already has the name you want to use, `mv` thoughtfully blows away the existing file (probably not what you want to do). You can use `mv -i` (like `cp -i`) to prevent inadvertent file clobbering.

Want to hide a file so that it doesn't appear in your directory listing? Use a period (.) as the first letter of the filename. To see all your files, including hidden files, type

```
ls -al
```

Looking at the Guts of a File

Although we have been slicing and dicing files for a while now, you still haven't seen what's inside one. Two basic types of files exist:

- ✔ Files that contain text that UNIX can display nicely on-screen
- ✔ Files that contain special codes that look like monkeys have been at the keyboard when you display the files on-screen

The first type of files are called *text files*. The second type is composed of spreadsheet files, database files, program files, and just about everything else. Text editors make text files, as do a few other programs.

To display a text file, type this line:

```
cat eggplant.recipe
```

If you want to see the guts of a file that isn't named *eggplant.recipe*, substitute your file's name. The `cat` stands for *cat*alog, or maybe *cat*enate — who knows? We're surprised that the lazy typists didn't call it something like q. If you try to use `cat` with a file that doesn't contain text, your screen looks like a truck ran over it — but you won't hurt anything. Sometimes the garbage in the file can put your terminal in a strange mode in which characters you type don't appear or appear as strange Greek squiggles. See Chapter 22 to learn how to "un-strange" your terminal.

If the file is long, the listing goes whizzing by. (You find out how to look at the file one screen at a time in Chapter 7.) To see just the first few lines of the file, you can type this line:

```
head eggplant.recipe
```

Most versions of the `head` command display the first ten lines.

You can ask UNIX to guess at what's in a file, by using the `file` command. If you type

```
file filename
```

(replacing *filename* with the name of the file you're wondering about), UNIX takes a guess at what's in the file, by looking at it. It says something like this:

```
letter.to.jordan:    ascii text
```

or this

```
unix4d:    directory
```

Is This a Printout I See Before Me?

If a file looks okay on-screen when you use the `cat` command, try printing the file. If you use UNIX System V, type this line to print your famous eggplant dish:

```
lp eggplant.recipe
```

If you use BSD UNIX or Linux, type

```
lpr eggplant.recipe
```

Assuming that you have a printer that's hooked up, turned on, has paper, and that your username is set up to use it, the `eggplant.recipe` file prints. If it doesn't, see Chapter 9 to straighten things out. If your computer is blessed with a network, the printed copy may come out down the hall or on another floor. In one inexplicable case, when users in New York printed any file, the copies ended up on a printer somewhere in Japan. If your printer isn't attached directly to your computer, you probably have to ask for advice about where to pick up the printout. If you can print files on more than one printer, you use the `-d` or `-P` option with the printer name to tell UNIX which printer you want to use, as described in see Chapter 9.

Who Goes There?

Unlike some operating systems we could name (such as . . . oh, Microsoft Windows, f'rinstance), UNIX was designed from the beginning to be used by more than one person. Like all multi-user systems, UNIX keeps track of who owns what file and who can do what with each file. *Permissions* attached to each file and directory determine who can use them.

Permissions come in three types:

- ✔ **Read permission:** Enables you to look at a file or directory. You can use `cat` or a text editor to see what's in a file that has read permission. You also can copy this type of a file. Read permission for a directory enables you to list the directory's contents.

- ✔ **Write permission:** Enables you to make changes to a file. Even if you can write (change) a file, you can't necessarily delete it or rename it; for those actions, you must be able to write in the directory in which the file resides. If you have write permission in a directory, you can create new files in the directory and delete files from it.

- ✔ **Execute permission:** Enables you to run the program contained in the file. The program can be a real program or a shell script. If the file doesn't contain a program, execute permission doesn't do you much good and can provoke the shell to complain bitterly as it tries (from its rather dim point of view) to make sense of your file. For a directory, execute permission enables you to open files in the directory and use `cd` to get to the directory to make it your working directory.

Rock groups, pop groups, and UNIX groups

Every UNIX user is a member of a group. When the system administrator created your username, she assigned you to a group. To see which group you're in, type

```
id
```

You see something like this:

```
uid=113(margy) gid=102(guest) groups=102(guest),101(book),
            103(cheese)
```

Groups usually indicate the kind of work you do. UNIX uses groups to give a bunch of people the same permissions to use a set of files. All the people who work on a particular project are usually in the same group so that they can look at and perhaps change each other's files.

If you are part of the accounting department, for example (it's a dirty job, but someone has to do it), you and the other accounting staff members may need read, write, and execute access to basically the same files. People in other departments should not have the same access to accounting programs and data. The system administrator probably made a group called something like acctg and put all you accounting boys and girls in it.

In Linux and BSD, you can be in several groups at a time, which is handy if you're working on several projects. To find out what groups you're in, type **groups**.

That's mine!

Every file and directory has an owner and a group owner. The *owner* is usually the person who made the file or directory, although the owner can sometimes change the ownership of the file to someone else. The *group owner* is usually the group to which the owner belongs, although the owner can change a file's group owner to another group.

If you use Linux or System V, you can change who owns a file with the chown command (described later in this chapter).

Who can do what?

To see who can do what to a file, use the ls command with the -l option. Type this line:

```
ls -l myfile
```

You see something like this:

```
-rw-r--r--   1 margy    staff    335 Jan 22 13:23 myfile
```

If you don't specify a filename (in this case, `myfile`), UNIX lists all the files in the directory, which is often more useful. For every file, this listing shows all the following information:

- ✔ **Whether it's a file, symbolic link, or directory.** The first character in the line is a hyphen (-) if it's a file, an *l* if it's a symbolic link, and a *d* if it's a directory.

- ✔ **Whether the owner can read, write, or execute it (as shown by the next three characters, 2 through 4, on the line).** The first character is an *r* if the owner has read permission or a hyphen (-) if not. The second character is a *w* if the owner has write permission or a hyphen (-) if not. The third character is an *x* (or sometimes an *s*) if the owner has execute permission or a hyphen (-) if not.

- ✔ **Whether the members of the group owner can read, write, or execute the file or directory (as indicated by the next three characters, 5 through 7).** An *r, w,* or *x* appears if that permission is granted; a hyphen (-) appears if that permission is not granted.

- ✔ **Whether everyone else can read, write, or execute the file or directory (as indicated by the next three characters, 8 through 10).** An *r, w,* or *x* appears if that permission is granted; a hyphen (-) appears if that permission is not granted.

- ✔ **The link count, that is, how many links (names) this file has.** For directories, this number is the number of subdirectories the directory contains plus 2 (don't ask).

- ✔ **The owner of the file or directory.**

- ✔ **The group to which the file or directory belongs (group owner).**

- ✔ **The size of the file in bytes (characters).**

- ✔ **The date and time the file was last modified.**

- ✔ **The filename** — at last!

Permissions by number

Figuring out which permissions a file has by looking at the collection of *r*s, *w*s, and *x*s in the file listing is not too difficult. Sometimes permissions are written another way, however: with numbers. Only UNIX programmers could have thought of this method. (It's an example of lazy typists at their finest.) Numbered permissions are sometimes called *absolute permissions* (perhaps because they are absolutely impossible to remember).

Why those numbers?

You may well ask why those particular numbers are assigned to permissions. They weren't assigned at random. For those of you who remember New Math from fourth grade, all this makes sense if you think in binary (base 2).

Think of every permission digit as a three digit binary number, like 010 (that's binary for 2). The first digit is 1 if you have read permission, or 0 if you don't. The second digit is 1 if you have write permission, or 0 if you don't. The third digit is 1 if you have read permission, or 0 if you don't.

So, the permission digit 6, which is 110 in binary, means that you can read and write, but not execute. If this subject still doesn't make sense, find a fourth-grader to work it out for you.

When permissions are expressed as a number, it's a three-digit number. The first digit is the owner's permissions, the second digit is the group's permissions, and the third digit is everyone else's permissions. Every digit is a number from 0 to 7. Table 5-1 lists what the digits mean.

Table 5-1	Absolute Permissions Decoded
Digit	**Permissions**
0	None
1	Execute only
2	Write only
3	Write and execute
4	Read only
5	Read and execute
6	Read and write
7	Read, write, and execute

If Mom says no, go ask Dad

If you own a file or directory, you can change its permissions. You use the chmod (for *change mode*) command to do it. You tell chmod the name of the file or directory to change and the new permissions you want the file to have for yourself (the owner), your group, and everyone else. You can either type the numerical absolute permissions (such as **440**) or use letters.

To use letters to type the new permissions, you use a cryptic collection of letters and symbols that consists of the following:

- ✔ **Whose permissions you are changing:** u for user (the file's owner), g for the group, o for other (everyone else), or a for all three.
- ✔ **If the permission should be on or off:** + (on, yes, OK) or - (off, no, don't let them).
- ✔ **The type of permission you're dealing with:** r for read, w for write, and x for execute.

Type the following line, for example, to allow everyone to read a file called announcements:

```
chmod a+r announcements
```

This line says that the user or owner, the group, and everyone else can read the file. To not let anyone except the user or owner change the file, type

```
chmod go-w announcements
```

You can also use numeric (absolute) permissions with chmod. To let the user or owner and associated group read or change the file, type

```
chmod 660 announcements
```

This line sets the owner permission to 6 (read and write), the group permission to 6 too, and everyone else's permission to 0 (can't do anything).

You can change the permissions for a directory in exactly the same way you do for a file. Keep in mind that read, write, and execute mean somewhat different things for a directory.

Finding a new owner

When someone gives you a file, he usually copies it to your home directory. As far as UNIX is concerned, the person who copied the file is still the file's owner. In Linux and System V, you can change the ownership of a file you own by using the chown command. (BSD users have to get the system manager's help to change a file's owner.)

You tell `chown` the new owner for the file and the filename or filenames whose ownership you are changing, as shown in this example:

```
chown john chapter6
```

This command changes the ownership of the file named `chapter6` to `john`. Keep in mind that only you can give away files you own; if you put a file in someone else's directory, it's polite to `chown` the file to that user.

Another way to change the owner of a file is to make a copy of the file. Suppose that Fred puts a file in your home directory, and he still owns it. You can't use `chown` to change the ownership because only the owner can do that (we have a chicken-before-the-egg problem here). You *can* get ownership of a file if you copy the file. When you copy a file, you own the new copy. Then delete the original.

File seeks new group; can sing, dance, and do tricks

If you own a file or directory, you can change the group that can access it. The `chgrp` command enables you to change the name of the group associated with the file, as shown in this example:

```
chgrp acctg billing.list
```

This command changes the group associated with the file `billing.list` to the group called `acctg`.

Chapter 6

Directories for Fun and Profit

. . . .

. . . .

*F*iles are great — they're where you store all your important information, as well as where UNIX itself and all your programs are stored. UNIX systems have, in fact, tens of thousands of files, even before you create a single one. Imagine typing your ls command and getting a list of 10,000 filenames. Not pretty (or fast).

To avoid this situation, UNIX has things called *directories,* which enable you to divide your files into groups. This chapter explains how to organize your UNIX files into directories and how to find things after you have done so.

Good News for Windows Users

We have good news about UNIX directories for you experienced Windows users who occasionally use commands in a DOS window. They work almost exactly the same as Windows directories do. Actually, it's the other way around: A guy named Mark added directories to DOS back in 1982 and ripped off . . . er, emulated the way UNIX did things — with a few confusing changes, of course.

Briefly, Windows users should know the following information about UNIX directories:

- All those backslashes (\ ) you learned to type in Windows turn into regular slashes (/) in UNIX. For some reason, Mark decided that DOS slashes should lean backward. We're sure that he had a very good reason, of course — maybe the / key on his keyboard was broken.

- The UNIX cd (change directory) command works (more or less) like the DOS window CD command; remember not to capitalize it in UNIX.

- The UNIX command for making a directory is mkdir rather than the DOS window MD command. To remove a directory in UNIX, you use the rmdir command rather than the DOS window RD command. Don't capitalize these commands, either.

- As always, UNIX believes that uppercase and lowercase letters have nothing to do with each other. Because the two types of letters are completely different, be sure to use the correct capitalization when you type directory names and filenames.

If you understand directories and paths intuitively from your vast experience with PCs, skip to the sidebar "Getting the big picture," later in this chapter.

What Is a Directory?

A *directory,* for the rest of you people, is a group of files or a work area. (Windows and Macintosh users may recognize it as a *folder.*) You give a directory a name, such as Budget or Letters or Games or Harold. You can put as many files in a directory as you want.

The good thing about directories (also sometimes called *subdirectories,* for no good reason) is that you can use them to keep together groups of related files. If you make a directory for all your budget files, those files are the only ones you see while you are working in that directory. Directories make concentrating on what you are doing easy so that you're not distracted by the zillions of other files on the hard drive.

You can make directories, move files into them, rename directories, and get rid of them. This chapter describes the commands that perform each of these stunts.

Divide and Conquer

Interestingly, a directory can contain other directories. You may have a directory called Budget, for example, for your departmental budget. The Budget directory may contain several other directories (also called subdirectories) such as Year2003, Year2004, and Estimates. If a directory contains so many files that you can't find things, you should create some subdirectories to divide things up.

Files and directories are stored on hard drive. Every hard drive has a main directory that contains everything on the disk. This directory is called the *root directory*. The designers of UNIX were thinking of trees here, not turnips. They imagined an upside-down tree with the root at the top and the branches reaching downward, as shown in Figure 6-1. This arrangement of directories is called a *tree-structured directory*.

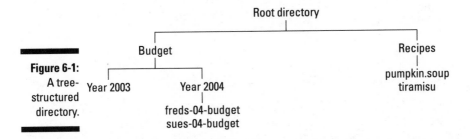

Figure 6-1:
A tree-structured directory.

Strangely, you don't type root when you're talking about the root directory. Rather, you press /. Just like that: A single slash means "root" in UNIX-ese.

Paths to power

Unfortunately, UNIX never shows you the directory structure as a nice picture, as shown in Figure 6-1. That would be too easy. Rather, to tell UNIX which file you want to use, you type its pathname. The *pathname* is the step-by-step map UNIX follows to get to a file, starting at the root. The pathname for the file named freds-04-budget in Figure 6-1, for example, contains these steps:

- ✔ /: The root, where you start.
- ✔ Budget: The name of the first directory you move to on your way to the file.
- ✔ /: Confusingly, this slash doesn't refer to another root; it's just the character used to separate one name from the next in a pathname.
- ✔ Year2004: The next directory on your way to the file.
- ✔ /: Another separator character.
- ✔ freds-04-budget: The filename you want.

When you type this pathname, you string it all together, with no spaces:

```
/Budget/Year2004/freds-04-budget
```

Luckily, you don't often have to type big, long pathnames like this one; it's devilishly hard to get all that right on the first try!

Family matters

You can also think of the tree structure of directories as a family tree. In this way of thinking, the `Year2004` directory is a *child* of the `Budget` directory, and the `Budget` directory is the *parent* of the `Year2004` directory. You see these terms sometimes if you read more about UNIX.

Names for directories

Choose names for directories in the same way as you choose names for files: Avoid funky characters and spaces, and don't make the name so long that you never type it correctly, for example. Some people capitalize the first letter of directory names to make it easier to tell what's a directory and what's a file. When you type `ls` to list the contents of a directory, the command lists both filenames and the names of subdirectories. When you use capitalization to distinguish between directory names and filenames, you can quickly tell which are which.

Getting the big picture

If you have a UNIX workstation that's all your own, most or all of the files on its hard drive are yours. If you connect from a PC and share a UNIX computer with others, the computer's hard drive has files that belong to all the users. As you can imagine, we are talking about oodles of files. To keep the files — and users! — organized, UNIX has lots of different directories.

UNIX has lots of directories for the UNIX program files themselves, program files for other programs, and other stuff you definitely are not interested in. The files that belong to users (such as yourself) usually are stored in one area. A directory called `/usr` (or sometimes `/home`) contains one subdirectory for every user. If your username is `zacyoung`, for example, the `/usr` directory contains a subdirectory called `zacyoung`, which contains your files.

There's No Place Like Home

Every user has a home directory (sweet, isn't it?) in which you store your personal stuff, mail, and so on. When you log in, UNIX starts you working in your home directory, where you work until you move somewhere else. Your home directory is your subdirectory in the /usr/home (or /home) directory, so Zac Young's home directory is /usr/home/zacyoung. (Although Zac is only 8 years old, he's got plenty of stuff to put in his home directory.)

Because most UNIX systems involve lots of people sharing hard drive space and files, UNIX has a security system to prevent people from reading each other's private mail or blowing away each other's work (accidentally, of course). Chapter 5 talks about the security system. In your home directory, you usually have the right to create, edit, and delete all the files and subdirectories. You can't do that in someone else's home directory unless the directory's owner gives you permission.

I've been working in the directory

Whenever you use UNIX, the directory you are working in is the *working* directory. Some people call it the *current* directory, which also makes sense.

When you first log in, your home directory is your working directory. Although you start in your home directory, you can move around. If you move to the /Budget directory, for example, the /Budget directory becomes the working directory. (Your home directory is still your home directory — it never moves.)

If you forget where you are in the directory structure, you can ask UNIX. Type the following line to ask UNIX where you are:

```
pwd
```

This line is short for *p*rint *w*orking *d*irectory. UNIX doesn't print the information on paper; it just displays it on-screen. You see something like this:

```
/Budget/Year2004
```

When you use the ls command (or most other UNIX commands), UNIX assumes that you want to work with just the files in the working directory. The ls command lists just the files in the working directory unless you tell it to look somewhere else.

To move to another directory to do some work (if you're tired of working on the budget and want to get back to that recipe for pumpkin soup, for example), you can change directories. To move from anywhere in the /Budget directory to the /Recipes directory, type this line:

```
cd /Recipes
```

Remember that cd is the change *d*irectory command. After the cd (and a space), you type the directory you want to go to. You can tell UNIX exactly which directory you want in two ways:

- ✔ Type a *full pathname,* or *absolute pathname* (the pathname starting at the root, as you did earlier). In the /Recipes example, the slash at the beginning of the pathname indicates that the pathname starts at the root.
- ✔ Type a *relative pathname* (the pathname starting from where you are now).

This stuff is confusing, we know, but UNIX has to know exactly which directory you want before it makes the move. Because the hard drive can have more than one directory called Recipes, UNIX has to know which one you want.

When you type a full pathname starting at the root directory, the pathname starts with a /. When you type a relative pathname starting at the working directory, the pathname doesn't start with a /. That's how UNIX (and you) can tell which kind of path it is.

If you are in the /Budget directory (on the /Budget branch of the directory tree) and want to go to the Year2004 subdirectory (a branchlet off the main /Budget branch), for example, just type **cd Year2004**. To go to a different branch or to move upward toward the root, you must type the slashes. To move from the /Budget/Year2004 branchlet back to the main /Budget branch, type **cd /Budget**. To move from the /Budget branch to the /Recipes branch, for example, type **cd /Recipes**.

If you try to move to a directory that doesn't exist or if you incorrectly type the directory name or pathname, UNIX says:

```
Budegt: No such file or directory
```

(or whatever directory name you typed).

I want to go home!

If you move to another directory (/0z, for example) and want to get back to your home directory (/Kansas, that is), you can do so as easily as clicking the heels of your ruby slippers three times. (Or were they glass slippers?) Just type this line:

```
cd
```

When you don't tell UNIX where you want to go, it assumes that you want to go home.

Putting Your Ducks in a Row

As with everything else in life (if we may be so bold as to suggest it), it pays to be organized when you're naming files and putting them in directories. If you don't have at least a little organization, you will never find anything. Think about which types of files you will make and use. (Word-processing files? Spreadsheet files?) Then make a directory for every type of file or for every project you're working on. This section shows you how.

Making directories

Before you create a directory, be sure that you put it in the right place. Remember that you type the following line to display your working directory (the current directory):

```
pwd
```

The most likely place to create a subdirectory is in your home directory. If you're not there already, type this line to go back home:

```
cd
```

When you create a directory, you give it a name. To create a directory called Temp to hold temporary files, type this line:

```
mkdir Temp
```

Many people have a directory called Temp to hold files temporarily. These files can be the ones you need to keep just long enough to print, to copy to a floppy disk or tape, or whatever. Anyway, you have one now, too. To confirm that the Temp directory is there, type this line:

```
ls
```

You can even go in there and look around by typing the following (and pressing Enter after typing the first line):

```
cd Temp
ls
```

When you create a directory, it starts out empty (it contains no files).

Most people have directories with names something like these examples:

- ✔ `Mail` or `Maildir`: For electronic mail (see Chapter 17).

- ✔ `Docs`: For miscellaneous documents, memos, and letters.

- ✔ `Temp`: For files you don't plan to keep. Use `Temp` to store files you plan to throw away soon. If you put them in some other directory and don't erase them when you finish with them, you may forget what they are and be reluctant to delete them later. Directories commonly fill up with junk in this way. Make a rule that any files left in the `Temp` directory are considered deletable. Most UNIX systems also have a directory called `/tmp` where anyone can stash temporary files for a while, which is emptied every time the system is restarted.

- ✔ `bin`: For programs that you use but that aren't stored in a central place. Your system administrator may have already made you your own `bin` directory. (See Chapter 12 for information about the `bin` directory and making your own programs.)

You can also make one or more directories to contain actual work.

Dot and dot dot

UNIX has two funny directory names you can use — especially with the `cd` and `ls` commands. One is `.` (a single dot), which stands for the current directory. You type the following line, for example, to tell UNIX to list the files in the current directory:

```
ls .
```

This command is pointless, of course, because typing the following line does exactly the same thing:

```
ls
```

Okay, forget about `.` (the single dot). But `..` (the double dot, or dot dot) is useful. It stands for the parent directory of the working directory. The *parent* directory is the one of which the working directory is a subdirectory. The parent is one level up the tree from where you are now. If you're in the directory /usr/home/zacyoung/Budget, for example, the .. (dot dot, or parent) directory is /usr/home/zacyoung.

Suppose that you type this line:

```
ls ..
```

You see a list of the files in the parent directory of where you are now. This command can save you from some serious typing (and the associated errors).

Neat operations you can perform on directories

After you have some directories, you may want to change their names or get rid of them. You also may want to move a file from one directory to another. This section shows you how to try that first.

Transplanting files

Chapter 5 describes the use of the mv command to rename a file. You can use the same command to move files from one directory to another. To get the mv command to move files rather than just rename them, you tell it two things:

- ✔ The name of the file you want to move
- ✔ The name of the path where you want to put the file

If you want, you can rename the file at the same time you move it, but we like to keep things (comparatively) simple. Suppose that you put the file sues.04.budget into the /Budget/Year2003 directory rather than in /Budget/Year2004. The easiest way to move it is to go first to the directory in which it is located. In this example, you type this line:

```
cd /Budget/Year2003
```

Use ls to make sure that the file is in the current directory. After you are sure that the file is there, you can move it to the directory you want by typing this line:

```
mv sues-04-budget /Budget/Year2004
```

Be sure to type one space after mv and one space between the name of the file and the place you want to move it to. If you use ls again, you discover that the file is no longer in the working directory (Year2003). You should change to the directory to which you moved the file and use `ls` to make sure that the file is there. Make one typing mistake in a `mv` command, and you can move a valuable file to some unexpected place.

Amputating unnecessary directories

You can use the `rmdir` command to remove a directory, but what about the files in the directory? Are they left hanging in the air with the ground blown out from under them? Nope; you must either get rid of the files in the directory (delete them) or move them elsewhere before you can hack away at the directory.

To erase a directory, follow these steps:

1. **Use the `rm` command to delete any files you don't want to keep.**

   (See Chapter 5 for the gory details of using this command.)

2. **If you want to keep any of the files, move them to somewhere else by using the `mv` command (as explained in the preceding section).**

3. **Move to some other directory when the directory you want to delete is empty.**

   Deleting your working directory is usually a poor idea. The easiest thing to do is to move to the working directory's parent directory:

   ```
   cd ..
   ```

4. **Remove the directory by typing this line:**

   ```
   rmdir OldStuff
   ```

   Replace *OldStuff* with the name of the directory you want to ax.

5. **Use `ls` to confirm that the directory is gone.**

You can delete a directory and all the files in it or even a directory and all the subdirectories and files in them, but this process is dangerous stuff. You usually are better off sifting through the files and deleting or moving them in smaller groups. If you're interested in a *really* dangerous command, which we shouldn't even be telling you about, you can type `rm -r` to remove a directory and all its files and subdirectories in one fell swoop.

Renaming a directory

If you have used DOS, you will be thrilled to learn that in UNIX you can rename a directory after you create it. (DOS didn't let you do that, at least not in early versions.) Again, the `mv` command comes to the rescue.

To rename a directory, you tell `mv` the current directory name and the new directory name. Go to the parent directory of the directory you want to rename, and then use the `mv` command. To rename the `/Budget` directory to the `/Finance` directory, for example, go to the `/` directory (type **cd /**) and then type this line:

```
mv Budget Finance
```

Make sure first that a directory with that name isn't already there. If it is, UNIX moves the first-named directory to become a subdirectory of the existing directory. In other words, if a `/Finance` directory is already there, `/Budget` moves to become `/Finance/Budget`. That could be handy, if that's what you have in mind. Then again, it could drive you out of your mind if that's not what you expect.

Putting Your Ducks on the Web

Web sites on UNIX systems use directories, too. Many ISPs organize their Web servers by user, so if your username is `fred`, your Web site is called `http://www.myisp.com/fred` or maybe `http://www.myisp.com/~fred/`. The site's home page is usually a file called `index.html` in the site's home directory, and the other pages are files whose names match their URLs, so a page named `http://www.myisp.com/fred/effluent.html` is stored in a file called `effluent.html`. If your site has more than a handful of pages, you should organize it into directories. Not by coincidence, the syntax of URLs is almost exactly the same as the syntax of UNIX filenames, so if you organize your site so that a page is called `http://www.myisp.com/fred/Greenstuff/Smelly/effluent.html`, the file is called `Greenstuff/Smelly/effluent.html`.

A few directory names are reserved for special Web server purposes, so you have to be careful to avoid them. The list varies from server to server (this is UNIX, after all), but the directory `cgi-bin` is invariably reserved for CGI scripts, programs that the Web server runs to produce pages on the fly. Check with your Web host to find out the reserved directory names on your system.

A Map of UNIX

Most UNIX systems have thousands, or even tens of thousands, of files. They are stored in hundreds of directories. Luckily, you don't care about most of these directories because they contain nothing other than the files that make up the murky technical underbelly of UNIX.

You may, however, need to find something in some directory other than your own safe, well-lit home directory. Table 6-1 is a guide to some directories that you're likely to find on your UNIX system. (Not every UNIX system has all these directories, but most do.)

Table 6-1	Popular UNIX Directories and What They Contain
Directory Name	*What It Contains*
/bin	Standard system commands.
/usr/bin	More standard system commands.
/usr/contrib/bin	Even more standard system commands (the ones contributed by third parties).
/usr/local/bin	Nonstandard, locally installed system commands.
/dev	Contains connections to devices, such as tape drivers, rather than real files. UNIX uses a terribly clever trick for referring to hardware devices as though they were files.
/etc	Miscellaneous system files. Not really interesting to nonweenies.
/home	Contains a home directory for each user. (If you don't see /home, try /usr/home.)
/lib	Program libraries and the like. (See our comment about /etc.)
/usr/lib	More program libraries and the like. (See our comment about /etc again.)
/tmp	Small temporary files.
/usr/tmp	Larger temporary files.
/usr/src	On systems that come with source code, the source code to the system. (Fascinating to programmers, but not so fascinating otherwise.)
/var/src	Another place where source code can be found.
/usr/man and /usr/catman	Text of online manual pages.

Chapter 7

The Shell Game

. . . .

. . . .

*I*f you read the preceding chapters in this book, you know how to work with files and how to type some commands to UNIX (you type them to the shell, as you know, but don't get bogged down in that here). UNIX has a clever way to increase the power of its commands: *redirection*. This chapter shows you how to use redirection and how to use wildcards to work with groups of files.

This Output Is Going to Havana: Redirection

When you use a UNIX command like ls, the result (or *output*) of the command is displayed on-screen. The standard place, in fact, for the output of most UNIX commands is the screen. The output even has a name: *standard output*. As you can imagine, there is also *standard input*, usually the keyboard. You type a command; if it needs more input, you type that, too. The result is output displayed on-screen — all very natural.

You can pervert this natural order by *redirecting* the input or output of a program. A better word is *hijacking*. You say to UNIX, "Don't display this output on-screen — instead, put it somewhere else." Or, "The input for this program is not coming from the keyboard this time — look for it somewhere else."

The "somewhere else" can be any of these sources:

- **A file:** You can store the output of ls (your directory listing) in a file, for example.

- **The printer:** It's useful only for output. Getting input from a printer is a losing battle.

- **Another program:** This one gets really interesting when you take the output from one program and feed it to another program!

A bunch of UNIX programs are designed primarily to use input from a source other than the keyboard and to output stuff to someplace other than the screen. These kinds of programs are called *filters*. Readers old enough to remember what cigarettes are may recall that the advanced ones had a filter between the cigarette and your mouth to make the smoke smoother, mellower, and more sophisticated. UNIX filters work in much the same way, except that they usually aren't made of asbestos.

The only exception to this redirection business is with programs, such as text editors and spreadsheets, that take over the entire screen. Although you can redirect their output to the printer, for example, you won't like the results (nor will your coworkers, as they wait for a pile of your garbage pages to come out of the printer). Full-screen programs write all sorts of special glop (they give instructions) to the screen to control where stuff displays, what color to use, and so on. These instructions don't work on the printer because printers use their own, different kind of glop. The short form of this tip is that *redirection and editors don't mix.*

Grabbing output

So how do you use this neat redirection stuff, you ask? Naturally, UNIX does it with funny characters. The two characters < and > are used for redirecting input and output to and from files and to the printer. You use another character (|) to redirect the output of one program to the input of another program.

To redirect (or *snag,* in technical parlance) the output of a command, use >. Think of this symbol as a tiny funnel *into which* the output is pouring (hey, we use any gimmick we can to remember which funny character is which). To make a file called list.of.files that contains your directory listing, for example, type this line:

```
ls > list.of.files
```

UNIX creates a new file, called list.of.files in this case, and puts the output of the ls command into it.

If `list.of.files` already exists, UNIX blows away the old version of the file. If you don't want to erase the existing file, you can tell UNIX to add this new information to the end of it (*append* the new information to the existing information). To do it, type this line:

```
ls >> list.of.files
```

The double `>>` symbol makes the command append the output of `ls` to the `list.of.files` file, if it already exists. If `list.of.files` doesn't exist already, `ls` creates it.

Some (but not all, of course) versions of the C shell check to see whether the file already exists and refuse to let you wreck an existing file with redirection. To overwrite the file if your C shell works this way, use `rm` to get rid of the old version. The command that tells the C shell not to clobber an existing file when you're creating a new file from redirection is `set noclobber`. To turn this protection off, you can use the `unset noclobber` command. We recommend turning on `noclobber` every time you run UNIX (or get a UNIX wizard to help you make this command execute automagically every time UNIX starts up).

Redirecting input

Redirecting input is useful less often than redirecting output, and we can't think of a single, simple example in which you would want to use it. Suffice it to say that you redirect input just like you redirect output except that you use the < character rather than the > character.

Gurgle, Gurgle: Running Data through Pipes

The process of redirecting the output of one program so that it becomes the input of another program can be quite useful. This process is the electronic equivalent of whisper-down-the-lane, with each program passing information to the next program and doing something to the information being whispered.

To play whisper-down-the-lane with UNIX, you use a *pipe*. The symbol for a pipe is a vertical bar (|). Search your keyboard for this character. It's often on the same key with \ (the backslash). Sometimes the key shows the vertical bar with a gap in the middle, although the gap doesn't matter. If you type two commands separated by a |, you tell UNIX to use the output of the first command as input for the second command.

Gimme just a little at a time

When you have many files in a directory, the output of the `ls` command can go whizzing by too fast to read, which makes seeing the files at the beginning of the list impossible before they disappear off the top of the screen. A UNIX program called `more` solves this problem. The `more` program displays on-screen the input you give it, and it pauses as soon as it fills the screen and waits for you to press a key to continue. To display your list of files one screen at a time, type this line:

```
ls | more
```

This line tells the `ls` command to send the file listing to the `more` command. The `more` command then displays the listing. You can think of the information from the `ls` command gurgling down through the little pipe to the `more` command (we think of it this way).

The cat and the fiddle . . . er, file

As we explain in Chapter 5, you can use the `cat` command to display the contents of a text file. If the text file is too long to fit on-screen, however, the beginning of the file disappears too fast to see. You can display a long file one screen at a time in these two ways:

- Redirect the output of the `cat` command to `more` by typing the following line (assuming, of course, that the file is called `really.long.file`):

```
cat really.long.file | more
```

- Just use the `more` command by typing this line:

```
more really.long.file
```

If you use the `more` command without a pipe (without the `|`), `more` takes the file you suggest and displays it on-screen a page at a time.

Sorting, sort of

A program called `sort` sorts a file line-by-line in alphabetical order. The program alphabetizes all the lines according to the beginning of each line. Each line in the file is unaffected; just the *order* of the lines changes.

Suppose that you have a file called `honors.students`, which looks like this:

```
Meg Young
Shelly Horwitz
Neil Guertin
Stuart Guertin
Sarah Saxon
Zac Young
Gillian Guertin
Tucker Myhre
Andrew Guertin
Megan Riley
Chloe Myhre
```

To sort it line by line into alphabetical order, type this:

```
sort honors.students
```

The result looks like this:

```
Andrew Guertin
Chloe Myhre
Gillian Guertin
Meg Young
Megan Riley
Neil Guertin
Sarah Saxon
Shelly Horwitz
Stuart Guertin
Tucker Myhre
Zac Young
```

The list appears on-screen, however, and nowhere else. If you want to save the sorted list, type

```
sort honors.students > students.sorted
```

You can also sort the output of a command:

```
ls | sort
```

Because ls displays filenames in alphabetical order anyway, of course, this example doesn't do you much good. If you want the filenames in *reverse* alphabetical order, however (we're stretching for an example here), you can use the -r option with the sort command:

```
ls | sort -r
```

If you are sorting numbers, be sure to tell UNIX. Otherwise, it sorts the numbers alphabetically (the sort of imbecilic and useless trick only a computer would do). To sort numbers, use the -n option:

```
sort -n order.numbers
```

Suppose that your file of honors students contains total test scores:

```
10000 Meg Young
8000  Shelly Horwitz
7000  Neil Guertin
5000  Stuart Guertin
9000  Sarah Saxon
5000  Zac Young
8000  Gillian Guertin
7000  Tucker Myhre
11000 Andrew Guertin
6000  Megan Riley
7000  Chloe Myhre
```

When you alphabetize things as letters, not as numbers, a 1 comes before an 8 no matter what, even if it's the first number of 10. When you alphabetize things as numbers, 10 comes after 8, not before it. If you sort this file as letters, with this command:

```
sort honors.students
```

you get

```
10000 Meg Young
11000 Andrew Guertin
5000  Stuart Guertin
5000  Zac Young
6000  Megan Riley
7000  Chloe Myhre
7000  Neil Guertin
7000  Tucker Myhre
8000  Gillian Guertin
8000  Shelly Horwitz
9000  Sarah Saxon
```

This output does not show the bonus amounts in any useful order. If you sort the file as numbers, with this command:

```
sort -n honors.students
```

you get this more useful listing:

```
5000   Stuart Guertin
5000   Zac Young
6000   Megan Riley
7000   Chloe Myhre
7000   Neil Guertin
7000   Tucker Myhre
8000   Gillian Guertin
8000   Shelly Horwitz
9000   Sarah Saxon
10000  Meg Young
11000  Andrew Guertin
```

If the file contains letters, not numbers, the -n option has no effect.

Can we get that on paper?

Being able to print the output of a command is terrifically useful when you want to send to a printer something that normally appears on-screen. To print a listing of your files, for example, type this line:

```
ls | lp
```

Users of Linux and BSD UNIX use the lpr command rather than lp. (Chapter 9 explains other stuff about printing.)

You can use more than one pipe if you want to be advanced. To print a listing of your files in reverse order, for example, you can use this convoluted command:

```
ls | sort -r | lp
```

Wild and Crazy Wildcards

When you type a command, you may want to include the names of a bunch of files on the command line. UNIX makes the typing of multiple filenames somewhat easier (as though we should be grateful) by providing wildcards. *Wildcards* are the two special characters (still more of them to remember!) that have a special meaning in filenames:

Wildcard	What It Means
?	Any single letter
*	Anything at all

Pick a letter, any letter

You can use one or more ? wildcards in a filename. Each ? stands for exactly one character — no more, no less. To list all your files that have two-letter names, for example, you can type this line:

```
ls ??
```

The command `ls budget??` lists all filenames that start with *budget* and have two — and only two — characters after *budget,* like `budget98` and `budget99`; the combination doesn't match `budget1` or `budget.draft` or `Budget98` (because of the uppercase *B*).

Stars (***) in your eyes

The * wildcard stands for any number of characters. To list all your files that have names starting with a *c,* for example, type

```
ls c*
```

This specification matches files named `customer.letter`, `c3`, and just plain `c`. The specification `budget.*` matches `budget.2004` and `budget.draft`, but not `draft.budget`. The name `*.draft` matches `budget.draft` and `window.draft`, but not `draft.horse` or plain `draft`. By itself, the filename `*` matches everything (watch out when you let the asterisk go solo!).

Are kings or deuces wild?

Unlike some other kinds of operating systems (we don't name any, although one system's initials are *DOS*), UNIX handles the ? and * wildcards in the same way for every command. You don't have to memorize which commands can handle wildcards and which ones cannot. In UNIX, they all can handle wildcards.

Wildcards commonly are used with the `ls`, `cp`, `rm`, and `mv` commands. For example, to copy all the files from the current directory to the `temp` directory, you can type

```
cp * temp
```

Look before you delete!

The combination of wildcards and the rm command is deadly. Use wildcards with care when you delete files. You should look first at the list of files you are deleting to make sure that it is what you had in mind. *Before* you type the following command, for example, to delete a bunch of files:

    rm *.03

type this line and look at the resulting list of files:

    ls *.03

You may see in that list of .03 files something worth keeping that you forgot about.

The most deadly typo of all is this one (*do not type this line!*):

    rm * .03

Notice the space between the * wildcard and the .03. Although you may have thought that you were deleting all files ending with .03, UNIX thinks that you have typed two filenames to delete:

* This "filename" deletes all the files in the directory.

.03 This filename deletes a file named .03 (yes, filenames can start with a period). By the time UNIX tries to delete this (nonexistent) file, it has, of course, already deleted all the files in the directory!

You end up with an empty directory and lots of missing files. Watch out when you use rm and * together!

Wildcards for Windows users

Although UNIX wildcards look just like Windows wildcards and they work in almost the same way, they have a few differences:

- ✔ Because UNIX filenames don't have to have the extensions that Windows filenames use, don't use *.* to match all files in a directory. That trick matches only files that have a dot in their names. A simple * does the trick.

- ✔ In Windows, you cannot put letters after the * wildcard — Windows ignores the letters following the asterisk. In Windows, *d*mb* is the same as *d**, for example. It's dumb, we know. The good news is that UNIX is not so dumb. In UNIX, *d*mb* works just the way you want it to.

History Repeats Itself

We make fun of the C shell a lot (and rightly so), but when Bill wrote it, he added a lovely feature called history. BASH does history too, even more nicely than the C shell. And the Korn shell has a way to do history that is clunky but serviceable.

The `history` command enables you to issue UNIX commands again without having to retype them, a big plus in our book. Bourne shell users may as well skip the rest of this chapter because it will just make you jealous (or it'll make you bite the bullet and switch to the BASH shell, by typing **bash**).

Here's how `history` works. The shell stores in a *history list* a list of the commands you've given. Then you can use the list to repeat commands exactly as you typed them the first time or edit previously used commands so that you can give a similar command.

History in the key of C

In the C shell, you can type **!!** and press Enter to repeat the last command you typed. The shell displays the command and then executes it.

You can also rerun the last command line that begins with a particular bunch of letters. If you type

```
!find
```

the C shell repeats the last command line that began with the text *find*. You don't have to type an entire command. If you type

```
!fi
```

it looks for the last command you typed that started with *fi*, which may be a `find` command or `file` command.

To see the history list, type **history**. You see a list like this:

```
1   20:26   ls
2   20:26   ls -l
3   20:26   ls -al
4   20:26   history
5   20:26   cat junk3
6   20:26   cat .term
7   20:26   history
8   20:27   history
```

This example shows the commands you just typed, in the order you typed them. Because the list is numbered, you can refer to the commands by number. After the number comes the time you gave the command (if you care), followed by the command you typed.

If you want to repeat a command, you can type **!** followed by the number of the command. For example, if you type

```
!3
```

TECHNICAL STUFF

Instant script — just add water

For those of you who know what a shell script is, you can use the `history` command to create an instant script. (For those of you who don't, read Chapter 12.)

Here's how to use the `history` command to create a script. Give the commands you want to include in the script, in the order in which you want them to occur. Then type **history** to display the list of commands. Note how many of the previous commands you want to include in the scripts; for this example, perhaps it's the last eight commands. Type a command like this (for the C shell):

```
history -h 8 >myscript
```

If you use BASH, type

```
history 8 > myscript
```

In the Korn shell, type

```
fc -l 8 > myscript
```

This command lists the last eight commands and stores the list in a file called `myscript`. Requesting from your history list more commands than you think you need is a good idea, because you can always delete them from your script. You have to use a text editor to clean up the script anyway, deleting the command numbers and times.

---

the C shell repeats command number 3 on the list (in this case, `ls -al`).

You can also repeat a command with a modification. Suppose that you just typed this command:

```
find . -name budget.04 -print
```

Now you want to give the same `find` command, but this time you're looking for a file named `budget.05`. Rather than tediously, arduously retype the line, character by character and keystroke by keystroke, worrying anxiously about a possible typo with every key you press, you can tell the C shell to repeat the last command, substituting *05* for *04*. The command is

```
^04^05
```

You type a caret (^), the old text, another caret, and the text to substitute. Voilà! The C shell displays the new command and then executes it.

BASHing through commands

BASH can do all the cool history tricks the C shell can, with some additional acrobatics. When BASH displays your history list, it usually stores the last 500 commands you typed, so the list can be huge. To see it a page at a time, type this command:

```
history | more
```

To see the last nine commands on the history list, type

```
history 9
```

Here comes the neat part — you can press the arrow keys to flip back through your commands. When you press the up-arrow key (or Ctrl+P, for *previous*), BASH shows you the previous command from the history list. You can press Enter to execute the command. You can keep pressing the up-arrow key (or Ctrl+P) until you get to the command you want. If you go past it, you can move back down your history list by pressing the down-arrow key (or Ctrl+N, for *next*).

This feature is downright useful and typo-saving! DOS windows in Windows have it too, of course, but who's counting?

After you display a command from your history list on the command line, you can edit the command before you press Enter to execute it. Press the left- and right-arrow keys (or Ctrl+B and Ctrl+F, for *backward* and *forward*) to move the cursor. When you type characters, BASH inserts them on the command line where the cursor is.

The folks at the Free Software Foundation who wrote BASH are big emacs fans (as are we) because you can use most emacs editing commands to edit the command on the command line. For example, pressing Ctrl+A moves your cursor to the beginning of the line, Ctrl+E moves it to the end of the line, Esc+F moves it forward by a word, and Ctrl+K deletes everything to the right of the cursor. For users who, for some reason, prefer vi to emacs, if you press Esc+Enter, BASH changes to a vi-like editor, where you search for history commands by pressing Ctrl+R and Ctrl+S.

Enough about BASH and history. You get the general idea!

A Korn-ucopia of commands

We don't use the Korn shell much because we've become rather fond of BASH, but the Korn shell can do history, too. The history command lists your history list, as does the more cryptic fc -l command. To repeat the last command, just type **r** and press Enter. That's it — just **r**. To repeat the last cat command, type

```
r cat
```

To repeat the last command, but replace *03* with *04*, type

> r 03=04

The Korn shell enables you to edit your previous commands in all kinds of fancy ways, although it's confusing to do, so we suggest that you switch to the BASH shell if you long to edit and reissue commands.

Do I Have to Type the Same Things Every Time I Log In?

Most users find that, every time they log in, they type the same commands to set up the computer the way they like it. You may typically change to your favorite directory, for example, and then change the terminal settings (see the following section), check your mail, or do any of a dozen other things.

The Bourne, Korn, and BASH shells look in your home directory for a file called .profile when you log in. If the .profile file exists, UNIX executes the commands in that file. The C shell has two corresponding files: .login (which it runs when you log in) and .cshrc (which it runs every time you start a new C shell, either at login time or when you type **csh**).

Your system administrator probably gave you a standard .profile or .login file when your account first was set up. Messing with stuff that's already there is *definitely* not a good idea. You may end up unable to log in and then have to crawl to your system administrator and beg for help. So don't say that we didn't warn you.

The standard .profile, .login, and .cshrc files vary considerably (why do we even finish this sentence — you know what we're going to say) from one system to another, depending on the tastes of the system administrator. These files usually perform this tasks:

 ✔ Set up the search path the shell uses to look for commands

 ✔ Arrange to notify you when you have new mail

 ✔ (Sometimes) change the shell prompt from the usual $ or % to something more informative

If you always type the same commands when you log in, adding new commands at the end of .profile or .login is fairly safe. If you do most of your work in the directory bigproject, for example, you may add the following three lines to the end of the file your shell uses to start up your UNIX session (.profile or .cshrc):

```
# change to bigproject, added 3/04
cd bigproject
echo Now in directory bigproject.
```

The first line is a comment the computer ignores but is useful for humans trying to figure out who changed what. Any line that starts with a pound sign (#) is a comment. The second line is a regular cd command. The third line is an echo command that displays a note on-screen to remind you of the directory you're in.

If you use the C shell, a frequently useful command to put in .login is this one:

```
set ignoreeof
```

If you press Ctrl+D in the shell, the shell normally assumes that you're finished for the day and logs you out — in keeping with the traditional UNIX "you asked for it, you got it" philosophy. Many people think that you should be more explicit about your intention to log out and use ignoreeof to tell the shell to ignore Ctrl+D (the following section tells you what eof has to do with Ctrl+D) and log out only when you type **exit** or **logout**.

Terminal Options

About 14 zillion different settings are associated with each terminal or pseudo-terminal attached to a UNIX system, any of which you can change with the stty command. More than 13 zillion of the 14 zillion shouldn't be messed with, or else your terminal vanishes in a puff of smoke (as far as UNIX is concerned), and you have to log in all over again or even get your system administrator to undo the damage. You can, however, safely change a few things.

All the special characters that control the terminal, such as Backspace and Ctrl+Z, are changeable. People often find that they prefer characters other than the defaults, for any of several reasons: They became accustomed to something else on another system, the placement of the keys on the keyboard makes some choices more natural than others, or their terminal emulator is dumb about switching Backspace and Delete. The special characters that control the keyboard are described in Table 7-1.

Table 7-1	Terminal-Control Characters	
Name	*Typical Character*	*Meaning*
erase	Ctrl+H	Erases (backspaces over) the preceding character
kill	Ctrl+U	Discards the line typed so far

Name	Typical Character	Meaning
eof	Ctrl+D	Marks the end of input to a program
swtch	Ctrl+Z	Pauses the current program (see Chapter 13)
intr	Ctrl+C	Interrupts or kills whichever program is running
quit	Ctrl+\	Kills the program and writes a core file

To tell stty to change any of these control characters, you give it the name of the special character to change and the character you want to use. If, as is common, you want to use a control character, you can type a caret (^— the thing above the 6 on the key in the row of keys across the top of the keyboard) followed by the plain character, both enclosed in quotation marks. As a special case, ^? represents the Del or Delete key. The Tab key is represented as ^I. The Backspace key is usually ^H. To make the Delete key the erase character and Ctrl+X the kill character, for example, type this line:

```
stty erase '^?' kill '^X'
```

If you're feeling perverse, you can set the various control characters to whatever you want. You can make the erase character q and the intr character 3, although doing so makes getting any work done difficult because you couldn't use *q* or *3* in anything you type.

The other thing you can change is *terminal output stop mode,* which controls whether background jobs can display messages on your terminal. (Chapter 13 explains what this statement means.) To allow output from background jobs to display on your terminal, turn off output stop mode by typing

```
stty -tostop
```

To prevent output from background jobs, or, more exactly, to make background jobs stop and wait when they want to display something, turn on output stop mode by typing this line:

```
stty tostop
```

All these stty commands usually go in the .login or .profile file so that the terminal is set up the way you want every time you log in.

Chapter 8

Where's That File?

Doncha love to set up lots of different directories so that you can organize your files by topic, program, date, or whatever suits you? We do. After you have files in all those directories, however, you can also easily lose them. Is that budget memo in your `Budget` directory, your `Memos` directory, your `ToDo` directory, Fred's `Budget.Stuff` directory, or somewhere else?

Two programs can help you find files: `find` and `grep`. Alternatively, you can use the `ln` command to create links to your files so that a file can appear in several directories at a time and you have that many more opportunities to find it.

The Search Is On

UNIX systems have lots of files. Lots and lots. Tens of thousands, to be more specific. So where's the memo you wrote last week?

Links to shadow files

You may run into a situation in which a file seems to be in several directories at one time (*Twilight Zone* music here, please). Mac users ought to be thinking of *aliases* here; Windows users ought to be thinking of *shortcuts.* UNIX has its own way of letting you keep a file in several places at the same time. To avoid excessive clarity, the file can even have several different names. Seriously, having a file in, for example, the home directories of several people at one time so that they all can easily share it is useful.

To achieve this magical feat, you use *links.* We discuss links in the section "A File by Any Other Name," later in this chapter. In the meantime, don't panic if you see a file lurking around in one place when you're sure that it belongs somewhere else.

Peering into every directory

The first approach to finding a lost file is to use the brute-force method. Starting in your home directory, use ls to search through each of your directories. In every directory, type this line:

```
ls important.file
```

Replace *important.file* with the name of the file you're looking for. If the file is in the current directory, ls lists it. If the file isn't there, ls complains that it can't find the file. This approach can take awhile if you have a large number of directories. An additional drawback is that you won't find the missing file if it has wandered off to someone else's directory.

If you know — or think that you know — that your file is nearby, you can use * (asterisk) wildcards in directory names. (Wildcards are covered in Chapter 7. They enable you to work with lots of files or directories at one time.) To find *important.file* in any of the subdirectories in the working directory, type this line:

```
ls */important.file
```

This technique doesn't work if you have directories within directories: It looks only one level down.

"Hey, I know the filename!"

With luck, you know the name of the file you have lost. If so, you can use the find program to find it. When you use find, you tell it the name of the file and the place to start looking. The find program looks in the directory you indicate and in all that directory's subdirectories.

Suppose that you're working in your home directory. You think that a file named tiramisu is in there somewhere. Type this line:

```
find . -name tiramisu -print
```

That is, you type these elements:

- ✔ **find** (just like you see it here).
- ✔ A space.
- ✔ The directory in which you want the program to begin looking. If it's the working directory, you can type just a period (which means "right here").
- ✔ Another space.
- ✔ **-name** (to mean that you will specify a filename).
- ✔ Another space.
- ✔ The name of the file you want to find (**tiramisu**, in this case).
- ✔ Another space.
- ✔ **-print** to tell UNIX to print (on-screen) the full name, including the directory name, to let you know where UNIX finds the file. If you omit this step and find finds the file, it doesn't tell you. (We know that this situation is stupid, but computers are like that.) If you use UNIX SVR4 or Solaris, you'll notice the find command is fixed so that it warns you rather than runs the command pointlessly.

The find program uses a brute-force approach to locate your file. It checks every file in all your directories. This process can take quite a while. After find finds the file, it prints the name and keeps going. If the program finds more than one file with that name, find finds them and reports them all. After find prints a found file, you usually will want to stop the program (unless you think that it will find more than one match). You stop find by pressing Ctrl+C or the Delete key.

If the find command doesn't work and you think that the file may be in some other user's directory, type the same find command and replace the . (dot) with a / (slash). This version tells find to start looking in the root directory and to search every directory on the hard drive. As you can imagine, this process can take some time, so try other things first.

"I know where to search (sort of)"

Rather than use a period to tell find to begin looking in the working directory, you can use a pathname. You can type this line, for example:

```
find /usr/margy -name tiramisu -print
```

This command searches Margy's home directory and all its subdirectories. (Her home directory name may be something different; see Chapter 6 to find out about home directories.) To search the entire disk, use the slash (/) to represent the root of the directory tree:

```
find / -name tiramisu -print
```

If your disk is large and full of files, a search from the root directory down can take a long time — as long as half an hour on a very large and busy system.

You can even type several directories. To search both Margy's and John's home directories for files named white.chocolate.mousse, for example, type this line:

```
find /usr/margy /usr/johnl -name white.chocolate.mousse
          -print
```

If you use the BASH or C shell, rather than type the home directory name, you can type a tilde (~) and the username; the shell puts in the correct directory name for you:

```
find ~margy ~johnl -name white.chocolate.mousse -print
```

"At least I know part of the filename"

You can use wildcard characters in the filename if you know only part of the filename. (Remember the * and ? characters that act as wildcards in filenames?) Use ? to stand for any single character; use * to stand for any bunch of characters. There's a trick to using wildcards, however: If you use * or ? in the filename, you have to put quotation marks around the filename to keep the shell from thinking that you want it to find matching names in only the current directory.

You can search the entire disk for files that start with budget, for example, by typing

```
find / -name "budget*" -print
```

If you leave out the quotation marks, the search may look like it worked, although find probably hasn't done the job correctly.

Remote searches

If your system uses NFS (Network File System, as described in Chapter 16), some or all the directories and files on your machine may really be on other computers. The find command doesn't care where files are and cheerfully searches its way into any directory it can get to. Because getting to files over a network is about half as fast as getting to files stored locally, telling find to look through a large number of files stored on a network can take a long time. Consider having a long lunch while find does its thing.

Suppose that you're looking for Dave's famous stuffed-squid recipe. The obvious way to look for it is with this line:

```
find ~dave -name stuffed-squid -print
```

If you know that Dave's files are stored on machine xuxa, however, this command can be much faster:

```
ssh xuxa "find ~dave -name stuffed-squid -print"
```

See Chapter 16 for details about the ssh command.

It's what's inside that counts

"Hmm . . . I don't remember what the file is called, but I'm looking for a letter I wrote to Tonia, so it should contain her mailing address in the heading. That's 1471 Arcadia. How do I find it?"

This situation is made for grep — a great program with a terrible name. It stands for, if you can believe it, *g*lobal *r*egular *e*xpression and *p*rint, or some such thing. The grep command looks inside files and searches for a series of characters. Every time it finds a line that contains the specified characters, it displays the line on-screen. If it's looking in more than one file, grep also tells you the name of the file in which the characters occur. You control which files it looks in and which characters it looks for.

Three grep programs exist: grep, egrep, and fgrep. They are similar, so we talk just about grep. (Fgrep is faster but more limited, and egrep is more powerful and more confusing.)

To look in all the files in the working directory (but not in its subdirectories) for the characters 1471 Arcadia, type this line:

```
grep "1471 Arcadia" *
```

That is, type these elements:

- ✔ **grep** (just as you see it here).
- ✔ A space.
- ✔ The series of characters to look for (also called the *search string*). If the string consists of several words, enclose it in quotation marks so that grep doesn't get confused.
- ✔ A space.
- ✔ The names of the files to look in. If you type * here, grep looks in all the files in the current directory.

The grep program responds with a list of the lines in which it finds the search string:

```
ts.doc: 1471 Arcadia Lane
tonia.letter: 1471 Arcadia La.
```

The program lists the name of the file and then the entire line in which it finds the search string.

You can do lots of things with grep other than look for files. In fact, one could write entire (small) books about using grep. For our purposes, however, here are some useful options you can use when you use grep to look for files.

If you want to see just the filenames and you don't want grep to show you the lines it found, use the -l (for *list*) option. (That's a small letter *l*, not a number one.) Suppose that you type this line:

```
grep -l "1471 Arcadia" *
```

The grep program responds with just a list of filenames:

```
ts.doc
tonia.letter
```

It may be a good idea to tell grep not to worry about uppercase and lower-case letters. If you use the -i (for *ignore* case) option, grep doesn't distinguish between uppercase and lowercase letters, as shown in this example:

```
grep -i DOS *
```

With this command, grep, which is extremely literal-minded, finds both references to DOS and some "false hits":

```
fruit.study: salads; in Brazil, avocados are used in
          desserts.
chapter.26: DOS vs. UNIX
chapter.30: Dos and Don'ts
```

Finally, if you don't know the exact characters that occur in the file, you can use grep's flexible and highly powerful (that is, cryptic and totally confusing) expression-recognition capabilities, known in nerdspeak as *regular expressions*. The grep program has its own set of wildcard characters, sort of but not much like the ones the shell uses to enable you to specify all kinds of amazing search strings. If you're a programmer, this feature is useful because you frequently need to find occurrences of rather strange-looking stuff.

The reason we mention this subject is that grep's wildcard characters include most punctuation characters — namely:

```
. * [ ] ^ $
```

Quick 'n' dirty database

You can use grep to treat a text file like a quick and dirty database. Using a text editor, for example, you can create a file named 411 that contains the names and phone numbers of your friends and associates, with one entry per line:

```
Jordan Young, 555-4673
Meg Young, 555-5485
Zac Young, 554-8649
```

To look up someone's phone number, you just type

```
grep Meg 411
```

The grep program displays the line or lines of the file containing the name or names you asked for.

The grep program is widely used by UNIX enthusiasts for searching all kinds of files for all kinds of information. As long as each item fits on one line, you can keep all sorts of data in this kind of cheap database file. One of our favorite files is called restaurants, which has lines that look like this:

```
Chef Chung's Cheap 555-3864
```

If you're in the mood for something cheap, you can say

```
grep -i cheap restaurants
```

Directory assistance

You can look for lost directories in addition to lost files. Give the `find` command the option `-type d`:

This command searches the entire hard drive for directories that begin with `Budget`.

```
find / -name "Budget*" -type d
    -print
```

If you include any of these characters in a search string, `grep` doesn't do what you expect. To type any of these characters in a search string, precede them with a backslash (\ ). To search for files containing *C.I.A.,* for example, type this line:

```
grep "C\.I\.A\." *
```

The period (.) is `grep`'s wildcard character, like the question mark (?) in the shell. In this example, if you don't precede the periods with backslashes, `grep` matches not only `C.I.A.` but also `CHIFAS` (a Peruvian dialect word meaning *Chinese restaurants,* in case you are wondering) and lots of other things. Don't press your luck — use the backslashes with punctuation marks to be safe.

What to Do with Files after You Find Them

After you find the file or files you are looking for, you can do more than just look at their names. If you want, you can tell the `find` command to do something with every file it finds.

Rather than end the `find` command with the `-print` option, you can use the `-exec` option. It tells `find` to execute a UNIX shell command every time it finds a file. The following command, for example, tells the `find` command to look for files with names beginning with `report`:

```
find . -name "report*" -exec lpr {} ";"
```

Every time the command finds that type of file, it runs the `lpr` program and substitutes the name of the file for the { }. (You type two curly braces, which was some nerd's idea of a convenient placeholder.) The semicolon indicates the end of the UNIX shell command. (You have to put quotation marks around the semicolon, or else the shell hijacks it and thinks that you want to begin a new shell command. If that didn't make sense, take our word for it and remember to put quotation marks around the semicolon when you use find.) Every time find finds a filename beginning with report, this command prints the file it finds.

You can use almost any UNIX command with the -exec option, so, after you find your files, you can print, move, erase, or copy them as a group. A slight variation is to use -ok rather than -exec. The -ok option does the same thing except that, before it executes each command, find prints the command it's about to run, followed by a question mark, and waits for you to agree to run the command. Press the y key if you want to do it, and press the n key if you want it to skip that particular command.

By using find and -exec rm, you can delete many unwanted files in a hurry. If you make the smallest mistake, however, you can delete many important and useful files equally as quickly. We don't recommend that you use find and rm together. If you insist, however, please use -ok to limit the damage.

Searching Is Slow!

Because the grep and find commands can take a couple of minutes to do their work, you may want to run them in the background, as described in Chapter 13. To do that, redirect their output to a file so that you can review the results of the search at your leisure. End the command with an ampersand (&), which tells UNIX to run the command in the background. For example, you can type these two commands, pressing Enter after each one:

```
find / -name "budget*" -print > budget.files &
grep "chocolate mousse" * > mousse.recipe.files &
```

When the jobs end, you can type these commands to see what they found:

```
cat budget.files
cat mousse.recipe.files
```

A File by Any Other Name

Sometimes, having a file in more than one place is nice (that budget file we keep mentioning, for example). If you are working on it with someone else, the file can be in both your home directory and your coworker's home directory so that neither of you have to use the cd command to get to it.

A nice feature of UNIX (and you thought there weren't any!) is that this situation is possible — even easy to set up. A single file can have more than one name, and the names can be in different directories.

Suppose that two authors are working on a book together (a totally hypothetical example). The chapters of the book are in John's directory: /usr/johnl/book. What about Margy? Having to type the following line every time work on the book begins is annoying:

```
cd /usr/johnl/book
```

Instead, the files could also be in /usr/margy/book.

How can you be in two places at once when you're not anywhere at all?

The way to let a file be in two places at once is with the ln (for *link*) command. You tell ln two things:

✔ The current name of the file or files you want to create links to

✔ The new name

Start with just one file. Margy wants to make a link to the chapterlog file (it contains the list of chapters). The file is in /usr/johnl/book. In her book directory, Margy types this line:

```
ln /usr/johnl/book/chapterlog booklog
```

UNIX says absolutely nothing; it just displays another prompt. (No news is good news.) It just created a *link,* or new name, however, to the existing chapterlog file. The file now appears also in /usr/margy/book as booklog. You have only one file (UNIX doesn't make a copy of the file or anything tacky like that) with two names.

Playing the links

After you create a link by using ln, the file has two names in two directories. The names are equally valid. It isn't as though /usr/johnl/book/chapterlog is the real name, and /usr/margy/book/booklog is an alias. UNIX considers both names to be equally important links to the file.

Deleting links

To delete a link, you use the same `rm` command you use to delete a file. In fact, `rm` always just deletes a link. It just so happens that, when no links to a file exist, the file dries up and blows away. When you use `rm` on a file that has just one name (link), the file is deleted. When you use `rm` on a file that has more than one name (link), the command deletes the specified link (name), and the file remains unchanged, along with any other links it may have had.

Renaming a link

You can use the old `mv` command to rename a link, too. If Margy decides that for the book-status file to have the same name in both places is less confusing (as it stands now, it's `chapterlog` to John and `booklog` to Margy), she can type this line:

```
mv booklog chapterlog
```

You can even use the `mv` command to move the file to another directory.

Linking a bunch of files

You can also use `ln` to link a bunch of files at the same time. In this case, you tell `ln` two things:

✔ The bunch of files you want to link, probably using a wildcard character such as `chapter*`. You also can type a series of filenames or a combination of names and patterns. (UNIX may be obscure, but it's flexible.)

✔ The name of the directory in which you want to put all the new links.

The `ln` command uses the same names the files currently have when it makes the new links. It just puts them in a different directory.

The `chapterlog` business in the preceding example, for example, works so well that Margy decides to link to all the files in `/usr/johnl/book`. To make links in `/usr/margy/book`, she types this line:

```
ln /usr/johnl/book/* /usr/margy/book
```

Linking once and linking twice

Here's one caveat. The `ln` command in the example in this section links all the files that exist at the time the command is given. If you add new files to either `/usr/margy/book` or `/usr/john1/book`, the new files are not automatically linked to the other directory. To fix this situation, you can type the same `ln` command every few days (or whatever frequency makes sense). The command tells you that lots of files are already identical in the two directories and makes links for the new files.

If you linked to someone else's files, you may have permission to read those files but not to change or write to them. When you ask `ln` to make the new links, if it tries to replace a file you can't write to, it says something like this:

```
ln: chapter13: 644 mode?
```

See Chapter 25 for the exact meaning of this uniquely obscure message. Press the y key if you want to replace the file, which you probably do in this case. Press the n key if you don't want to replace the file.

This command tells UNIX to create links for all the files in `/usr/john1/book` and to put the new links in `/usr/margy/book`. Now every file that exists in `/usr/john1/book` also exists in `/usr/margy/book`. Margy uses the `ls` command to look at a file listing for her new `book` directory. It contains all the book files. This arrangement makes working on the files much more convenient.

Linking across the great computer divide

All this talk about links assumes that the files you're linking to are on the same file system (that's UNIX-speak for *disk* or *disk partition*). If your computer has several hard drives or if you're on a network and use files on other computers (through NFS or some other system, as explained in Chapter 16), some of the files you work with may be on different file systems.

Here's the bad news: The original `ln` command couldn't create links to files on other file systems. Bummer. But all modern UNIX systems have things called *soft links,* or *symbolic links* (*symlinks,* for short) that are almost as good.

Soft links enable you to use two or more different names for the same file. Unlike regular links (or *hard links*), however, soft links are just imitation links. UNIX doesn't consider them to be the file's real name.

Making soft links

To make a soft link, add the -s option to the ln command.

Suppose that you want a link in your home directory to the recipe.list file in /usr/gita. In your home directory, you type this line:

```
ln /usr/gita/recipe.list gitas.recipes
```

Rather than respond with serene silence, UNIX responds with this line:

```
ln: different file system
```

Drat! Gita's home directory is on a different file system from yours, perhaps even on a different computer. So you make a soft link by sticking an -s into the command:

```
ln -s /usr/gita/recipe.list gitas.recipes
```

As usual, no news is good news; ln says nothing if it works. Now a file called gitas.recipes seems to be in your home directory — all through the magic of soft links. You still have only one file, but you have an extra link to it.

Using soft links

You can look at, copy, print, and rename a soft-linked file as usual. If you have the proper permissions, you can edit it. If Gita deletes her file, though, the file vanishes. Your soft link now links to an empty hole rather than to a file, and you see an error message if you try to use the file. UNIX knows that the soft link isn't the file's real name. When you see a soft link in a long ls listing, UNIX gives the name of the soft link and also the name of the file it refers to.

If you try to use a file and UNIX says that it isn't there, check to see whether it's a dangling soft link (a link to a nonexistent file). Type ls -l to see whether the file is a soft link. If it is, use another ls -l on the real filename to make sure that the file really exists.

To get rid of a dangling soft link, use the rm command to delete it.

Chapter 9

Printing (The Gutenberg Thing)

• •

• •

*U*nless you happen to work in the paperless office of the future (reputed to be down the hall from the paperless bathroom of the future), from time to time you will want to print stuff. The good news is that doing so is usually easy. The bad news is that nothing is as easy as it should be.

The major extra complication is that the way to print things is different on UNIX BSD and System V systems. (Remember which one you have? Refer to Chapter 2 if you don't. You may have written it on the Cheat Sheet in the front of this book.) We start by explaining how you print something already in a file; then we go on to the fancy stuff.

Printing Stuff: Daemons at Work

From a human being's point of view, printing stuff in UNIX is simplicity itself: You use either the lp command or the lpr command, depending on your flavor of UNIX. Many office suite packages have built-in printing commands, but they're all lp or lpr underneath.

From your computer's point of view, this arrangement is, of course, way too simple. To make things suitably complex, the print command doesn't print the file. What it does is leave a note for another program buried deep inside UNIX, and this buried program prints your file. This buried program is called a *daemon* (pronounced "demon"). The theory behind this arrangement is that a bunch of people may want to use the printer, and waiting for the printer to be free is a pain. The print command puts your file on a list, and the daemon runs down the list and does the printing so that you don't have to wait. The *request ID* is the name the print command gives to the note it leaves for the daemon. You can ignore the request ID unless you change your mind and decide that you don't want to print that file after all.

Printing in System V

If you use UNIX System V, you print stuff with the `lp` command. If you have a file named `myletter`, for example, you print it by typing this line:

```
lp myletter
```

UNIX responds with this important information:

```
request id is dj-2613 (1 file)
```

Usually, that's all you need to do. UNIX responds to your request to print by telling you the request ID of the print job, which you probably don't care about. Sometimes you want to pretty up the way the printout looks by leaving wider margins; we talk about that subject later in this chapter.

Printing in BSD and Linux

If you use Linux or BSD UNIX, printing is just as easy as printing with System V, except that you use the command `lpr` rather than `lp`. If you have a file named `myletter`, for example, you print it by typing

```
lpr myletter
```

Some systems, notably SVR4 and Solaris, have both the `lp` and `lpr` commands. If you have these versions of UNIX, either command works equally well. Note that the `lpr` command doesn't report a request ID.

Finding Your Printout

As far as UNIX is concerned, its only job is to send your file to the printer. Now the real work begins: *finding* your printout.

If your UNIX system is attached to a network, chances are that your printer is attached to some other computer rather than to yours. You may have to go looking for it to find your printouts.

You may have to ask people in nearby cubicles or stand still in the center of the office and listen for the sound of printing (a gentle whir and click from most laser printers). If all else fails, ask your system administrator. Because your UNIX system may be capable of using more than one printer, your system administrator may be the only person who can tell you which printer your printout is on.

Aha! There's the printer! If you're lucky, no one else printed anything recently, so the paper on top of the printer is all yours. More likely, lots of people printed stuff, and a pile of paper is on top of the printer — only some of which is yours.

With luck, every printout has in front of it a sheet that identifies the file that's printed, with the username, time, and other odds and ends that seemed relevant to the person who configured the printer. Rooting through the stack, picking out your own pages, and leaving the rest in a heap is considered tacky. Instead, separate the printouts and leave them on the table or in printout racks (if available) with the usernames visible. With luck, others do the same for you. If you can't find your printout on the printer, maybe someone else already separated and stacked the printouts. Or maybe other users decided that your printout looked more interesting than theirs and took it off the printer to read it.

Printers, printers, everywhere

A reasonably large installation probably has several printers, either because one printer can't handle all the work or because the installation uses different kinds of printers. When you use the lp or lpr command, UNIX picks one printer as the default. If you use lp, you use the -d option (that's a lowercase *d* — remember that UNIX cares about these things) to identify the printer. To print your file on a printer named draft, for example, you type

```
lp -ddraft myletter
```

If you use lpr, the analogous option is -P (that's an uppercase *P*), so the command you type is

```
lpr -Pdraft myletter
```

In either case, don't type a space between the -d or -P and the printer name.

Calling all printers

The list of available printers depends entirely on the whims of the system administrator. Typically, one day she gets tired of putting up with the slow, illegible, or chronically broken previous printer, storms into the boss's office, gets the necessary signature, and buys the first printer available. Sometimes the old printer is thrown away, sometimes not.

Getting a list of printers known to the system is generally not too difficult. If you use the `lp` command to print, type this line to get a list of available printers:

```
lpstat -a all
```

This line means roughly, "Show me the status of all printers that are active." The `lpstat` program lists the status of all available printers, one per line, like this:

```
dj accepting requests since Thu Apr 26 13:43:50 2001
```

In this case, only one printer, whose name is `dj`, is available. The listing also shows you the vital fact that it was installed on a Thursday afternoon in April 2001. Whoopee.

If you use the `lpr` command to print, try typing this line to get the same information:

```
lpq -a
```

Woodsman, spare that file!

When you tell UNIX to print a file, the file doesn't print immediately. UNIX makes a note to print the file and remembers its filename.

What if you delete the file before UNIX has a chance to print it? If you print with `lp`, you get a nasty message because UNIX can't find the file. If you print with `lpr`, the file prints normally because UNIX makes a copy of the material to print.

To force `lp` to copy the file, use the `<` command-line operator. To send a copy of the file `myfile` to the printer, for example, type

```
lp < myfile
```

You can then delete or change `myfile` and not affect the printout.

If you are printing a large file, `lpr` can take a long time to make the copy of the file (which it doesn't really need to do because it's already in a file in the first place, isn't it?). You can use `lpr -s` to tell UNIX to print from the original file to save time and hard drive space. If you use the `-s` option, be sure not to delete or change the file until it's printed.

You can tell `lpr` to delete the file when it finishes printing it. This capability is sometimes useful when you made the file in the first place only so that you could print it. Use the `-r` option to remove the file after printing:

```
lpr -r myfile
```

For large files, you can use `-r` and `-s` together:

```
lpr -s -r myfile
```

The lpq program responds with a similar list:

```
lp:
      Rank        Owner  Job  Files        Total Size
      1st         johnl  7    longletter   4615 bytes
      ps:
      no entries
```

The lpq command stands for something like *l*ine *p*rinter *q*uery, and -a means *a*ll printers. In this case, two printers are available, named lp and ps, and something is printing on the first one.

Keep in mind that not every printer the lpstat and lpq commands report to is usable. System administrators frequently put in the table of printers some test entries that don't really represent printers you can use.

"Help! I've Printed, and It Won't Shut Up!"

The first time you print something large, you suddenly will realize that you don't really want to print the file because you have found a horrible mistake on the first page. Fortunately, you can easily tell UNIX that you have changed your mind.

If you tell UNIX to print a file that does not contain text, such as a file that contains a program or a database, in most cases UNIX prints it anyway. In a classic example of Murphy's Law (anything that can go wrong will go wrong), files like that tend to print about 12 random letters on each of 400 pages. Every page has just enough junk on it that you can't use that piece of paper again. As you may expect, people who print a large number of files like that tend to become unpopular, particularly with coworkers whose 2-page memos are in line behind the 400 pages of junk.

Cancel the order, System V

If you used lp to print the file in the first place, you use cancel (we don't know how that name slipped past the lazy typists) to cancel the print job. You have to give the cancel command the request ID that lp assigned to the job. If you're lucky, the lp command is still on-screen, and you can see the request ID. If that information has vanished from your screen, remain calm. Remember that the lpstat command lists all the requests waiting for the printer. Type this command:

```
lpstat
```

This command displays a list like the following:

```
dj-2620    john1    34895        Dec 23 21:12 on dj
```

This list tells you that your request was named `dj-2620`, it was done on behalf of a user named `john1`, the size of the file to be printed is 34895, and the print command was given on December 23. You can cancel the request with this command:

```
cancel dj-2620
```

UNIX responds with this line:

```
request "dj-2620" cancelled
```

UNIX has a surprisingly convenient (surprising for UNIX, anyway) shortcut you can use. If you give the name of a printer, UNIX cancels whatever is printing on that printer. If you remember that the local printer is named `dj`, you can type the following line to cancel whatever `dj` is printing:

```
cancel dj
```

Cancel the order, BSD

If you made your printing mistake with the `lpr` command, you use `lpq` to find out the request ID, which — to add confusion — is called a *job number* here. Just type this command:

```
lpq
```

UNIX responds with a list of print jobs:

```
Rank    Owner     Job   Files                    Total Size
1st     john1     12    blurfle                  34895 bytes
```

You need to note the job number (12, in this case). Use that number with the `lprm` command, which, despite its name, removes the request to print something and not the printer itself:

```
lprm 12
```

The `lprm` command usually reports something about "dequeued" lines; this information is meant to be reassuring, although it's not clear to whom. In response to the `lprm 12` command, for example, UNIX displays this message:

```
dfB012iecc dequeued
cfA012iecc dequeued
```

TECHNICAL STUFF

Why you don't want to know about PostScript

You may have what's known as a PostScript printer. Two general camps of laser-printer design exist: the Hewlett-Packard (HP) camp and the PostScript camp. Printers in the Hewlett-Packard camp are based on the design of the HP LaserJet line of printers. Printers in the PostScript camp use the PostScript programming language designed by Adobe Systems. LaserJet printers are said to speak PCL, although PCL is not nearly as complicated or flexible (depending on how you look at it) as PostScript. To add to the confusion, most laser printers produced in recent years speak both PostScript and PCL.

You may reasonably ask, "What does a programming language have to do with a printer?" If you send to the simpler LaserJet a file that contains the text *Your mother wears army boots,* the printer prints `Your mother wears army boots`. If you send the same file to a PostScript printer, the printer doesn't print anything. The reason is that a PostScript printer is a powerful computer with a built-in programming language (that's PostScript) that can print stuff sort of as a sideline. To make a PostScript printer print anything, you have to send it a program to do the printing. Fortunately, this type of program is widely available.

This arrangement isn't quite as deranged as it sounds. To print simple files of text, it's a pain; for fancy typeset documents with lots of typefaces and figures and line drawings and such things, however, PostScript is considerably more flexible than PCL, enough so that people use PostScript to typeset entire books (such as this one).

PostScript has two problems that may bite you. The first is sending a regular file to a PostScript printer. UNIX printer software is usually smart enough to figure out automatically that it must PostScript-ize the file in order to print it. If the printer software is not that smart, another program can do the PostScript-ization. Adobe, the originator of PostScript, sells a widely used package named Transcript. It includes a program named `enscript` that prints plain files. If the plain `lp` or `lpr` command doesn't work, try using the `enscript` command or its freeware clone `nenscript` before you run for help.

The other problem you may encounter is that a file contains PostScript but prints like a regular file. PostScript files look like incomprehensible programs written in an obscure programming language because that's what they are. The tipoff is that the first two letters on the first line are `%!`. To see what the file is supposed to look like, you must send it to a PostScript printer that can run the program in the file and print whatever the file contains. If your printer prints the PostScript program instead, most likely your printer doesn't speak PostScript.

Lacking a PostScript printer, you still may not be out of luck. A program from the Free Software Foundation named Ghostscript can read PostScript files and translate them into something your local printer can print. Later in this chapter — in "Printing for the PostScript-Challenged," to be precise — we discuss Ghostscript and its cousin Ghostview, which lets you preview PostScript documents on-screen.

Some final words about stopping the printer

Most printers have something called an *internal buffer,* which is where data to be printed resides before the printer prints it. An internal buffer is good and bad: It's good because it keeps the printer from stopping and starting if the computer is a little slow in passing your file to it. It's bad because, after data is in the buffer, the computer cannot get it back. So, even after you cancel something you want to print, some of it may still be in the buffer: as much as 2 pages of normal text or about 20 pages of the junk that results from printing a non-text file.

You have no easy way to keep from printing the stuff in the printer buffer. One really bad idea is to turn the printer off in the middle of a page: This method tends to get the paper stuck and, on laser printers, lets loose a bunch of black, smeary stuff that gets all over your hands and on the next 1,000 pages the printer prints. If you insist, press the printer's Stop or Off-line button and wait for the paper to stop moving. Then you can turn the printer off relatively safely. Or, with luck, a button on the printer provides a Cancel option to discard what's waiting in the printer.

After you cancel your print request, the printer probably still has half a page of your failed file waiting to print. You can eject that page by pressing a button on the printer labeled something like Form Feed or Print/Check or even Reset.

Prettying Up Your Printouts

If you send a file full of plain text to a printer, the result can look ugly: no margins, titles, or anything else. You can use the pr command to make your file look nicer. Use it only with plain text files, however, not with files full of PostScript code, document files from your favorite word processor, or a desktop publishing program.

Titles and page numbers look so official

The simplest thing you can do with the pr command is to add titles and page numbers to your printout. By default, the title is the name of the file and the date and time it was last changed. You can use a pipe (defined in Chapter 7 as the vertical bar, |) to format with pr and print on a single line:

```
pr myfile | lpr
```

(Remember to use the lp command rather than lpr, if appropriate.) This command tells the pr program to pretty up the file and pass the results to the lpr program.

You can set your own heading by using the -h option with the pr command:

```
pr -h "My Deepest Thoughts" myfile | lpr
```

The pr command assumes that printer pages are 66 lines long. If that's not true for you, rather than the title's appearing at the top of every page, it sort of oozes down from page to page. You can override the length of the standard page with the -l option. Suppose that the page length is 60 lines. You type this line:

```
pr -l 60 myfile | lpr
```

If you want to use pr and not have any heading at the top of the page, use the -t option:

```
pr -t myfile | lpr
```

(This example doesn't do anything interesting to myfile. In the next section, however, you see that it really is useful when you combine it with the margins and stuff.)

Marginally yours

You may frequently put printouts in three-ring binders. Normally, because printing starts very close to the left side of the page, the hole punch may put holes in your text and make the page difficult to read — not to mention make it look stupid. The -o option (that's a lowercase letter *o*, not a zero, for *o*ffset) pushes the stuff you print to the right, leaving a left margin. To leave five spaces for a left margin, for example, type this command:

```
pr -o5 myfile | lpr
```

Sometimes leaving a wider margin at the bottom of the page is nice. You can do that by combining the -l option (to set the page length, as described in the preceding section) with the -f option that tells pr to use a special form-feed character to make the printer start a new page. (Normally, the -l option uses blank lines to space to the next page, like a typewriter.) Use the following command if you're in this situation:

```
pr -o5 -l 50 -f myfile | lpr
```

This command tells UNIX to print just 50 lines per page, indented five spaces. That amount of space in the margin should be enough for anyone.

Seeing double

The -d option tells pr to double-space the printout. Type this command:

```
pr -d myfile | lpr
```

This command also puts a title on every page. Use -d -t to avoid that:

```
pr -d -t myfile | lpr
```

One column can't contain me

If the lines in your file are short, you can save paper by printing the file in multiple columns. To print your file in two columns, for example, type

```
pr -2 myfile | lpr
```

Astute readers probably can guess what the options -3, -4, and up to -9 do. (If you're not feeling that astute today, these options specify the number of columns you want.) Columns normally run down and then across the page, as they do in newspapers. If your file contains a list of items, one per line, and you want to print them in columns, you may want to change the order in which the lines print. If you want to print items across the page and then move down to the next line, and so on (which is nowhere near as cool), use the -a option in addition to the -2 or -3 option.

For a truly baffling effect, you can arrange to print several files side by side with the -m option:

```
pr -m firstfile secondfile | lpr
```

This command prints the first line of every file on the first line of the print-out, the second line of every file on the second line, and so on. You can specify as many as nine filenames and have them print side by side in skinny little columns. We never have been able to figure out much of a use for this option, although it is definitely a way to produce odd printouts.

Troff, Nroff, Groff!

No, it's not a rabid dog. It's a typesetting program. The troff program is the "typesetter *runoff*" that has been part of UNIX since the 1970s. The nroff program is "new *runoff*" (new as of about 1972), which formats documents for simple printers without fancy fonts. The groff program is the GNU (refer to Chapter 2) version of troff, which, like every GNU program, does all the stuff the originals do and about 47 other things, too. Because groff is free, whereas nroff and troff are subject to expensive licenses from whoever owns the original UNIX licensing rights this year, groff is all you see these days.

All the "roff" programs are *batch formatters*. In these programs, you type your document with formatting codes into a text file and then run the text file through groff, which produces a beautifully typeset version of your document, give or take all your typos and coding errors. Then you fix the document, re-groff, and so on. These programs are the antithesis of WYSIWYG (What You See Is What You Get) formatting.

People still use groff, partly because it's free and partly because you can do fancy stuff with highly structured documents that's difficult or impossible with WYSIWYG formatters. We don't expect that you'll write a great many groff documents yourself, but you'll probably run into some on the Internet or in software packages.

With a bit of effort, you can turn groff documents into something legible. Assuming that you have a PostScript printer available, type a command like this one:

```
groff filename
```

Replace *filename* with the name of the text file you want to print. The groff program interprets the typesetting codes in the text file and tells the printer how to print your document.

As you probably figured out if you got this far in this book, principle yields to hideous complication after you add a few practical details. This section describes some of the details and the ensuing complications.

Macro mania

Formatting a document by using troff and its cousins requires rather low-level detailed instructions using incomprehensible two-letter codes in the documents — instructions so detailed that even UNIX weenies find them tedious (and that's saying a great deal). To relieve the tedium, most troff documents take advantage of *macro packages* that define higher-level instructions, which people use rather than the low-level stuff. (These macro packages serve roughly the same function as style sheets in Microsoft Word.) The troff program has been around for more than 25 years, and many macro packages have come and gone, although a few have stood the test of time. Because lazy typists have written all of them, each has a cryptic two- or three-letter name, all starting with -m, the flag code that tells groff to use the macro package. Table 9-1 lists a few popular macro packages.

Table 9-1		Macro Packages
Name	*Description*	*Origin*
-ms	Manuscript macros	Bell Labs
-mm	Different manuscript macros	Another part of Bell Labs
-me	Eric's macros	Somebody's Ph.D. thesis at Berkeley (must have been a good thesis because he's now the head of Google)
-man	Manual page macros	Same place as -ms

To tell `groff` to format a document with the -ms macros, for example, you type

```
groff -ms filename
```

Telling *a priori* what macros are used in what document is difficult, unless the author took pity and gave you a clue by naming the file `mobydick.ms` or the like. Fortunately, the worst that happens if you use the wrong macro package is that the document looks ugly. (It's not totally illegible: The text is still there, but it's formatted incorrectly.) You can try different macro packages and see which one works least badly. As a general rule, documents from academia usually use the -me macro package, whereas those from industry usually use -mm or -ms. Documents about the UNIX system itself usually use -ms because -ms was written by some of the same guys who did the original UNIX work, and pages from the online manual (what the `man` command shows you) use -man.

Let's sneak a peek

One of the nicest things about `groff` is that it's *device independent,* which means that it can reformat your document for any of several output devices. To format your document and display it on a normal, text-only terminal, use the `nroff` command:

```
nroff -ms filename | more
```

(This command actually calls `groff`, but tells it to format for plain-text output. Change the -ms to one of the other macro packages if necessary.) The `more` command displays the result a screen at a time. Press the spacebar to move from screen to screen, or press Q when you see enough.

Why UNIX succeeded

Back in the mid-1970s, the whole idea of computerized document formatting and typesetting was much less established than it is now. Within AT&T, however, troff and the UNIX system it ran on rapidly became the standard for document preparation. Why? Two words: line numbers. AT&T files a large number of patents, and patent applications must have every fifth line numbered. The troff program was the first text formatter that could do that. The patent typists embraced troff (patent applications are revised and retyped about a thousand times before they're finally sent to the patent office), and the rest, as they say, is history.

If you're running X Windows, you can tell groff to display a page at a time, beautifully typeset in an X window, by typing this command:

```
groff -TX75 -ms filename
```

In the window that groff creates, press the spacebar to move from screen to screen or press Q when you see enough. If the type is too small to read, use -TX100 rather than -TX75 to make the text bigger. (You can't use any other numbers; X comes with one set of fonts for 75 dot-per-inch screens and another for 100 dot-per-inch screens, so that's what groff uses.)

Printing for the PostScript-Challenged

Earlier in this chapter, we talk about PostScript, the fabulously complicated printer language that enables you to print fabulously complex documents on PostScript printers. But what if you don't have a PostScript printer?

These days, the short answer is "Get one." Although PostScript printers used to cost much more than other kinds of printers, these days you can buy a perfectly decent PostScript laser printer for less than $500. Nonetheless, there are still lots of PostScript-free sites, where Ghostscript comes to the rescue.

Ghostscript is a free, GNU version (see Chapter 2) of PostScript, written by L. Peter Deutsch, a skillful programmer from way back who surely should have been doing something else when he wrote it. When Ghostscript runs, it reads its PostScript input from either a file or the keyboard (not very useful unless you're trying to learn PostScript) and produces its output on one of a zillion possible output devices. If you want to see what the PostScript document looks like, you can tell it to send its output to an X Windows system window. If you want to print the document, you can send its output to your printer.

Printing PostScript with Ghostscript

If you're lucky, your system manager installed Ghostscript so that it's semi-automatically called when you print a PostScript file. You typically use the `-v` flag, something like this:

```
lpr -v floogle.ps
```

Failing that, in order to run Ghostscript, you type its name (**gs**) and the name of the PostScript file to display:

```
gs floogle.ps
```

If you just type that line, Ghostscript opens a new X window and displays the first page of `floogle.ps` in that window — probably not what you want. Press Ctrl+C once or twice to stop Ghostscript from displaying the page in a window. To get Ghostscript to do something useful, you have to use switches — lots and lots of switches:

```
gs -sDEVICE=deskjet -dNOPAUSE -sOutputFile=floogle.lj
            floogle.ps quit.ps
```

What's going on here is that we set the output device (`DEVICE`) to a popular ink-jet printer. We tell it not to pause between pages, we tell it what output file to create and which PostScript file to print, and then we give it another file from the Ghostscript library (`quit.ps`). The `quit.ps` file contains a one-line command, which tells Ghostscript that it's finished. You can tailor this command as needed; run `gs -h` to see the available printers.

We expect that you find this subject a wee bit complicated. In practice, unless your system manager has set up Ghostscript to run automatically, your best bet is to find a local expert who can tell you the exact command to use. Lacking an expert, you can still look at PostScript on-screen by using a slick little program named Ghostview.

Part III
Getting Things Done

The 5th Wave   By Rich Tennant

FELDMAN NOVELTY ITEMS

"We can monitor our entire operation from one central location. We know what the 'Wax Lips' people are doing; we know what the 'Whoopee Cushion' people are doing; we know what the 'Fly-in-the-Ice Cube' people are doing. But we don't know what the 'Plastic Vomit' people are doing. We don't want to know what the 'Plastic Vomit' people are doing."

In this part . . .

*I*n the first two parts of this book, we talk about the computer, files, mice, printers, and the shell — you name it. But what about getting some real work done?

To do useful work, you need software. This part talks about using text editors, word processors, e-mail programs, and other useful programs. We also talk a little about installing software and (for you Linux users) doing a tiny bit of system administration.

Chapter 10

Writing Deathless Prose

. . . .

In This Chapter

▶ What is a text editor?

▶ What is a text formatter?

▶ What is a word processor?

▶ What is a desktop publishing program?

▶ Using `vi` if you absolutely have to

▶ Using `emacs`, which is not that bad, really

▶ Using `pico`, which works rather well

▶ Using `ed` if you don't have anything better

. . . .

*I*n the land of UNIX, many programs handle text. Where you come from, you may be accustomed to the idea of using a word processor when you want to type something and print it. Not in UNIX. It has four kinds of programs for this task, just to keep things interesting.

UNIX Has Its Way with Words

The four kinds of UNIX programs that handle text are

✔ Text editors

✔ Text formatters

✔ Word processors

✔ Desktop publishing programs

Before describing the most commonly used text editors in gory detail, we thought that you would want to know the differences among these four kinds of programs, in case you plan to impersonate a geek at the next meeting of your local UNIX users' group.

Just the text, ma'am

A text editor enables you to

- ✔ Create a file full of text
- ✔ Edit the text

You can print a file by using the lp or lpr programs, as described in Chapter 9, although text editors can't do boldface, headers or footers, italics, or all that other fancy stuff you need in order to produce modern, overformatted, professional-quality memos.

You may want to use a text editor to write letters and reports. You certainly will use one to send electronic mail, as described in Chapter 17.

The most commonly used text editors in the land of UNIX are vi, emacs, and pico. We have strong opinions about these editors, which becomes abundantly clear in the later sections in this chapter, where we tell you how to use each of them.

Text formatters aren't really editors

Text formatters are programs that read text files and create nice-looking formatted output. You use a text editor to make a text file that contains special little commands only the formatter understands; the .IT command, for example, makes something italic. When you run the text formatter, it reads the text file, reads the special little commands, and creates a formatted file you can then print. You use lp or lpr to print the output of the text formatter.

The most common UNIX text formatter is TeX, pronounced "tecccch" (like yecccch), an arcane language popular among mathematicians and physicists because of its capability to format large, complex equations, and because it produces more aesthetically pleasing results than any of its competitors. A companion program, LaTeX, is designed to make TeX easier to use (relatively speaking, of course). (See the nearby sidebar, "Howdy, TeX!" for more info about TeX and LaTeX and where to get them.)

Another common text formatter is troff. Some people use nroff (an older version of troff), or groff, a newer GNU version of the program. With luck, you never have to use any of them. If your luck has run out, you may want to check out the section about troff, nroff, and groff in Chapter 9.

Howdy, TeX!

Donald E. Knuth created the popular TeX text formatter way back in the late 1970s. According to Knuth himself, TeX is a "typesetting system . . . intended for the creation of beautiful books — and especially for books that contain a lot of mathematics."

Like troff and its cousins nroff and groff, TeX uses *macros* (prewritten bits of formatting code) to shield you (theoretically) from painful, low-level programming chores. In practice, TeX is hard to handle because it can do many, many things in a variety of ways, all proudly anti-intuitive. For people overwhelmed by the sheer complexity of TeX, Knuth created something called plain TeX, which is a slim and trim, stripped-down version of TeX. Because TeX overwhelms almost everyone, almost everyone uses plain TeX rather than TeX itself.

Over the years, various intrepid UNIX hackers have taken it upon themselves to write their own sets of macros that work with TeX. The best known is probably LaTeX (the La part comes from the last name of its creator, Leslie Lamport). To make a long story short, LaTeX simplifies TeX by letting you describe the structure of a document without making you worry about the way the document looks (sort of like using the built-in styles in a word processor, such as Microsoft Word). Other macro packages for TeX include Eplain, Lollipop, pdfTeX (for creating books in Adobe Acrobat), and HyperTeX (for creating hypertext documents, such as Web pages, with TeX).

Like many things UNIX, TeX and the TeX source code and documentation are available for free; you can download them from various FTP and Web sites on the Internet. Also, you can buy one of a number of commercial versions of TeX; you get technical support and, in some cases, additional features in exchange for your money.

The best source of information about TeX, LaTeX, and related subjects is The TeX Users Group home page on the World Wide Web (at www.tug.org/) or one of the many TeX Usenet newsgroups, such as comp.text.tex.

Cuisinarts for text: Word processors

Word processors combine the capabilities of text editors and text formatters. Most word processors are (or try to be) WYSIWYG (an acronym for What You See Is What You Get), which enables you to see on-screen how the document (that's what they call their files) will look when you print them.

Several surprisingly good, free word processors are available for UNIX. KWord, which comes with the KDE desktop package, is a simple but quite usable word processor. AbiWord is quite similar to Microsoft Word, and OpenOffice.org contains equivalents to most of the Microsoft Office. When writing this original version of this book in 1993, we used troff, but for the current edition we used OpenOffice.org Writer, which produced files that, to our editor's relief, work fine in Microsoft Word.

Most UNIX users think that word processors are for wimps (*what you see is all you've got*) because they like the unintelligible and unmemorable commands used by text formatters and prefer to imagine what their text will look like when it is printed rather than be able to see it on-screen. Text formatters can do more complex things than word processors can, such as format complicated mathematical expressions, lay out multi-page tables, and neatly organize sections and headers of huge, book-length documents. But that's probably not your problem.

Desktop publishing does it all

A desktop publishing (DTP) program resembles a fancy word processor. It can do everything a word processor can, plus things you need only if you are printing a book, newsletter, or something else that looks fancy. DTPs have facilities for creating tables of contents and indexes, maintaining cross-references — you name it. For writing an occasional memo, a desktop publishing program is definitely overkill.

The most popular desktop publishing program for UNIX is Adobe FrameMaker (available for PCs and Macintoshes also).

TeX and some versions of troff are available for free, which explains why they remain so popular (big surprise, eh?). All desktop publishers are commercial products that cost extra. Lots extra.

vi and emacs and pico are your friends

The rest of this chapter explains how to use each of the Big Three text editors (vi, emacs, and pico), along with some words about how to use the prehistoric but not yet extinct ed (who, as you will see, is *not* your friend). Even if you use a word processor or desktop publishing program, you may need to use a text editor to do some things, such as these tasks:

- ✔ Write electronic mail (see Chapter 17).
- ✔ Create or edit text files called *shell scripts,* which enable you to create your own UNIX commands (see Chapter 12).
- ✔ Create or edit special text files that control the way your UNIX setup works (see Chapter 7).
- ✔ Write C programs (just kidding!).

Shy vi, the Princess of Text Editors

The vi text editor can claim a unique status among UNIX editors: Almost every UNIX system in the universe has vi. This fact makes it a good editor to know if you plan to be moving around from system to system, because you can always count on it being there. Someone may have other reasons for using vi, but ease of use is not foremost among them.

To run vi, type **vi**, a space, and the name of the file you want to edit, and then press Enter.

If you get an error message when you try to run vi, talk to your system administrator. If the screen looks weird, your terminal type may not be set right — another reason to talk to your system administrator.

Editor à la mode

The most distinctive feature of vi (and the one that has spawned legions of vi-haters, along with a few devotees) is that it is a *modal* editor. The vi program is always waiting for one of two things: commands or text (also known as input). When vi is waiting for a command, it is in *command mode.* When it is waiting for text, it is in *input mode.* Normally, it is up to you to figure out which mode vi is in at any particular moment — it doesn't give you a clue.

Most vi commands are one letter long. Some are lowercase letters, and others are uppercase letters. When you type vi commands, be sure to use the correct capitalization.

If you are in input mode and want to give a command, press the Esc key.

Emergency exit from vi

To escape from vi, follow these steps:

1. **Press Escape at least three times.**

   The computer should beep. Now you are in command mode, for sure.

2. **Type the following line and press Enter:**

   :q!

   This line tells vi to quit and not save any changes.

Whenever we tell you to type a command, it works only if you are in command mode. If you are not sure which mode you're in, press Esc first. If you are already in command mode, pressing Esc just makes vi beep.

To switch from command mode to input mode, you tell vi to add the text after the character the cursor (the point at which you are working) is on (by using the a command) or to insert the text before the current cursor position (by using the i command).

Help! I need somebody!

The guy who wrote vi (remember Bill, the grouchy guy who's 6'4" and in excellent physical condition? — same guy) didn't believe in help, so there wasn't any.

Fortunately, vi has been used in so many introductory computing courses that Bill eventually relented and added "novice" mode. Rather than type **vi** to run the editor, type **vedit** to get the same editor with some allegedly helpful messages. In particular, whenever you're in input mode rather than command mode, vi displays, at the bottom of your screen, a message such as INPUT MODE, APPEND MODE, CHANGE MODE, or OPEN MODE. All these messages mean the same thing (except to Bill, evidently): Text you type when these messages are visible is added to the file rather than interpreted as commands.

Easy text-entry techniques

Make a new file with some deathless prose so that you can practice entering text in vi. Run vi with a new filename:

```
vi madeline
```

To add text after the current position of the cursor, type the letter **a** (you do *not* press Enter after a command):

We tell you in a minute how to move the cursor, when you have some text to move around in. You can type **a**, for example, to add this text to the newly created xanadu file:

```
In Xanadu did Kubla Khan
        A stately pleasure-dome decree:
        Where Alph, the sacred river, ran
        Through caverns measureless to man
            Down to a sunless sea.
```

To get back to command mode, press Esc. Press Esc whenever you finish typing text so that you are ready to give the next command.

Other commands you can use to enter text include i to insert text *before* the current cursor position, A (that's an uppercase A, which to vi is totally unrelated to a lowercase a) to add the text at the end of the line the cursor is on, and 0 to add the text on a new line before the current line.

The vi program shows you a full-screen view of your file. If the file isn't long enough to fill the screen, vi shows tildes (~) on the blank lines beyond the end of the file. Figure 10-1, for example, shows a text file called eating.peas (created in a later discussion about ed) as it appears in vi.

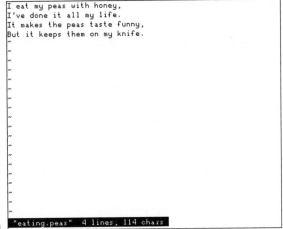

Figure 10-1:
Tildes fill up
the blank
lines on the
vi screen.

The cursor appears at the beginning of the first line of the file.

All kinds of ways to move the cursor

You can use dozens of commands to move the cursor around in your file, but you can get to where you want with just a few of them:

✔ The arrow keys (←, →, ↑, and ↓) usually do what you expect: They move the cursor in the indicated direction.

Sadly, on some terminals vi does not understand the arrow keys. If this statement is true for you, press h to move left, j to move down, k to move up, and l to move right. Bill chose these keys on the theory that, because those keys are a touch typist's home position for the fingers on the right hand, you can save valuable milliseconds by not having to move your fingers. Really. In some versions of vi, the arrow keys work only in command mode; in other versions, they also work in input mode.

✔ Enter or + moves the cursor to the beginning of the next line.

✔ The hyphen (-) moves the cursor to the beginning of the preceding line.

✔ G (the uppercase letter) moves the cursor to the end of the file.

✔ 1G moves the cursor to the beginning of the file. (That's the number 1, not the letter *l*. Why ask why?)

Giving your text a makeover

To modify the text you typed, follow these steps:

1. **Move the cursor to the beginning of the text you want to change.**

2. **To type over (on top of) the existing text, press the R key.**

3. **Type the new text. What you type replaces what is already there. Press Esc when you finish replacing text.**

4. **To insert text in front of the current cursor position, press the i key.**

5. **Type the new text. What you type is inserted without replacing any existing text. Press Esc when you finish inserting text.**

Removing unsightly text

To delete text, follow these steps:

1. **Move the cursor to the beginning of the text you want to delete.**

2. **To delete one character, type** x. **To get rid of five characters, type** xxxxx. **You get the idea.**

3. **To delete text from the current cursor position to the end of the line, type an uppercase D.**

4. **To delete the entire line the cursor is on, type** dd **(the letter *d* twice).**

Nobody undoes it better

Like many text editors, vi has a way to undo the most recent change or deletion you made. Type the letter **u** to undo the change. If you type an uppercase **U**, vi undoes all changes to the current line since you moved the cursor to that line.

Write me or save me — just don't lose me

To save the updated file, type the following (be sure that you press Esc first so that you're in command mode):

```
:w
```

That's a colon and a *w*, and then press Enter. You should give this command every few minutes, in case the confusing nature of vi commands makes you delete something important by mistake.

Good-bye, vi

To leave vi, type

```
ZZ
```

Be sure to press Esc a few times so that you are in command mode before giving this command. To quit and not save the changes you have made, type this line:

```
:q!
```

Then press Enter. This line means, "Leave vi and throw away my changes. I know what I'm doing."

Most other letters, numbers, and symbols are also vi commands, so watch what you type when you are in command mode. Table 10-1 lists the most common commands you use with vi.

Table 10-1	Commands in vi
Command	*Description*
Esc	Return to command mode
Enter	Move to beginning of next line
+	Move to beginning of next line
-	Move to beginning of preceding line
a	Add text after cursor

(continued)

Table 10-1 *(continued)*

Command	Description
A	Add text at end of current line
dd	Delete entire current line
D	Delete from cursor to end of line
G	Move (go) to end of file
1G	Move to beginning of file
h	Move one space left
i	Add text before cursor
j	Move down one line
k	Move up one line
l	Move right one space
O	Add text on new line before current line
:q! (followed by Enter)	Quit vi, even if changes aren't saved
R	Replace text
u	Undo last change
U	Undo changes to current line
x	Delete one character
:w (followed by Enter)	Save (write) file
ZZ	Quit vi and save changes

A Novel Concept in Editing: emacs Makes Sense

We don't want to get your hopes up, but emacs is much easier to use than vi. The reason is that it doesn't have the mysterious modes that require you to remember at every moment whether the program is expecting a command or text.

On the other hand, commands in emacs aren't exactly intuitive. Still, we like them better. In case you are wondering, the name *emacs* comes from *editor macros* because the original version of emacs was written as an extension to an early text editor called teco, an editor that makes ed (see the section "Talk to Mr. ed," at the end of this chapter) look like the winner of the Nobel prize for user-friendliness. (Scary thought, isn't it?)

To run emacs, type this line:

```
emacs eating.peas
```

You replace *eating.peas* with the name of the file you want, of course. If the file you name doesn't exist, emacs creates it. Like vi, emacs displays a full-screen view of your file, as shown in Figure 10-2. On the bottom line of the screen is the *status line,* which tells you the name of the file you are editing and other, less interesting information.

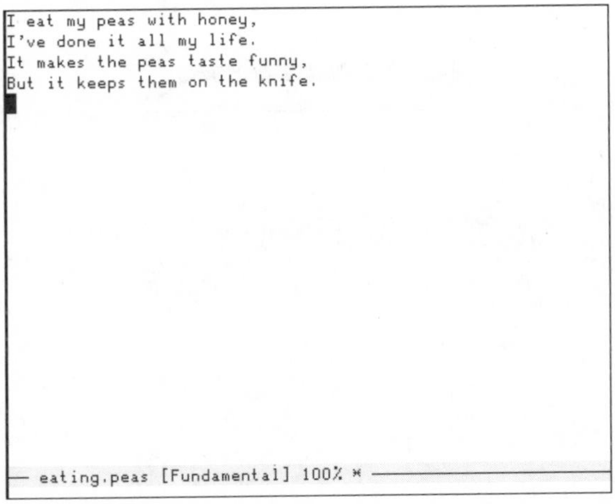

Figure 10-2:
The GNU
Emacs
display in
a text
console. At
the bottom
of the
screen,
emacs
displays on
the status
line the
filename
and other
mysterious
information.

```
I eat my peas with honey,
I've done it all my life.
It makes the peas taste funny,
But it keeps them on the knife.




















— eating.peas [Fundamental] 100% *
```

A tale of two emacs

Unlike vi, emacs does not automatically come with UNIX. Because most versions of emacs are distributed for free, however, most systems have it or can get it. By far the two most common versions of emacs are GNU Emacs and XEmacs. Despite the name, XEmacs runs under both X Windows and text-based consoles, and so does GNU Emacs. The basic commands are the same for both versions, and the most obvious differences between the two are the button bars and more sophisticated 3-D look to the windows in XEmacs. (Compare the difference in Figures 10-3 and 10-4.) Other than that, it really doesn't matter which you use.

Figure 10-3:
The GNU Emacs display in an X window includes pull-down menus for most common commands, including save, search, undo, and help.

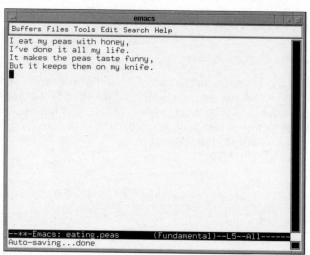

Figure 10-4:
The XEmacs display in an X window includes a toolbar in addition to pull-down menus and a 3-D look to the interface.

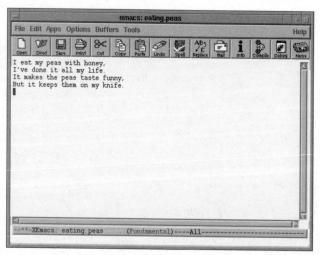

More than just a text editor

The `emacs` program is a cornucopia of bells and whistles, including two different e-mail packages, a newsreader, a file manager, color text highlighting, and countless other fun and unnecessary features. These features make `emacs` a much larger package than any other editor (it has been somewhat accurately called an operating system disguised as an editor) and has been known to cause some system administrators to balk at installing it on their UNIX machines. For others, it's almost a way of life, so whether you have access to `emacs` may depend on how strongly your system administrator feels about those types of things.

✔ If you get an error message when you try to run `emacs`, ask your system administrator what's up. The `emacs` program may have another name on your system. If your system administrator says that you don't have `emacs`, plead with him or her to get it.

✔ If `emacs` looks or acts weird (weirder than usual, that is), your terminal type may not be set correctly. Again, ask your system administrator to straighten it out.

To run XEmacs on the `eating.peas` file, type the command **xemacs eating. peas**.

Telling emacs what to do

Rather than have two modes, as does `vi`, `emacs` treats normal letters, numbers, and punctuation as text and sticks them in your file when you type them. (Pretty advanced concept, huh?) Commands are usually given by pressing combinations of the Ctrl (Control) key and a letter. You also give some commands by pressing the Meta key and a letter.

On most computers, the Meta key is the Esc key. If your keyboard has an Alt key, it may be the Meta key. Try Alt to see whether it works. If it doesn't, use Esc. Unlike with Alt, if you use Esc you must release the Esc key before you type the subsequent letter (Esc, release, letter). In the following section, we tell you to press Esc.

Another novel concept: Type to enter text

To enter text, just start typing! The text is inserted wherever your cursor is.

Getting around in emacs

To move the cursor around in your text, use these keys:

- Arrow keys usually move the cursor up, down, left, and right.

  In a few situations, emacs doesn't understand the arrow keys. If that's true for you, press Ctrl+B to move backward one character, Ctrl+F to move forward one character, Ctrl+P to move to the preceding line, and Ctrl+N to move to the next line. At least they tried to make them mnemonic.

- Ctrl+A moves to the beginning of the line.

- Ctrl+E moves to the end of the line.

- Esc+< (press Esc and then hold down Shift and press the comma key) moves to the beginning of the file.

- Esc+> (press Esc and then hold down Shift and press the period key) moves to the end of the file.

Making changes in emacs

Even though emacs is a better text editor, you still make typos, change your mind, and think of brilliant improvements to your text. To change text, follow these steps:

1. **Move the cursor to the beginning of the text you want to change.**

2. **Type the new text. The text is inserted wherever the cursor is.**

3. **Delete any text you don't want.**

It's that simple. No weird commands required.

Emergency exit from emacs

To stop using emacs, press Ctrl+X followed by Ctrl+C.

This command doesn't save any changes you made to the file in emacs. It just gets you out. Some versions of emacs may ask whether you want to save the file the editor was looking at or say something like "Buffers not saved. Exit?" (Translation: "Do you really want to quit without saving your changes?") Press Y for yes or N for no, as appropriate. If you just want to get out, press N to the "Do you want to save" question or Y to the "Buffers not saved" question.

TIP

Moving text in emacs

Although this subject is beyond the scope of this quick introduction to emacs, we tell you how to move text from one place to another in a file. It turns out that when you press Ctrl+K to kill the text from the cursor to the end of the line, the killed information is stored in a temporary place called the *kill buffer.* You can copy the information from the kill buffer back into your file by pressing Ctrl+Y (yank it back into the file). To move some text, kill it with Ctrl+K, move the cursor to the new location, and press Ctrl+Y to insert the text where your cursor is. (*Kill* and *yank* in emacs-ese correspond to *cut* and *paste* in the regular world.) If emacs is running in an X window, the kill buffer is connected to X's cut-and-paste system, which means that you can cut and paste between emacs and other programs.

Deleting stuff in emacs

emacs has several commands for deleting stuff:

- ✔ To delete the character the cursor is on, press Ctrl+D. Or, on many terminals, press the Del key.
- ✔ To delete text from the cursor to the end of the word (up to a space or punctuation mark), press Esc and then D.
- ✔ To delete from the cursor to the end of the line, press Ctrl+K.

Save that file before it's too late!

To save the text in the file, press Ctrl+XS (press and hold down the Ctrl key, press X and S, and then release the Ctrl key). You should save your work every few minutes. Even though emacs isn't as frustrating as vi (or ed, for that matter), lots can still go wrong.

Bidding emacs adieu

When you finish editing and want to leave emacs, press Ctrl+XC (press and hold down the Ctrl key, press X and C, and then release the Ctrl key). You leave emacs and see the UNIX shell prompt.

If you didn't save your work, emacs politely points out that your buffers
stuff you have been working on) aren't saved and asks whether you really
want to exit. It suggests pressing the n key as the safe default in case you
want to return to emacs to save the file. To leave without saving, press the y
key and then Enter.

It takes many fewer emacs commands to make a file and type some stuff,
make a few changes, and then save the file and leave than it does with ed or
vi. The emacs program has tons of commands, most of which are utterly useless. Table 10-2 lists the commonly used emacs commands.

Table 10-2	Commands in emacs
Command	**Description**
Ctrl+A	Move to the beginning of the line
Ctrl+B	Move back one space
Ctrl+D	Delete one character
Ctrl+E	Move to the end of the line
Ctrl+F	Move forward one space
Ctrl+K	Delete to the end of the line
Ctrl+N	Move to the next line
Ctrl+P	Move to the preceding line
Ctrl+XC	Leave emacs
Ctrl+XS	Save the file
Esc+<	Move to the beginning of the file
Esc+>	Move to the end of the file
Esc+D	Delete to the end of the word

A Peek at pico

One other editor has become popular: pico. As the Pine e-mail program has
spread like wildfire, the editor that comes with it, pico, has taken off, too.
pico is the easiest to use of the four text editors we describe in this chapter,
albeit not the most powerful. Folks at the University of Washington wrote it.

To run `pico`, type this command:

```
pico eating.peas
```

As usual, type the name of the file you want to edit rather than *eating.peas*. If you type a filename that doesn't exist, `pico` creates a file with that name just for you.

Your system may not have `pico` — if not, ask your system administrator if she can get it for you. Assure her that if she doesn't, you'll pester her ten times a day for the next year for help with `ed` or `vi`.

The `pico` screen looks like the one shown in Figure 10-5. Amazing — `pico` shows you at the bottom of the screen a menu of the most commonly used commands! What will they think of next?

Figure 10-5: The `pico` editor is easy to use, with a small menu at the bottom of the screen.

You're my type

Typing text into a file by using `pico` is a breeze. Just type. That's all. No modes, commands, or anything strange.

You move me

If your cursor keys work in `pico`, great. If not, you can use Ctrl+F to move forward one character, Ctrl+B to move back one character, Ctrl+N to move to the next line, and Ctrl+P to move to the preceding line. The following keys also move you around the screen:

✔ Ctrl+A moves to the beginning of the line.

✔ Ctrl+E moves to the end of the line.

✔ Ctrl+V moves forward one screen of text (F8 does this, too).

✔ Ctrl+Y moves back one screen of text (as does F7).

You're a big help

To get help with the `pico` commands, press Ctrl+G. If your keyboard has an F1 key, that should work, too. You see pages of helpful information about the program. Press Ctrl+V to see more or Ctrl+X to return to `pico`.

Time for a change

Editing your text in `pico` is also easy. Whatever you type is inserted wherever the cursor is. You can use these commands to edit stuff:

✔ Ctrl+D deletes the character the cursor is on.

✔ Ctrl+^ (that's Ctrl+Shift+6) marks the beginning of some text you want to work with. You use this command to select a bunch of text to delete or move.

✔ Ctrl+K (or F9) deletes (cuts) the text from the mark to the current cursor position. Blammo! — the text is gone and is stored in an invisible holding tank somewhere.

✔ Ctrl+U (or F10) uncuts or pastes the last text you cut, making it reappear where the cursor is now.

Thanks for saving my file

To save the text in a file, press Ctrl+O (or press F3). `pico` asks for the filename to write the text into, suggesting the filename you used when you ran `pico` in the first place. You can change the name so that the text is written to a new file or leave it as is, to update the existing file. When you press Enter, `pico` writes the information into the file.

I'm outta here

When you finish editing and want to leave `pico`, just press Ctrl+X. If you haven't already saved your file, `pico` asks whether you really want to leave, because leaving will lose any changes you made to the file since you last saved it. Tell it that you do. Then you're out, and you see the shell prompt.

Editors galore

UNIX being UNIX, you could use many more text editors in addition to the Big Three (and reluctant Fourth) described in this chapter, including such alien-sounding programs as sed, perl, and awk. The popular vim editor is a souped-up, X-ified version of vi. KDE comes with two editors, KEdit (a relatively simple one) and Kate (a fancier one), GNOME comes with gedit (a relatively simple, as far as anything in GNOME is simple, editor), and Cream (a GNOME-ized version of vim). A little searching around will find you more editors than you could try out in your lifetime. We suggest that unless you have a compelling reason to use a different editor, such as everyone else in your company uses another editor, stick with one of the Big Three. Someday you'll switch to another version of UNIX, and if your favorite editor isn't there, you'll either waste a lot of time finding and installing a copy of your editor, or else relearning one of the editors that it does have. But the Big Three are all either there, or easily added.

pico doesn't claim to be an editor with the power of emacs or vi. After all, you can't edit ten files at a time, read your mail, and rename files from pico. Who cares? It's a nice, easy program for editing text. Isn't that what a text editor is supposed to be?

Table 10-3 lists the top pico commands.

Table 10-3	Commands in pico
Command	*Description*
Ctrl+A	Move to the beginning of the line
Ctrl+B	Move back one character
Ctrl+D	Delete one character
Ctrl+E	Move to the end of the line
Ctrl+F	Move forward one character
Ctrl+G (or F1)	Get help (display online help information)
Ctrl+K (or F9)	Kill (delete) selected text (text between the mark and the cursor)
Ctrl+N	Move to the next line
Ctrl+O (or F3)	Output (save) the file
Ctrl+P	Move to the preceding line

(continued)

Table 10-3 *(continued)*

Command	Description
Ctrl+U (or F10)	Uncut (paste) the last text that was deleted by using the Ctrl+K command
Ctrl+V (or F8)	Move down one screen
Ctrl+X (or F2)	Exit from pico
Ctrl+Y (or F7)	Move up one screen
Ctrl+^ (Ctrl+Shift+6)	Mark the beginning of selected text

Talk to Mr. ed

The vi editor may seem like a quaint throwback to prehistoric software, but in the early days of UNIX vi didn't even exist. In the pre-CRT era of Teletype terminals, *line editors* ruled, and the standard among line editors was (and still is) ed. A *line editor,* such as ed, is one that assigns line numbers to the lines in a file. Every time you do something, you must tell ed which line or lines to do it to. If you use the EDLIN program in DOS, ed should look familiar. The ed program has been a part of UNIX since the beginning of time. When you use it, you begin to appreciate how far software design has progressed since 1969.

If you can get another text editor to use in *any way* @@repeat — *any way,* do it. If you don't think that ed can really be that bad, just peruse the rest of this section, and you will run screaming to your system administrator for vi , pico, or emacs (preferably pico or emacs).

Some systems have a program called ex that is similar to but not quite as horrible as ed. Try typing **ex** to see what happens.

To run ed, type this line:

```
ed important.letter
```

(Type the name of your file rather than *important.letter.*) If no file has the name you specify, ed makes one. UNIX responds to this command with a number, which is the number of characters (letters, numbers, punctuation, and spaces) in the file, just in case you are being paid to write by the letter.

If you receive an error message when you try to run ed, talk to your system administrator. Congratulate her on getting rid of that Neanderthal text editor and find out which text editor you *can* use.

Emergency exit from ed

To get the heck out of ed — in case someone used your computer and left it running — follow these steps:

1. Type a period on a line by itself and press Enter.

This step gets you into command mode, in case you're in input mode. If you are already in command mode, a line of the file prints on-screen. Ignore it.

2. Type q and press Enter.

If changes to the file have been saved or if there were no changes, this step quits ed

and you see a UNIX shell prompt. If changes to the file haven't been saved, ed displays a question mark, meaning, "Yo, you're about to throw away your changes. Are you cool with this?" Press the q key and press Enter again. This time, ed exits. If someone has used your computer and ran ed and didn't save the work, to heck with it. If *you* ran ed by mistake and are fighting to get out, you probably don't want to save any changes anyway.

In most versions of ed, you can also use the capital Q command, which means, "*Quit* — and don't ask any questions!"

Hey, Wilbur, which command was that?

All ed commands are one-letter long (such as h).

Remember *not* to capitalize ed commands unless we specifically say to. ed commands are almost all lowercase letters.

Relatively recent versions of ed (since, oh, about 1983) have a P command (that's a capital *P,* one of the few uppercase commands) that turns on a prompt. If you type **P** and press Enter, ed prompts you with an asterisk when it's in command mode and waiting for a command. Is that incredibly user-friendly or what? This P command enables you to determine when you're in command mode! Must have snuck that one in when the lazy typists weren't looking.

If you're in input mode and want to give a command, type a single period on a line by itself, which switches ed to command mode.

In the remainder of this discussion about using ed, whenever we tell you to type a command, it works only if you're in command mode. If you're not sure, type a period and press Enter first.

If you're in command mode and want to type some text, you switch to text-input mode. First, however, you must decide whether you're going to *append* (by using the a command) after the current line the lines of text you will type or *insert* (by using the i command) the lines of text before the current line. More about the current line and the a and i commands in a minute.

Feeding text to Mr. ed

When you want to create a file and feed some text to it start the process by typing this line:

```
ed eating.peas
```

You can name your file something other than *eating.peas*, if you want. UNIX responds with a question mark, just to keep you on your toes. (This time, the question mark tells you that ed just created a new file for you.)

To add (append) new lines of text to the end of the file — in this case, the end of the file is the same as the beginning because the file is empty — type **a** and press Enter. UNIX responds by saying nothing, which is your indication that ed is now in input mode and waiting for you to type some text. Type some pearls of wisdom, like this:

```
I eat my peas with honey,
I've done it all my life.
It makes the peas taste funny,
but it keeps them on the knife.
.
```

When you finish typing text, type a period on a line by itself to switch ed from input mode back to command mode. Not that ed gives you a hint that this process is going on, unless you have used the P command to tell it to prompt you.

The lines of text are now in your file. Now is a good time to save the file, just in case you kick your computer's plug from the wall in your frustration at having to use such a brainless program.

Getting Mr. ed to save your text

The following command saves your text in a file with ed. If you are in input mode, remember to type a period on a line by itself to switch to command mode before typing **w** (followed by Enter). That's w for *write*. UNIX responds with the number of characters now in the file. Be sure to give this command before leaving ed so that your deathless prose is saved in the file, in this case, eating.peas (or whatever filename you used when you ran ed).

What if ed commands end up in my text?

If you are in input mode and type an ed command, ed doesn't perform the command. Instead, it thinks that you are typing text and stores the letter or letters of the command as just some more text in your file.

If this happens, delete the lines you don't want (we explain how to delete lines later in this chapter). The next time you want to enter a command, first be sure to type a period on a line by itself.

Show me the file, please

Now that you have text in the file, how can you see it or change it? By using the p (print) command. This command doesn't print anything on the printer; it just displays it on-screen — another example of superb software engineering. (Well, it printed on those old Teletypes.) If you type the p command by itself, as follows, ed displays the current line. In the case of the sample eating.peas file, the current line is the last line in the file. You can also tell ed which lines to display by typing their line numbers. To display lines 1 through 4, for example, type this line:

```
1,4p
```

You can also use the symbol $ to stand for the line number of the last line in the file (in case you don't know how many lines are in the file). The following command always displays the entire file:

```
1,$p
```

A miserable way to edit

You can change the contents of a line of text with ed, but it involves giving commands that look like this:

```
12,13s/wrong/right/
```

This command substitutes right for wrong in lines 12 through 13, inclusive. Totally primitive and painful, isn't it? For the amount of editing you probably do in ed, it's almost easier to delete the line with the typo and insert a new line. We recommend that you immediately ask your system administrator for a better text editor.

Undo your thing, ed!

Wait — ed has one useful, humane command, after all! The u command enables you to "undo" the last (and only the very last) change you made to the file. If you delete a line by mistake with the d command, for example, you can type **u** and then press Enter to undo the deletion.

Be sure that you don't make any other changes before using the u command. It undoes only the last thing you did.

Time to ed out

When you finish making changes and you want to leave ed (or even if you're not finished making changes and you want to leave ed anyway), type **q** and then press Enter. If you are in input mode, first type a period on a line by itself to get into command mode. Then press the q key to quit.

If you haven't saved your work by using the w command, ed just doesn't quit. Instead, it displays a question mark to tell you that it was expecting a w command first. To save your changes, type these two commands, pressing Enter after each:

```
w
q
```

If you don't want to save the changes to the file, press the q key again at the question mark. This time, ed believes that you really want to leave and thus exits. Not a moment too soon!

As a review, Table 10-4 lists the commands you use most commonly with ed.

Table 10-4	Commands in ed
Command	*Description*
a	Add lines after the current line and enter input mode
d	Delete line or lines
h	Display extremely terse help message right now
H	Display terse help messages whenever anything goes wrong
i	Insert lines before the current line and enter input mode

Command	Description
n	Display line or lines with line numbers
p	Display line or lines
P	Display an asterisk whenever ed is in command mode
q	Quit the whole thing
Q	Quit regardless of whether changes have been saved
u	Undo last change
w	Write (save) the file

Chapter 11

Umpteen Useful UNIX Utilities

. . . .

In This Chapter

▶ A grab bag of useful programs

▶ Sorting and comparing files

▶ Stupid calendar tricks

▶ Squashing files to make them smaller

▶ Some other odds and ends

. . . .

*I*n spite of the fact that we have been making fun of UNIX in this book, we are well aware that UNIX actually has some fairly handy programs lying around. In this chapter, we look briefly at some of them. All these programs have a severe case of what is known as Feature Disease (closely related to the greasy fingerprints mentioned in Chapter 2): They all are bristling with features and options. Most of the features and options aren't worth mentioning, however, so we don't.

Comparing Apples and Oranges

When you have used your UNIX machine for a while, you have piles of files (say that six times quickly) lying around. Often, many of the files are duplicates, or near duplicates, of each other. Two programs can help sort out this mess: cmp and diff.

The simplest comparison program is cmp; it just tells you whether two files are the same or different. To use cmp to compare two files, type this line:

```
cmp onefile anotherfile
```

You replace *onefile* and *anotherfile* with the names of the files you want to compare, of course. If the contents of the two files are the same, cmp doesn't say anything (in the finest UNIX tradition). If they're different, cmp tells how far into the files it got before it found something different. You can compare any two files, regardless of whether they contain text, programs, databases, or whatever, because cmp cares only whether they're identical.

A considerably more sophisticated comparison program is diff. This program attempts to tell you not only whether two files are different but also how different they are. The files must be plain text, not word processor documents or anything else, or else diff becomes horribly confused. Here's an example that uses two versions of a story one of us wrote. We compared files tse1 and tse2 by typing this command:

```
diff tse1 tse2
```

Enter the name of the older file first and the name of the new, improved second file. The diff program responds:

```
45c45
< steered back around, but the sheep screamed in panic and
        reared back.
-
> steered back around, but the goats screamed in panic and
        reared back.
46a47
> handlebars and landed safely in the snow.
```

The changes between tse1 and tse2 are that, in line 45, the *sheep* changed to *goats,* and a new Line 47 was added after Line 46.

diff reports, in its first line of output (45c45) that changes (that's what the *c* stands for) were made in lines 45 through 45 (that is, just line 45). Then it displays the line in the first file, starting with a <, and the line in the second file, starting with a >. We think of this as diff's way of saying that you took out the lines starting with < and inserted the lines starting with >. Then diff reports that a new line is between lines 46 and 47 in the original file, and it shows the line that was inserted. This is a great way of seeing what changes were made when you get a new revision of a document you wrote. Most versions of diff can also show you the context — a few lines around each change — by giving an option like -3 (which shows three lines of context).

BSD versions of diff (including the version that usually runs under Linux) can compare two directories to tell you which files are present in one and not in the other, and to show you the differences between files with corresponding names in the two directories. Run diff and give it the names of the two directories.

Assorted Files

Computers are good at putting stuff in order. Indeed, at one time a third of all computer time was spent sorting. UNIX has a quite capable sorting program, cleverly named `sort`, that you may remember meeting briefly in Chapter 7. Here, we talk about some other ways to use the program.

The `sort` command sorts the lines of a file into alphabetical order. From the `sort` point of view, a line is anything that ends with a carriage return (that is, you pressed Enter). If you have a file containing a list, with one item per line, this command alphabetizes the list.

The easiest way to use `sort` is to sort one file into another. In other words, you tell `sort` to place the sorted version of the original file in another file. This way, you don't risk screwing up the original file if the sort runs amok. To sort the original `myfile` into a second file named `sortedfile`, type this command:

```
sort myfile > sortedfile
```

Although you can sort a file back into itself, you can't do it in the obvious way. The following line, for example, doesn't work:

```
sort myfile > myfile
```

The problem with this command is that the UNIX shell clears out `myfile` before the sort starts (with the result that, when `sort` tries to sort something, it finds that `myfile` is empty). You can use the `-o` (for *o*utput) option to tell `sort` where to put the results, like this:

```
sort myfile -o myfile
```

This command works because `sort` doesn't start to write to the output file until it has read all its input.

Normally, `sort` orders its results based on a strict comparison of the internal ASCII codes the computer uses for storing text. The good news is that this command sorts letters and digits in the correct way, although some peculiarities exist: Normally, uppercase letters are sorted before lowercase letters, so *ZEBRA* precedes *aardvark*. You can use the `-f` (for *f*old cases together) option to sort regardless of uppercase and lowercase letters:

```
sort -f animals -o sortedanimals
```

Although we could use the > redirection symbol in this example, with the sort command using the -o option is safer. You can use several other options also to tell it to sort:

-b	Ignore spaces at the beginning of the line.
-d	Use dictionary order and ignore any punctuation. You usually use this option with -f.
-n	Sort based on the number at the beginning of the line. With this option, 99 precedes 100 rather than follows it, as it does in usual alphabetical order. (Yes, the normal thing the computer does is pretty dumb. Are you surprised?)
-r	Sort in the reverse order of whatever would have been done otherwise. You can combine this option with any of the others.

We find sorting to be particularly useful in files in which every line starts with a date, as shown in these examples:

```
0505      Tonia's birthday
1204      Meg's birthday
1102      Zac's birthday
0318      Sarah's birthday
```

We could type sort -n to sort this file by date. Notice that we wrote May 5 as 0505 (not 55, for example) so that a numeric sort works.

You can do much more complex sorting and treat every line as a sequence of "fields" that sort uses to decide the final sorted order. If you really need to do complex sorting, talk to someone who knows something about sorting or, if you're feeling adventurous, type man sort.

Time Is Money — Steal Some Today!

All UNIX systems have internal clocks. You can ask the system what the date and time are with the date command:

```
date
```

UNIX responds with this information:

```
Thu Dec  4 15:43:50 EST 2003
```

Many options enable you to tailor the date format any way you want. Don't waste your time. UNIX has an idea about the time zone too, and even does daylight savings time automatically.

You can schedule things to be done later by using the `at` command. You say something like this:

```
at 5:15pm Jul 4
sort -r myhugefile -o myhugefile.sort
pr -f -2 myhugefile.sort | lp
```

Then you press Ctrl+D to indicate that you finished giving commands.

You give the `at` command and specify a time and date. Then you enter the commands you want to run at that date and time. Press Ctrl+D on a separate line to tell UNIX that you're finished listing tasks. In this example, we sort a huge file and then print it in two columns, all on the Fourth of July, when presumably no one is around to complain that it's taking too long. If you omit the date, UNIX assumes that you mean today if the time you give is later than the current time; otherwise, UNIX assumes that you mean tomorrow.

Any output that normally goes to the terminal is sent back to you by electronic mail, so you should at least skim Chapter 17 to find out how to read your mail.

Squashing Your Files

One problem common to all UNIX systems — indeed, to nearly all computer systems of any kind — is that you never have enough hard drive space. UNIX comes with a couple of programs that can alleviate this problem: `compress` and `gzip`. They change the data in a file into a more compact form. Although you can't do anything with the file in this compact form except expand it back to its original format, for files you don't need to refer to often, compressing can be a big space-saver.

Compress without stress

You use `compress` and `gzip` in pretty much the same way. To compress a file named `confidential.txt`, for example, type this line:

```
compress -v confidential.txt
```

The optional `-v` (for *verbose*) option merely tells UNIX to report how much space it saved. If you use it, UNIX responds with this information:

```
confidential.txt: Compression: 49.79% — replaced with
        confidential.txt.Z
```

The `compress` program replaces the file with one that has the same name with `.Z` added to it. The degree of compression depends on what's in the file, although 50 percent compression for text files is typical. For a few files, the compression scheme doesn't save any space, in which case `compress` is polite enough not to make a `.Z` file.

To get the compressed file back to its original state, use `uncompress`:

```
uncompress confidential.txt.Z
```

This command gets rid of `confidential.txt.Z` and gets back `confidential.txt`. You can also use `zcat`, a compressed-file version of the `cat` program, which sends an uncompressed version of a compressed file to the terminal, without storing the uncompressed version in a file. The command is rarely useful by itself but can be quite handy with programs, such as `more` or `lp`. You use it this way:

```
zcat confidential.txt.Z | more
```

This command enables you to see one page at a time what's in the file. Unlike `uncompress`, `zcat` does not get rid of the `.Z` file.

The GNU crowd weighed in with its own `compress`-like program named `gzip`. It works the same way that `compress` does, but uses a different, slightly better, compression scheme. The `gzip` program is analogous to `compress`. `gunzip` and `gzcat` uncompress stuff. Use them this way:

```
gzip -v confidential.txt
gunzip confidential.txt.gz
zcat confidential.txt.gz | more
```

Note that the files end with lowercase `gz` rather than uppercase `Z`.

Fortunately, `gzip` knows how to uncompress files produced by `compress` as well as those produced by several other compression programs, so you can use `gunzip` as your one-stop uncompression utility.

Yet another compression program, called `bzip2`, comes with companions `bunzip2` and `bzcat`. You use it the same way as `gzip`, except that the files it makes end with `bz2` and are a little smaller than the equivalent `gz` files. Downloaded files from the Web are sometimes compressed with `bzip2`. If your system doesn't have `bzip2` installed, you (or maybe your local helpful nerd) can find it at `http://sources.redhat.com/bzip2`. Here's how you use them:

```
bzip2 -v confidential.txt
bunzip2 confidential.txt.bz2
bzcat confidential.txt.bz2 | more
```

How does file compression work, anyway?

This discussion is pretty technical. Don't say that we didn't warn you.

The issue of *optimal codes* (codes that use the least number of bits for a particular file — or *message* because at that time they were thinking in terms of radioteletypes) was a hot topic in the late 1940s, challenging the deepest thinkers in the field. In 1952, a student named David Huffman published a paper that any high-school student could understand showing how to use simple arithmetic techniques to construct optimal codes. Oops. Ever since then, this kind of code has been known as *Huffman coding.* For many years Huffman coding was the best available, and a UNIX program named `pack` used it.

Normally, every character in a file is stored by using 8 bits (binary digits, 1s and 0s, the smallest unit of data a computer can handle). Suppose that a file contains 800 *As* followed by 100 *Bs*, and 100 *Cs*. That's 1,000 characters, at 8 bits apiece, or 8,000 bits. For this particular file, a compression program can use much shorter codes. It can use a 1-bit code for *A* and 2-bit codes for *B* and *C.* That makes the total size 800 bits for the *As*, and 200 bits apiece for the *Bs* and the *Cs* — a total of 1,200 bits rather than 8,000. The packed file is a little larger than that (1,408 bits) because a table at the front of the packed file indicates which codes correspond to which letters.

The `compress` program uses a dictionary-compression scheme, which is kind of backward from Huffman coding. Rather than try to find the shortest code for every letter, `compress` runs through the file trying to find frequently occurring groups of letters it can encode as a single dictionary entry, or *token.* To compress the same file we packed in the previous paragraph, `compress` reads letter by letter and notes that it has seen *AA* more than once; then it notices that it has seen *AAA* more than once, and so on. It enters longer and longer runs of *A*'s into its dictionary until it has runs of more than 300 *As*, each represented by a single dictionary entry and a single token in the compressed file. When `compress` runs into the *Bs* and then the *Cs*, it does the same thing and also enters long runs of *Bs* and *Cs* in the dictionary.

Using a clever technique (at least, it's clever to data-compression wonks), `compress` doesn't have to store the dictionary in the compressed file because `uncompress` can deduce the contents of the dictionary that `compress` was building from the sequence of tokens in the compressed file. As a result, `compress` does a fantastic job on this file and squashes it to a mere 640 bits from the original 8,000.

Compression techniques are still a hot topic in the computer biz, and many techniques have been patented. The particular technique `compress` uses is known as LZW, after *L*empel, *Z*iv, and *W*elch, the three guys who thought of it. Welch, who works for Unisys and made some improvements to an earlier scheme designed by Lempel and Ziv, has a patent on it. It's such a cool technique, in fact, that two other guys named Miller and Wegman, who work for IBM, invented it at about the same time, and they also have a patent on it. Because the patent office is not supposed to grant two patents on the same invention, some people use this situation to suggest that issuing patents on software isn't a good idea. Fortunately, neither Unisys nor IBM has ever objected to the `compress` program, and the patent expired in June 2003, so you can go ahead and use it. `Gzip`, `zip`, and `bzip2` use techniques that are somewhat similar to LZW but not covered by patents.

Zippedy day-tah

WinZip and PKZIP are widely used compression programs among Windows and DOS users to create ZIP files containing one or more files compressed together. You may run into ZIP files if you get information from the Internet or on a disk from a DOS or Windows system. Fortunately, a number of volunteers (led by a perfectly nice guy who goes by the enigmatic handle of Cave Newt) have written free zipping and unzipping programs named `zip` and `unzip`. Because they're both available for free over the Internet, no UNIX system should be without them.

To unzip a ZIP file, you use `unzip`:

```
unzip video-list.zip
```

The `unzip` command has a bunch of options, the most useful of which is `-l`, which tells the program to list the contents of the ZIP file without extracting any of the files. To find out what all the options are, run `unzip` with no arguments.

If you need to create a ZIP file, you can use the equally boringly named `zip` program:

```
zip video-list *.txt
```

This command says to create a file named `video-list.zip` (it adds the `.zip` part if you don't) containing all the files in the current directory whose names end in `.txt`. The `zip` program has a number of options, the most useful of which are `-9`, meaning to compress as well as possible even though it's slow (`-1` means as fast as possible; other digits give results in between), and `-k`, which means to make the file look just like one created on a DOS system, not using any lowercase filenames or other UNIX-isms. We use `zip -9k` to create ZIP files to copy to DOS systems.

Incidentally, `gzip` bears only the vaguest connection to `zip` and `unzip`. `gzip` compresses single files, whereas `zip` compresses multiple files into a single archive.

What's in That File?

Sometimes you have a bunch of files and no recollection of what they contain. The `file` command can give you a hint. It looks at the files you name on the command line and makes its best guess about what's in the files.

To have file try to figure out what's in the files in the working directory, type this line:

```
file *
```

UNIX responds with this bunch of seemingly incomprehensible information:

```
sleuth1.doc: Microsoft Office Document
sleuth1.ms: [nt]roff, tbl, or eqn input text
tse1: ascii text
pictures.zip: Zip archive data, at least v2.0 to extract
```

This mess says that file figured out that sleuth1.doc was a Microsoft Word document, sleuth1.ms is a text file coded for input to the troff text formatter (those other programs are some of troff's helpers), that tse1 contains text, and that pictures.zip is compressed using zip. The file program guesses "data" whenever it has no idea what's in a file, usually because it was created by an application not commonly used on UNIX.

Chapter 12

Installing Software Can Be Tricky

. . . .

In This Chapter

▶ Where does software come from (the software stork)?

▶ Where to put software

▶ Writing shell scripts, or files full of commands

▶ Writing aliases for your favorite commands

▶ Grabbing software from the Internet

▶ Uncompressing, uudecoding, and otherwise fooling with files that contain programs

. . . .

*I*f you are a Windows or Macintosh user, you probably are thinking: "I can install new programs. What's the big deal? I just stick in a disk or a CD-ROM and type INSTALL, right?" No. In UNIX, it's not that simple, of course. You face issues of paths, permissions, and other technical-type stuff we have been protecting you from.

On the other hand, we're not about to train you to be a system programmer. Every user has a few favorite programs, and you wear out your welcome quickly if you go off to your local wizard every time you want to use a new program. Although installing new UNIX programs is much trickier than installing PC or Mac programs, in many cases you *can* do it yourself.

The Software Stork

Interesting software comes from many places:

✔ Some other user on the same machine already has it for his or her own use, and you want to use it, too.

✔ Some other machine on the network has a program you want for yourself. See Chapter 16 for the gory details of copying the program from other machines on the network.

✔ Someone sends you programs through e-mail. (Yes, it's possible, although you should be really, really sure that it's from someone you trust before you install it.)

✔ You create files that contain frequently used commands so that you don't have to type them repeatedly. In UNIX-speak, these files are called *shell scripts.* In essence, you make your own multipurpose UNIX commands.

First, we talk about where you should put your own software. Then we go into more detail about the mechanics of putting it there.

You've bin had

Every UNIX user should have a bin directory. It's just a directory named bin in your home directory. If it's not there, you can make it by going to your home directory and typing this line:

```
mkdir bin
```

The thing that's special about bin is that the shell looks for programs there. Most system administrators automatically set up a bin directory for users. If not, and you had to create it yourself, you may have to do some fiddling to tell the shell to look for programs there. See the sidebar "Your search path," later in this chapter, for the bad news.

To put programs in your bin directory, you just copy them there by using the cp command. Alternatively, you can move them there by using the mv command, a text editor, or any other way to create or move a file.

TIP

Why is it named bin?

Early on, bin was short for *bin*ary because most programs that people put there were, in fact, compiled binary code. In the late 1970s, a famous professor of cognitive science at the University of California published a paper titled "The Trouble with UNIX," in which he complained bitterly about how difficult it was to use UNIX. One of the items on his list was that bin was difficult to remember. One of the UNIX guys at Bell Labs published a witty rebuttal and pointed out that many of the allegedly "more natural" command names the professor suggested were merely the names the computer system at his university used. The UNIX guy reported that many Bell Labs users thought that a bin was the obvious place to stash their programs. So, it's still a bin.

The famous professor, who subsequently worked at Apple and Hewlett-Packard and is now back in academia, has come around somewhat and is reputed to even use UNIX now and then, although he probably shuts his office door so that no one can see.

You Too Can Be a Script Writer

You can make your own commands (that is, shell scripts) and put them in your `bin` directory. A *shell script* is a text file that contains a list of shell commands — the same commands you type at the shell prompt. You can store a list of commands as a shell script and run the commands any time by typing the name of the shell script. This section tells you how.

Shelling a script

To create a shell script, use any text editor (refer to Chapter 10). Enter the commands one per line, just as you type them at the shell prompt. Save the file in your `bin` directory.

Here's an example — if you frequently search for files with names that begin with `budget`, you probably are tired of typing this command over and over:

```
find . -name budget* -print
```

(Check out Chapter 8 to see how the `find` command works.) Instead, you can put this command in a shell script and perhaps name the script `findbud`. To do it, create a text file named `findbud` that contains just one line: the command.

First you move to your `bin` directory because that's where your programs live:

```
cd bin
```

Then you use a text editor to create a text file containing the commands you want in your script. In this example, we use `ed`, a creepy editor, but you can use the editor of your choice instead. Type

```
ed findbud
```

UNIX responds with this line:

```
?findbud
```

or maybe

```
findbud: No such file or directory
```

Either way, you are editing the `findbud` file. Type this command:

```
a
```

This command tells ed to start appending text to the end of the findbud file. (Remember that because you're using ed, you have to type weird commands.)

Then type these two lines:

```
find . -name budget* -print
.
```

The dot on a line by itself tells ed to return to command mode. To save the file, type

```
w
```

UNIX responds with the information that you saved a file with 29 (or so) characters:

```
29
```

Quit ed by typing this command:

```
q
```

You see the shell prompt again. Great! You created a shell script!

Getting your script to play

After you create the text file, you must tell UNIX it is executable — that it's more than a mere text file. Type this line:

```
chmod +x findbud
```

This line marks the findbud file as *executable* (it's a script the shell can run).

Running and rehashing your script

To run the shell script, just type its name:

```
findbud
```

Voilà! You just created your own UNIX command! UNIX runs the find command to look for your budget files.

Your search path

You can ignore this section unless you have put a command in your `bin` directory, and the shell can't find it. Still reading? Sorry to hear it. The shell has a list of directories that contain commands; this list is known as the *search path*. On any sensible UNIX system, the `bin` directory is already in your search path. If not, you have to put it there. You do it in two stages: putting it in once and putting it in permanently.

To see what your current search path is, type the following line if you are using the C shell:

```
echo $path
```

If you have BASH or the Bourne or Korn shell, type this line:

```
echo $PATH
```

Yes, one's uppercase and one's lowercase. Arrgh! The C shell responds with something like this:

```
/bin /usr/bin /usr/ucb/bin
   /usr/local/bin
```

BASH or the Bourne or Korn shell shows something like this:

```
/bin:/usr/bin:/usr/ucb/bin:/usr
   /local/bin:.
```

What you have to do is add your bin directory to the path.

If you use the C shell, type this magical incantation:

```
set path=($path ~/bin)
```

That's a tilde (~) in the middle. This line tells the C shell to set the path the same as the current path (`$path`), plus the `bin` subdirectory of your home directory (~).

If you use BASH or the Bourne or Korn shell, type this even more magical incantation:

```
PATH=$PATH:$HOME/bin
export PATH
```

Note that the second time you type **PATH** and **HOME** in the first command, you include a dollar sign ($) in front of them. This line tells the Bourne or Korn shell to set the path the same as the current path ($PATH), plus the `bin` subdirectory of your home directory ($HOME). Same song, different words.

Now you should be able to run your new script regardless of which directory you're using.

This new, improved path lasts only until you log out. To put your `bin` directory on the path every time you log in, you must add the incantation to the end of the shell script that runs automatically whenever you log in. If you use the C shell, add it to the `.login` file. If you use the Bourne or Korn shell, add it to the `.profile` file.

Yes, these filenames begin with periods. Filenames that start with periods usually don't show up in file listings, which is why you haven't noticed these files in your home directory. Type the following line to list all your files, including these hidden ones:

```
ls -a
```

In principle, you only have to edit the file, go to the end, and add the necessary lines. In practice, screwing up is easy, so — unless you're feeling particularly brave — you're probably better off asking for expert assistance.

You're not quite finished, though. Observe what happens when you go to another directory. Type the following two commands to go to your home directory and give the findbud command there:

```
cd
findbud
```

UNIX may respond with this message:

```
findbud: Command not found.
```

If so, type one of these commands to get UNIX to do what you want:

```
hash findbud
```

or

```
rehash
```

(Try the first; if it doesn't work, try the second.) Now when you type findbud, it works.

What's going on? Well, it's Mr. too-smart-for-his-own-good Shell. Because programs don't appear and disappear very often, when the shell starts up, it makes a list of all the commands it can access and where they are. Because five or six command directories frequently exist, this process saves considerable time (the alternative is to check every directory for every command every time you type one). The hash and rehash commands tell UNIX to rebuild its list (known in geekspeak as a *hash table*) because you have added a new command (the findbud file is really a command, remember?). If the command still doesn't work, you have to fiddle with your search path — not a pretty job. See the nearby sidebar, "Your search path."

Type **hash** or **rehash** to tell the shell that you have added a new command and that you want it to rebuild its list of available commands to include this one. If you don't give the **hash** or **rehash** command and you change directories, you can't use the newly created shell script during this login session.

One could write an entire book about shell scripts (others have done so, in fact). The finer points naturally vary depending on which shell you use, although this explanation gives you the general idea. Shell scripts aren't limited to one line: They can be as long as you want, which is handy when you have a long list of commands you want to run regularly.

TIP

Don't give me any arguments!

Shell scripts can be complete programs. Every shell program has lots of swell programming features you don't want to know about. One is so useful, however, that we're going to tell you anyway: Your shell scripts can use information from the command line. That is, if you type `foogle dog pig`, your script named `foogle` can see that you ran it saying `dog` and `pig`. The things on the line after the name of the command are called *arguments*. The word *dog* is the first argument, and *pig* is the second one. In shell scripts, the first argument is named `$1`; the second, `$2`; and so on. In shorthand, `$*` means "all the arguments."

Suppose that you want to write a script named `2print` that prints files in two-column format. (You do that by using the `pr` command, described in Chapter 9.) Create a file named `2print` that contains this line:

```
pr -f -2 $* | lp
```

Then use the `chmod` and, if necessary, `hash` or `rehash` commands to make `2print` an executable script. If you want to print several files, one right after the next, in two-column format, you can type this line:

```
2print onefile anotherfile
    yetanotherfile
```

In reality, you are saying

```
pr -f -2 onefile anotherfile
    yetanotherfile | lp
```

This line prints all three files in two-column format. (Note that you may need to use `lpr` rather than `lp` in this shell script. Refer to Chapter 9.)

Borrowing Other People's Programs

Lots of times, someone else has a cool program you want to be able to use. You have two approaches to getting what you want, and both are pretty easy. Suppose that your friend Tracy has a program named `pornotopia` in the `bin` directory. (No, we don't know what it does, either.) How can you run it?

The long way

If you use the C shell, you can run the program from Tracy's directory by typing this line:

```
~tracy/bin/pornotopia
```

If you use BASH or the Bourne or Korn shell, you can type this line:

```
/usr/tracy/bin/pornotopia
```

The easier way

Typing this long string of letters and symbols every time you want to run the program is a pain. A better way is to put in your `bin` directory a *link* to the cool program so that you can run it directly. (Links are described in Chapter 8.) You use the `ln` command to create a link, which makes the file appear to be in your own `bin` directory, too.

Try the direct approach. Move to your home directory and create a link:

```
cd
ln ~tracy/bin/pornotopia bin/pornotopia
```

With any luck, this method works, creating a link from Tracy's file to your `bin` directory. Give or take a quick `hash` or `rehash`, you're all set.

The `ln` command doesn't work, however, if you and Tracy have files on different hard drives. (All this stuff is explained in Chapters 8 and 16.) In this case, you may get this unhelpful message:

```
ln: different file system
```

If you get this message, it's time for Plan B. UNIX systems have *symbolic links* that work across different hard drives (these links also are explained in Chapter 8). Try this line:

```
ln -s ~tracy/bin/pornotopia bin/pornotopia .
```

If it works, it makes a symbolic link to the file you want. You're all set: The link to `pornotopia` refers to Tracy's version. After a `hash` or `rehash`, you're ready to go.

Using an alias

If you were named pornotopia, you probably would want an alias, too. Fortunately, the BASH, Korn, and C shells give you the ability to invent a short name for a long command. (Bourne shell users, you're out of luck. Skip to the next section.)

Time for Plan C. In the BASH and Korn shells, type

```
alias dobudget='/usr/tracy/bin/pornotopia'
```

This line tells the shell that, when you type `dobudget`, you really want to run Tracy's program. Heh, heh. To avoid inadvertent ease of use, the C shell's `alias` command works in almost the same way, but it is punctuated slightly differently:

```
alias dobudget '/usr/tracy/bin/pornotopia'
```

(In both cases, the single quotes are optional if the command doesn't contain any spaces or special characters, although it never hurts to use them.)

You can define aliases for any frequently used one-line command. The alias can contain spaces, pipes, and anything else you can type on a command line. In BASH, for example, you can type

```
alias sortnprint='sort -r bigfile | pr -2 | lpr'
```

This line makes the new `sortnprint` command sort your `bigfile` in reverse alphabetical order, format it in two columns with `pr`, and send the result to the printer. Aliases can also be useful if you are subject (as we are) to chronic miswiring of the nerves in your fingers. We always type `mroe` when we mean `more`, and the following alias fixes it:

```
alias mroe=more
```

(That's the BASH version; the C shell has a space rather than an equal sign between `mroe` and `more`.)

Aliases you type directly to the shell are lost when you log out. If you want them available permanently, you must put the `alias` commands in your `.login` or `.profile` file, in the same way we mentioned earlier in this chapter, in the "Your search path" sidebar.

Using a shell script

If this method doesn't work either, try Plan D to use Tracy's program: a one-line shell script. Although we use the `ed` program because it's easier to show in a book, you should use a real editor. Start by revving up `ed`:

```
ed bin/pornotopia
```

You get the following helpful response, or something like it:

```
?bin/pornotopia
```

Now tell `ed` to add some text to the file, by typing this command:

```
a
```

You are now in append mode. Type the command line you want to include in the shell script, followed by a dot (period) on a line by itself:

```
/usr/tracy/bin/pornotopia
.
```

The dot on a line by itself switches back to ed's command mode. Then type this command:

```
w
```

This command writes the new shell script file and prints the size of the file. Then type the following to quit ed:

```
q
```

Type the next command to make your new shell script runnable:

```
chmod +x pornotopia
```

If necessary, give this command to tell UNIX to redo its hash table:

```
rehash (or hash, if that's what your shell needs)
```

Now your script named pornotopia runs Tracy's original program named pornotopia. At least one of these three plans should work for any program lying around anywhere on your system.

We don't even discuss software copyrights, licenses, and ethics here, but, if you use a copyrighted program, you should pay for it unless you like to think of yourself as a thief.

Stealing Software from the Network

If you are on the Internet, you can get zillions of programs free for the taking. You can get copies of programs in the same way you get copies of anything else on the Internet — by either using FTP or downloading files from a Web browser, such as Netscape, Opera, or Mozilla. See Chapter 19 for the inside scoop on downloading files from the Internet.

On many UNIX systems, this process is the most common way to get new software. Although most of it is shareware or freeware, even some commercial outfits are now selling their programs that you can download from the Internet.

Tar pits

When you download UNIX software from the Internet, nine times out of ten the filename ends in either .tar, .tar.Z, or .tar.gz. (We get to the most common exception in the next section.) Named, oddly enough, *tar files,* they don't have anything to do with black, goopy paving material; *tar* is short for *t*ape *ar*chive. You use this command for backing up (what used to be called "archiving," in the days when people went out of their way to make computers Look Important) UNIX systems to tape. (We discuss this use of `tar` in Chapter 23.)

In this section, though, you're seeing `tar` in its other role, where it moonlights as a software-packaging command. The people who distribute the software use `tar` to glom into one big `tar` file all the files that make up the software package (it can have anywhere from just a few to as many as hundreds of files). This way, you download only one big file rather than hundreds of little files. Because `tar` files are generally so big, the software distributors then squish them even more, using either the `compress` command (which results in a file ending in `.tar.Z`) or the `gzip` command (which results in a file ending in `.tar.gz`). Using `compress` used to be the standard, but because `gzip` results in smaller files, it's the compression program most people use these days.

If you're familiar with the Microsoft Windows world, you may have come across *zip files,* which end in `.zip`. These files are the Windows equivalent of `tar` files, except that zip combines the glomming and squishing phases into one command, an example of efficiency that true UNIX die-hards would never stand for.

Suppose that you find a really cool editor that you decided you can't live without, and you download the `tar` file. It probably looks something horrendous, like `really_cool_ed_unix_v.3.4p16.tar.gz`. To unpack your newly acquired `tar` file, first you have to unsquish it. If the file ends in `.tar.Z`, type this command:

```
uncompress really_cool_ed_unix_v.3.4p15.tar.Z
```

Otherwise, type this command:

```
gunzip really_cool_ed_unix_v.3.4p15.tar.gz
```

Either way, you end up with a file named `really_cool_ed_unix_v.3.4p16.tar`. Notice that the `.Z` or `.gz` is gone? This file is much bigger now that it's unsquished.

Now you have to *untar* the file (that's really the way the UNIX gurus phrase it). This step blows up your `tar` file into potentially hundreds of little files and puts them into whatever your current directory is. Make sure that your working directory is the directory where you really want all those files to be rather than someplace where you'll have to move them later. (Moving one tar file where you want it is considerably easier than waiting until after you've blown it up into multitudes of files.) Okay, ready? Type this command:

```
tar xvf really_cool_ed_unix_v.3.4p15.tar
```

The *x* in xvf stands for extract, the *v* means verbose so that you can see all the files being created, and *f* is for file and is followed by the name of the tar file.

Don't get too excited yet, because you still have more to do. Included in the bunch of files you just created should be a file usually named README or INSTALL. This file has the rest of the installation instructions specific to the package you just downloaded.

Revving up RPM

For years, the tar file method has been the only game in UNIX-land for distributing software over the Internet. For UNIX administrators who are accustomed to installing software packages, this method works just fine. Among everyone else, though, a growing number of disgruntled users have clamored for an easier way to install and maintain software. Their calls were answered by Red Hat Linux, which came up with the Red Hat Package Manager (RPM).

RPM is a software-management system that is a substitute for tar. Rather than download a file ending in .tar.gz, you download one that ends in .rpm. The RPM utility unpacks the file, puts all the resulting little files in their correct places, and updates a database of installed software on the computer. If you later want to install an upgrade, RPM remembers that an older version is already installed and saves any existing configuration files while upgrading the necessary files. This feature is enough to generate grumbling from traditionalists about user-friendliness infiltrating UNIX.

An important caveat about RPM is that you can install software this way only if you are the system administrator, which for most people happens only if they have a PC running Linux, as described in Chapter 14. So far, its use has been limited mainly to versions of Linux, although the use of RPM is not necessarily restricted to Linux, and we've heard of people using it on other UNIX systems, too.

Unwrapping packages

If you use one of the BSD varieties of UNIX, including FreeBSD (which happens to be the version that Mac OS X is based on, so Mac users should keep reading), NetBSD, or OpenBSD, and if you're the system administrator and know the superuser password, you can use the *package* system to install software on your computer. It's the same general idea as RPM, except of course that it's different because we wouldn't want to be excessively compatible.

The program to install packages is called `pkg_add`. You give it the name of the package, which is a `.tar.gz` or `.tgz` (same thing for lazy typists) file. If you already downloaded the package or it's on a CD-ROM, you give it the actual name of the package file. If not, you can give a URL that says where the package is on the Internet. Either way, type **su** and enter the password to become the superuser, then run `pkg_add`:

```
pkg_add pornotopia-1.1.tgz
pkg_add
ftp://ftp.FreeBSD.org/pub/FreeBSD/ports/packages/multimedia/
          pornotopia-1.1.tgz
```

Unless someone sends you the URL of a package in an e-mail message or a Web page, the URL can be kind of hard to guess. Many versions of `pkg_add` have a `-r` option that looks in some likely places on the Internet to find the package:

```
pkg_add -r pornotopia
```

Because `pkg_add` runs as the superuser, you have no protection against software that turns out to be buggy or malicious. The packages from the main distribution site for each system, like `www.freebsd.org` for FreeBSD, should be fine, but otherwise be very sure of what you're getting.

Real Software Installation

In case you're wondering, purchased software has official software-installation procedures. To install these pieces of software, you must be the superuser — the one who can clobber anyone's files anywhere — by logging in as `root` or running `su`, and run a program named something like `install`. The `install` program directs you to load tapes, CD-ROMs, or disks as appropriate; reads in the programs; and then asks a bunch of configuration questions, such as "Does this system support DES-protected NFS mounts across router boundaries?" We suggest that you leave this procedure to trained professionals.

Chapter 13

Juggling a Bunch of Programs

· ·

· ·

*I*f you have a plain old terminal with no windowing system, you may be envious of users with fancy window systems who can pop up a bunch of windows and run umpteen programs at a time.

Don't. Any UNIX system enables you to run as many programs simultaneously as you want. Nearly all the systems let you stop and restart programs and switch around among different programs whenever you want.

If you're used to an old-fashioned, one-program-at-a-time system, such as DOS (without Windows) or the pre-System 7 Mac, you may not see the point of doing several things at a time. Suppose, however, that you're doing something that takes awhile and the computer can manage with little or no supervision from you, such as copying a large file over a network (which can take 10 or 15 minutes). You have no reason to sit and wait for that process to finish — you can do something useful while the copy runs in the background.

Or, suppose that you're in the middle of a program and you want to do something else: You're writing a memo in a text editor and need to check some e-mail you received to make sure that you spelled someone's name right. One way to do that is to save the file, leave the editor, run the mail program, leave the mail program, start the editor again, return to the same place in the file, and pick up where you left off. What a pain. UNIX enables you to stop the editor, run the mail program, and resume the editor exactly where you left it. For that matter, you can run both the editor and the mail program and flip between them as necessary.

Lots of X Windows

If you're running Motif or any other X Window Graphical User Interface (GUI), you probably already figured out how to run many programs at a time: Open several `xterm` windows and run a program in each one. You create a new window by moving the mouse outside of any window, holding down the left mouse button to get a menu and selecting New Window or something similar. If you're running a version of CDE, running many programs at a time is even easier: Just double-click the icon for each program you want to run. That's it. You don't even have to deal with opening `xterm` windows.

Read this chapter anyway, however, particularly the sidebar "Do windows and job control mix?" later in this chapter.

In the interest of fairness, we must point out that *job control,* the feature that enables you to flip back and forth, was written by Bill, the same guy who wrote the C shell, `vi`, and NFS (Network File System, described in Chapter 16). In contrast to our opinion of some of his other efforts, we think that job control is pretty cool.

If you have a process that has run amok, see Chapter 24 to find out how to kill it.

So What Is a Process, Anyway?

All the work UNIX does for you is done by UNIX *processes.* When you log in, the shell is a process. When you run an editor, the editor is a process. Pretty much any command you run is a process.

Processes called *daemons* lurk in the background and wait to do useful things without manual intervention. When you use `lp` or `lpr` to print something, for example, a daemon does the real work of sending the material to the printer.

Normally, all this process stuff happens automatically, and you don't have to pay much attention to it. Sometimes a program gets stuck, however, and you can't make it go away. If you use a personal computer running Windows 98 or a pre-OS X Macintosh, the usual response to a stuck program is to restart the computer. When you run UNIX, resetting the computer is a little extreme for a single stuck program. For one thing, other running programs and other people who are logged in do not appreciate having their computer kicked out from underneath them. Also, UNIX may take awhile to restart from a forced reboot (our system takes about 5 minutes to check all the hard drive), and you run the risk of losing files that were being updated.

Why processes are not programs and vice versa

Although programs and processes are similar, they're not the same. A *process* is, more or less, a running program. Suppose that you're using X Windows, have two windows on-screen, and are running vi in both of them. Although the same program is running in both windows, they're different processes doing different things (in this case, editing different files).

To add to the confusion, some programs use more than one process apiece. The terminal program cu, for example, uses two processes: one to copy what you type to the remote computer and the other to copy stuff from the remote computer back to your screen. Sometimes, hidden processes take place: Many programs have a way you can execute any UNIX command from inside the program. (In vi and ed, for example, you type ! and the command you want to run.) In addition to the command, a shell process usually interprets the command.

In most cases, identifying in a list of processes which one is which is easy because each one is identified by the command that started it.

Any Processes in the House?

The basic program you use to find out which processes are around is ps (for *process status*). Although the details of ps (wait! — how did you know?) vary somewhat from one version of UNIX to another, two main kinds of ps exist: the System V kind and the BSD kind. (SVR4 uses the System V kind of ps, even though SVR4 has a great deal of BSD mixed in. Linux uses a ps that looks more or less like BSD.)

Mind your ps (and qs)

If you run plain ps, no matter which version of UNIX you have, you get a list of the processes running from your terminal (or window, if you're using X Windows). The list looks something like this:

```
PID    TTY      TIME COMMAND
24812 ttyp0    0:01 -csh
25973 ttyp0    0:00 ps
```

The PID column gives the *process identification*, or *process ID*. To help keep processes straight, UNIX assigns every process a unique number as an identifier. The numbers start at 1 and go up. When the PIDs become inconveniently large (about 30,000 or so), UNIX starts over again at 1 and skips numbers that are still in use. To get rid of a stuck process, you have to know its PID to tell the system which process to destroy.

The TTY column lists the terminal from which the process was started. In this case, ttyp0 is the terminal, which happens to be pseudoterminal number 0. (Because UNIX systems are written by and for nerds, they tend to start counting at 0 rather than at 1.) UNIX uses a *pseudoterminal* when you're logged in from a window on your screen or from a remote system through a network rather than through a real, actual, drop-it-on-your-foot-and-it-hurts terminal. For our purposes, all terminals act the same, whether they're real, pseudo, or whatever.

The TIME column is the amount of time the computer has spent running this program. (The time spent waiting for you to type something or waiting for disks and printers and so forth doesn't count.)

The COMMAND column shows, more or less, the name of the command that started the process. If the process is the first one for a particular terminal or pseudoterminal, the command name starts with a hyphen.

The Linux ps

The Linux ps command has one additional column:

```
PID  TTY STAT   TIME COMMAND
1797 pp5 S      0:00 -bash
1855 pp5 R      0:00 ps
```

The STAT column shows the status of the process. According to the man page (online documentation) for the command, *R* means runnable, *S* means sleeping, *D* means uninterruptible sleep, *T* means stopped or traced, and *Z* means a zombie process. Wow! For our purposes, *R* means that it's a command you ran, and the other stuff doesn't matter much.

Fancier ps (and qs)

The System V version of ps has lots of options, most of which are useless. One of the more useful is -f, which produces a "full" listing:

```
UID    PID    PPID   C    STIME TTY        TIME COMMAND
johnl 11764   3812   0 14:06:02 ttyp3      0:00 /usr/bin/emacs
johnl 11766  11764   0 14:06:05 ttyp3      0:00 /bin/sh -i
johnl 11769  11766  10 14:06:15 ttyp3      0:00 ps -f
johnl  3812   3804   0   Jan 18 ttyp3      0:04 -sh
```

(We did it from a different window, which you can tell because the PID of the shell is different.)

This listing has a few more columns than does the basic ps listing, and a few columns are different. The UID column is the username — just what it looks like. PPID is the *parent PID,* the PID of the process that started this one. We had run emacs from the shell and then told emacs to start another shell to run a ps command.

The parent PIDs reflect the order in which the processes started each other: The login shell process (number 3812) is the parent of emacs, which in turn is the parent of the shell /bin/sh, which is the parent of ps. (We could explain why the processes aren't listed in order, but — trust us — you don't want to know.) All processes in a UNIX system are arranged in a genealogical hierarchy based on which process started which. The grand ancestor of them all is process number 1, which is named init. You can trace the ancestry of any process back to init. "Hark! I am yclept Ps, son of Bourne Shell, daughter of Emacs, son of Dash-shell (or is that Dashiell?), great-great-grandson of the ancient and holy Init!"

The C column is a totally technoid number relating to how much the process has been running lately. Ignore it. STIME is the *start time,* the time of day the process began. If it began more than 24 hours ago, this column shows the date. TTY is the name of the terminal the process is using. If you run a GUI, such as X Windows, and you run the xterm program in a window (as we did in this example), the entry for TTY doesn't show the terminal you are using. Instead, it lists the pseudoterminal assigned to the window (a useless piece of information). Sometimes the TTY column shows a ?, which means that the process is a daemon that doesn't use a terminal.

The COMMAND column shows the full command that began this process, including (in some cases) the full pathname of the program. (Because standard system programs live in the directories /bin and /usr/bin, you see them frequently in ps listings.)

If you're logged in on several terminals or in several windows, you may want to see all your processes, not just the ones for the current terminal. With the System V version of ps, you can ask to see all processes for a given user by using this command:

```
ps -u tracy
```

This command lists all processes belonging to user tracy. You can ask to see any user's processes, not just your own. You can get a full listing for that user, too:

```
ps -fu tracy
```

System V has other, less useful switches for ps, notably -e, which shows every process in the entire system.

Berkeley ps (and qs)

The basic report from the BSD version of ps looks like this example:

```
PID TT STAT   TIME COMMAND
7335 p4 S     0:00  -csh (csh)
7374 p4 R     0:00 ps
```

The PID, TIME, and COMMAND columns are the same as those you already know about. (In the COMMAND column, the true name of the program is listed in parentheses if a dash or something is in the regular name.) The TT column lists a short form of the terminal name (pseudoterminal 4, in this case). STAT lists the status of the process: R means that the process is running right now; anything else means that it isn't. Usually, you don't care unless you have a stuck process and you wonder whether it's sitting there waiting for you to type something (then its status is I or IW) or running off into the woods (then its status is R).

Adding the -u switch gives a user-oriented report, although perhaps they had a different kind of user than you and we in mind, as you may gather from this example:

```
USER      PID %CPU %MEM  SZ  RSS TT STAT START  TIME COMMAND
john1    7375 0.0  0.9  196  436 p4 R    14:59  0:00 ps -u
john1    7335 0.0  0.6  196  316 p4 S    14:56  0:00 -tcsh (tcsh)
```

The %CPU and %MEM columns list the percentage of the available central processor time and system memory the process has taken recently (these numbers are usually close to 0). RSS is Resident Set Size, a measure of how much memory the process is using right now, measured in thousands of bytes (abbreviated as K). The ps command, for example, takes 436K bytes (which is horrifying when you consider that the *entire* UNIX system used to fit into 64K total bytes). The START column lists the time of day the process began.

You can ask for a particular terminal's process list by using the -t option, as shown in this example:

```
ps -tp4
```

With the -t option, you have to use the same two-letter terminal abbreviation ps uses. Have fun guessing it. Try the two-letter abbreviations that appear in the TT column of the ps listing.

The BSD version of ps has lots of other useless options, including -l for a *long* technoid listing; -a for *all* processes, not just yours; and -x to show processes not using a terminal. You have no way to ask for all processes belonging to a particular user.

To see all the processes you started, type this incantation:

```
ps -aux | grep tracy
```

Replace Tracy's name with your own username. This line redirects the output of the ps command to the grep command (described in Chapter 8), which throws away all the lines except those that contain your username.

Why cd isn't a process

People always ask us (well, someone asked once) why the cd command doesn't always act the way they expect it to. The problem is what is called in erudite circles *Lamarckian Heritability* and what we call "you look like your mother."

When a parent process creates a child process, the child inherits many characteristics from its parent, such as the username, terminal, and (this one is important) current directory. The child, ungrateful for its heritage — as all children are — can change many of these things. Because inheritance goes only one way, changes in the child don't affect the parent. Suppose that you create a new process (type **sh** to start a new shell as the second process). Then go to some directory other than the one you are using, such as /tmp, by typing **cd /tmp**. Then type **pwd** to make sure that you are in /tmp. Leave the new shell by typing **exit**, and then type **pwd** back in the old shell to prove that you're back in the original directory.

This example proves that cd can't be a normal command executed in its own process. If it were, the new directory would apply to only that process. As soon as the process was finished, you would be back in the shell with the directory unchanged.

The authors of the various shells finessed this problem using what's technically known as a *kludge* (something that works but that you're not proud of; it rhymes with "huge," not with "fudge.") The kludge checks especially for the cd command and handles it itself in the shell. The exit and logout commands also are handled in the shell for the same reason.

Here's an example of where you may run into this stuff: If you make a shell script (see Chapter 12) that contains a cd command, the cd affects only subsequent commands in that script. After your shell script finishes running, you find yourself back in the original directory as though the cd never occurred. Although you can write a script that does change the directory, doing so is so complicated that even wizards shrink from the task.

Starting Background Processes

Starting a background command is simplicity itself. You can run any program you want in the background: When you type the command, stick a space and an ampersand (&) at the end of the line just before you press Enter.

Suppose that you want to use `troff` to print a file (even though we warned you not to use it). Because this process is bound to take a long time, for example, typing the ampersand to run it in the background is wise:

```
troff a_really_large_file &
```

The shell starts the command and immediately comes back to ask you for another command. It prints a number, which is the *process ID* (or PID) assigned to the command you just started. (Some shells print a small number, which they call the *job number,* and a larger number, which is the PID.) If you know the PID, you can check up on your background program with the `ps` command. If you get tired of waiting for the background process, you can get rid of it with the `kill` command and the PID, as you see in Chapter 24.

You can start as many programs simultaneously as you want in this way. In practice, you rarely want more than three or four. Because only one computer is switching back and forth among the various programs, the more simultaneous things you do, the slower each one runs.

When your background program finishes, the C, Korn, BASH, and SVR4 Bourne shells tell you that the program is finished; older versions of the Bourne shell say nothing.

If you know that a program will take a long time (a program that crunches for a long time to produce a report, for example), you can use the `nice` command with that program. The `nice` command tells the program to run in a nice way so that it gets a smaller share of the computer than it would otherwise. Although the `nice` program takes longer to run, other programs run faster, which is usually a good trade-off if the `nice` program was going to take a long time anyway. To use it, you just type **nice** followed by the command to run:

```
nice genreport Tuesday.raw &
```

You almost always use `nice` to run programs in the background because only an inexplicably saintly user wants to slow down a program he was going to sit and wait for.

If you want to wait for background programs to finish, the `wait` command waits for you until they're all finished. If you become impatient, you can interrupt `wait` by pressing Ctrl+C (or Del, depending on your system). These keystrokes interrupt only the `wait` and leave the background processes unmolested.

The Magic of Job Control

Quite awhile ago (in about 1979), people (actually, our pal Bill) noticed that, many times, you run a program, realize that it will take longer than you thought, and decide that you want to switch it to a background program. At the time, the only choices you had were to wait or to kill the program and start it over by using an & to run it in the background. Job control enables you to change your mind after you start a program.

The job-control business requires some cooperation from your shell. In SVR4, all three shells handle job control. In some earlier versions of UNIX, only the C shell, or sometimes the C shell and Korn shell, handled job control.

Suppose that you start a big, slow program by typing this line:

```
bigslowprogram somefile anotherfile
```

The program runs in the foreground because you didn't use an ampersand (&). Then you realize that you have better things to do than wait, so you press Ctrl+Z. The shell responds with the message Stopped. (If it doesn't, you don't have a job-control shell. Sorry. Skip the rest of this chapter.) At this point, your program is in limbo. You can do three things to it:

- ✔ Continue it in the foreground as though nothing had happened, by typing **fg** (which stands for *f*oreground).

- ✔ Stick it in the background by typing **bg** (for *b*ackground), which makes the program act as though you started it with an & in the first place.

- ✔ Kill it if you decide that you shouldn't have run it. This method is slightly more complicated. Details follow.

Take this job and . . .

UNIX calls every background program you start a *job*. A job can consist of several processes (which, as you know, are running programs). To print a list of all your files in all your directories with titles, for example, you can type this line:

```
ls -lR | pr -h "My files" | lp &
```

This command lists the files with ls, adds titles with pr, and sends the mess to the printer with lp, all in the background. Although you use three different programs and three separate processes, UNIX considers it one job because each of the three programs needs the other two in order to get work done.

Every regular command (those you issue without an &) is also a job, although, until you use Ctrl+Z to stop it, that's not an interesting piece of information. You can use the `jobs` command to see which jobs are active. Here's a typical response to the `jobs` command:

```
[1] - Stopped (signal)   elm
[2] + Stopped            vi somefile
```

This listing shows two jobs, both of which have been stopped with Ctrl+Z. One is a copy of `elm`, the mail-reading program; the other job is the `vi` editor. (The difference between `Stopped (signal)` and plain `Stopped` is interesting only to programmers, so we don't discuss it much.) One job is considered the *current job* — the one preceded by a plus sign (+); it's the one most recently started or stopped. All the rest are regular background jobs, and they can be stopped or running.

. . . stick it in the background

You can tell any stopped job to continue in the background by using the `bg` command. A plain `bg` continues the current job (the one marked by a plus sign) in the background. To tell UNIX to continue some other job, you must identify the job. You identify a job by typing a percent sign (%) followed by either the job number reported by `jobs` or enough of the command to uniquely identify it. In this case, the `elm` job is called %1, %elm, or %e because no other job uses a command starting with an *e*. As a special case, %% refers to the current job. Although some other % combinations are available, no one uses them. Typing **bg %e**, for example, continues the `elm` job in the background.

. . . run it in a window in the foreground

To put a process in the foreground, where it runs normally and can use the terminal, you use the `fg` command. Continuing a job in the foreground is so common that you can use a shortcut: You just type the percent sign and the job identifier. Typing **%1** or **%e**, for example, continues the `elm` job in the foreground. Typing **%v** or **%%**, however, continues the `vi` editor in the foreground.

Do windows and job control mix?

If you use a GUI system such as KDE or GNOME, you can run lots of programs in lots of windows. Is there any need for this Ctrl+Z nonsense? By and large, the answer is no; popping up three windows to run three programs is much easier than flipping the programs around in one window. (Chapter 4 shows you how to pop up new windows.)

Even if you use a GUI, it doesn't hurt to learn about job control, though. It's not hard to use, and someday you may be stuck in a single window (when you use `telnet` to access another system) or be banished to a regular non-X terminal. Then you will appreciate what job control has to offer.

. . . shove it

To get rid of a stopped or background job, use the kill command with the job identifier or (if it's easier, for some reason) the PID. You can get rid of the vi editor job by typing this line:

```
kill %v
```

Typically, you start a job, realize that it will take longer than you want to wait, press Ctrl+Z to stop it, and then type **bg** to continue that process in the background.

Alternatively, you interrupt a program by pressing Ctrl+Z, run a second program, and, when the second program is finished, type **fg** or %% to continue the original program.

You don't often bring in the gangster kill to turn out the lights on a program, although knowing that you have friends in the underworld who can put a nasty program to sleep for good is nice to know. Chapter 24 talks more about it.

What happens when two programs try to use the terminal?

Suppose that a program running in the background tries to read some input from your terminal. Severe confusion can result (and did, in pre-job-control versions of UNIX) if both the background program and a foreground program — or even worse, two or three background programs — try to read at the same time. Which one gets the stuff you type? Early versions of UNIX did the worst possible thing: A gremlin inside the computer flipped a coin to decide who got each line of input. That was, to put it mildly, not satisfactory.

With the advent of job control, UNIX enforced a new rule: Background jobs can't read from the terminal. If one tries, it stops, much as though you had pressed Ctrl+Z. Suppose that you try to run the ed editor in the background by using this command:

```
ed some.file &
```

UNIX responds:

```
[1]   + Stopped (tty input)   ed
```

As soon as ed started and wanted to see whether you are typing anything it should know about, the job stopped. You can continue ed as a foreground program by typing **fg** or %% if you want to type something for ed. You can kill it (which is all that ed deserves) by typing **kill %%**.

Taming background terminal output

Any program, foreground or background, usually can scribble on-screen anything it wants at any time it wants. More often than not, that's okay because most programs are well behaved about not blathering when they're in the background.

In some cases, however, particularly when you use a full-screen editor, the interspersed output gets on your nerves. Fortunately, job control lets you solve this problem. You can put your terminal into *terminal output stop* mode: When a background program wants to send something to the terminal, it stops, just as it does when it wants to

read something. You then have the same alternatives to continue that program in the foreground if you want to see what it has to say or kill it if you don't. To turn on output stop mode, type this command:

```
stty tostop
```

To turn off output stop mode, type this line:

```
stty -tostop
```

The stty command is used to make all sorts of changes to the setup of your terminal.

Full-screen programs and job control

Programs that take over the entire screen (or the entire terminal window), notably the vi and emacs editors and mail programs such as elm, treat the Ctrl+Z interrupt in a slightly different way. Just stopping the program and starting it again later isn't adequate; the screen shows the results of what you did in the meantime. To solve this problem, full-screen programs make arrangements with UNIX to be notified when you press Ctrl+Z and again when you continue them so that they can do something appropriate, such as redraw the screen when you continue. This process generally is all automatic and obvious, although people occasionally are confused when the screen is magically returned after they give the fg command.

Chapter 14

Taming Linux

. . . .

In This Chapter

▶ A few basics for the reluctant system administrator

▶ How a Linux system is structured

▶ Where to get help

. . . .

*Y*eah, we know that it's pronounced "linn-ux" or "leen-ux," not "line-ux," but it still needs taming, and if you look around the office and find nobody other than yourself to fix things, you're the Linux tamer.

Congratulations! You're a System Administrator!

Using Linux is no different from using any other UNIX, as long as it's on someone else's computer, and he or she has set you up with an account. When *your* computer is running Linux, however, and *you* are responsible for maintaining it, things become much more complicated. Although we have no way to teach all the complexities of Linux system administration in a book like this one, we can describe a few key points to get you started.

Linux For Dummies, 5th Edition, by Dee-Ann LeBlanc (published by Wiley Publishing) is a great introduction to Linux and Linux administration. *Running Linux,* by Welsh and Kaufman (published by O'Reilly & Associates), has most of the information you need to *really* administer a Linux system. Also, the World Wide Web is awash in sites devoted to Linux. A good place to start is the popular Linux site at www.linux.org/. (See Chapter 18 for more information about the World Wide Web if you're uncertain what it means.) Chapter 26 lists a number of other places to go Linux hunting on the World Wide Web.

The root of all UNIX

UNIX is a multi-user world, and that includes Linux: Lots of people can use the computer at the same time, by connecting from remote locations. The first thing you need to know about administering a Linux system is the difference between the user called root and every other user. Root (also grandly called the superuser) is the system administrator. This account has all the privileges to change things on the system. If you want to add users, install some software, or even turn off the computer, you must be logged in as root. If you're logged in as someone other than root and you try to do anything related to system administration, your computer responds with a barrage of "permission denied" messages. It's nothing personal. It's just the computer's way of telling you that in a multi-user environment, it doesn't want just anyone messing around with it — only the one person it trusts, which is root.

"Fine," you say. "I'll just log in as root all the time and not have to worry about running into those pesky permission problems." Bad idea! Using the root account to do non-system-administration tasks is dangerous because sometime — eventually, when you least expect it — you type a command you really didn't want to — oh, say, deleting all the files on the hard drive (it happens more frequently than you may think). If you're logged in as someone other than root, the computer replies with a simple "permission denied." If you're root, though, the damage is done, and Linux (or any other version of UNIX) does not have an undelete command! Remember that permissions are your friends!

Adding a user

Assuming that you're convinced about not logging in as root unless you really must, you have to add a user account for yourself (or for others) to use for everyday tasks. Suppose that you want to create the username bobbyjoe for yourself. To add this user, log in as root (because adding users is one of those special, privileged tasks that only root can perform) and at the shell prompt type the command adduser bobbyjoe. The computer creates the new user and then, if you're lucky, reminds you to set the password for the new user. Whether or not the computer reminds you, you have to add the password by typing passwd bobbyjoe. Then enter the password when the computer asks for it. It asks you to enter the password twice, just to make sure that you typed it correctly.

Windows users of the world, unite!

Users who bring experience with other flavors of UNIX to their first encounters with Linux will probably find getting Linux up and running relatively easy. The large (and growing) community of Windows users who want to add or switch to Linux will likely encounter some fairly rough sledding.

One of the great things about Linux is that it can run on PCs with Intel chips in them. Disgruntled Windows users can therefore switch to Linux without having to buy a new computer. Windows users who are still sufficiently gruntled can check out Linux by installing it, cheek by jowl, on the same computer with Windows (as long as it has enough free disk space, of course).

All well and good, in theory. In practice, however, you can get yourself into trouble with startling efficiency. Even if it's going to coexist on your computer with Windows, Linux needs its own separate file system, which in turn needs its own separate area of your computer's disk. These separate areas are called *partitions*, or *drives*, and you have to have at least two

partitions, one for Windows and one for Linux, to get Windows and Linux to live together in peace and harmony.

If you have only one big drive or partition on your computer, you have to create a second partition before you can even begin installing Linux. To do so, you have to run a DOS utility named `fdisk` on your computer. The trouble with `fdisk` is that if you make one false move, everything that's already on your computer gets wiped out, no questions asked. If you already have Windows installed on your computer, do yourself a favor and back up your system before even *thinking* about using `fdisk`. Then carefully follow whatever instructions you have for setting up a computer that can run both Windows and Linux (known as a *dual-boot* system). *Linux For Dummies* (mentioned earlier in this chapter), for example, describes the whole process in gory detail. If you already have Windows installed, you can also use Partition Magic, a popular (but not free) disk utility to repartition your hard drive without having to reinstall everything from scratch.

With some versions of Linux, your computer gives you remedial password advice if it thinks that you need it. If you create a user named `noah` and then try to add the password `ark`, your computer may say BAD PASSWORD: It's WAY too short. If you try to fake the computer out by adding the password `arkarkark`, it may say BAD PASSWORD: it does not contain enough DIFFERENT characters. If you're not sure what constitutes a good password, go back and read the section in Chapter 1 about password smarts. As a system administrator, you're responsible for the security of the system, so don't say that you haven't been warned.

How do I turn this thing off?

UNIX and Linux are very sensitive to impolite treatment on the part of the operator. If you just log out and turn off the machine with the power switch, it reminds you of this rude treatment with a flood of error messages when you next restart the computer. To turn the machine off, you first must execute the shutdown command. While logged in as root, enter the command shutdown now to turn the machine off gracefully. If other users are logged in and you want to give them some warning, you can type the number of minutes until shutdown: shutdown +10, for example, waits ten minutes before shutting down and warns any users who are logged in. To reboot the computer, shutdown -r now (-r for *reboot*) shuts down the machine and then restarts it. Some Linux systems also let the "three-finger salute" (Ctrl+Alt+Del, familiar to DOS and Windows users) serve as a shortcut for shutdown -r now.

A Pride of Linuxes

Complete Linux systems are packaged into *distributions,* which describe not how Linux is distributed but rather how the operating system and the GNU programs are bundled. A few distributions are in common use: Slackware, Red Hat, Mandrake, and Debian. All are available for free via the Internet or for a small charge on CD-ROM. As a user, which distribution you use doesn't matter because they all behave in much the same way. As a system administrator, though, you should consider the important differences the distributions have among them.

Slackware, the oldest of the three, has been around since the beginning of Linux. It is the most traditional distribution (traditional in the UNIX sense, as in not particularly user-friendly) and has relatively little in the way of utilities to facilitate the management of a Linux system. For this reason, those who have been around UNIX systems for a while tend to favor it.

Linux: Not just for PCs

Although Linux was originally developed for Intel-based PCs, you can now find versions of Linux for just about every kind of computer currently in production. Most of the popular distributions have versions for the PowerPC (the chip inside modern Macs), and Yellow Dog Linux (www.yellowdoglinux.com) has a version designed just for Macs. If you have $10 million to spare, IBM will be happy to sell you a high-end mainframe computer running Red Hat, SuSE, or Turbolinux, or, if you want, all three at the same time.

Linux goes commercial

The freely available, "alternative" image of Linux discouraged commercial enterprises from adopting Linux in its early days. Understandably, many companies did not want to deal with an operating system that did not have a corporate entity standing behind it, no matter how reliable or trouble-free the product. To fill this need, a number of companies have stepped in to provide commercial support for Linux. Red Hat Software, Inc., for example, provides a commercial version of its Linux distribution in addition to the free version. Organizations that purchase the commercial Red Hat distribution can therefore turn to Red Hat for support rather than (or in addition to) Usenet. Most other distributions also have support companies that support them for a monthly or yearly subscription.

Red Hat Linux is the most popular distribution. It features plenty of tools to make the life of a system administrator easier, most notably the Red Hat Package Manager (RPM), which eases the installation, upgrade, and deletion of software packages, and even the operating system itself. For about $40, you can get a CD set with the Mozilla Web browser, OpenOffice office suite, KDE, GNOME, and about a hundred other packages. The $40 is for the CDs, not the software on them (which is free), and one month of Web-based software support. (More support — Red Hat's main business — is available for more money.)

The *Debian* and *Mandrake* distributions, like Red Hat, also provide interfaces that ease the task of a system administrator. Although these distributions are not as popular as Red Hat, they both have plenty of followers.

If you enjoy editing lots of configuration files and moving them around by hand, the old-fashioned way (believe it or not, some people like to do it that way), you should go with Slackware. Everyone else will find life easier with Red Hat, Debian, or Caldera.

Many other Linux distributions are out there, of course, so you may want to do a little more investigating before deciding on a package:

- **Knoppix:** For PC users without much free space, this version of Linux can run (kind of slowly) directly from its CD-ROM without needing to be installed on a regular disk. (See www.knoppix.org.)

- **Lindows:** A combination of Linux and proprietary add-ons intended to be easy to set up and easy for Windows users to use. Costs about $50 at www.lindows.com.

- **SuSe Linux:** Comes with all kinds of preconfigured software packages, X servers, and graphical utilities for novice users.

- **Turbolinux:** Primarily intended for larger businesses and servers; developed in Japan and popular in Asia.

"I Need Help!"

What happens when you have a problem with Linux? (It has been known to happen.) If you shelled out for a commercially distributed CD version, you get possibly a few months of free support if the company has the wherewithal to offer it. Otherwise, no technical-support hotline exists to call when things go wrong.

There *is* a huge base of Linux users around the world, though, most of whom have access to the Internet. Usenet is the best place to find help with Linux, as described in Chapter 18. For someone accustomed to calling a commercial entity on the phone for tech support, the idea of posting questions on Usenet may seem foreign, even hopelessly naive. Questions are generally read by so many thousands of people, though, that the odds are overwhelming that someone familiar with your problem will read the question and respond, usually within a day or so. (In fact, many people claim that Usenet-based support is faster and more reliable than some technical-support hotlines!) The Linux community as a group still maintains an attitude of "we're all in this together," and the Usenet support system has mostly worked. The Linux groups, which tend to be some of the most active computer groups on all of Usenet, are listed at the end of Chapter 26.

Part IV
UNIX and the Net

The 5th Wave   By Rich Tennant

"Guess who found a Kiss merchandise site on the Web while you were *gone?*"

In this part . . .

Most computers that run UNIX are connected to other computers. Many are parts of office-wide networks, many have network connections to UNIX systems in other places, most are connected to computers running operating systems other than UNIX, and nearly all are connected directly or indirectly to the biggest network of all: the Internet.

This part of the book reveals how to use your UNIX system to send and receive e-mail, browse the World Wide Web, transfer files, and log in to other computers over the Internet. We even tell you a few things about how to set up your own Internet site so that you can make files and Web pages on your own computer available to your cohorts in cyberspace.

Chapter 15

Your Computer Is Not Alone

In This Chapter

▶ Discovering who else is using your computer by using the `finger` command

▶ Fingering people who use other computers on the Internet

▶ Communicating with other user computers by using the `write` and `talk` commands

▶ Talking to everyone at the same time

▶ Getting your UNIX box on the Net

*F*rom the beginning, UNIX was designed as a multi-user system. In the early years of UNIX computing, keeping an entire PDP-11/45 (a 1972 vintage minicomputer about the speed of a Palm Pilot but the size of a trash compactor) to yourself was considered greedy. It was also kind of expensive. These days, the cost argument is much less compelling — unless your computer is a Cray supercomputer or the like — although UNIX remains multi-user partly because it always was and partly because multi-user systems make sharing programs and data easier.

Even if you have your own workstation but are attached to a network, your machine is potentially multi-user because other people can log in to your machine over the net, as we technoids call a network. (On the other hand, you can log in to their machines, too. See Chapter 16 for details.)

Don't confuse *net* — any network of computers — with *the* Net, which is what we technoids call the Internet. In this day and age, all anyone ever talks about is the Internet. If your computer is attached to the Internet, you can talk to literally millions of computers.

In this chapter, you see how you can nose around and find out who's on your system and on other systems to which you're connected. For the most part, we talk about the net — the computer network to which your machine is attached. If we mean *the* Net (also known as the Internet), we say so. After you find out who's out there, you can look into getting in touch with them.

If you are the only person who ever uses your computer and you don't have a network or a phone line (your computer is all alone in the world), skip this chapter — in fact, skip this entire part of the book.

You Don't Need to Be In Who's Who to Know What's What

If you have an account on a UNIX machine, UNIX knows a great deal about you. (Not that we're paranoid.) It knows your username, when you last logged on, which terminal you are using, and possibly additional facts, such as your real name and office extension, and it writes a short essay about what you are up to. (No, we're not kidding. Read on.) Other people can see this information, including people who use the same computer as you, and (if your UNIX system is on a network) people who use other computers.

Finding Out Who's on Your Computer

You can use three main commands to find out who's using your machine: who, w, and finger. The simple way to use either one is just to type **who**.

The typical response is something like this:

```
john1          console Sep  3 14:57
john1          ttyp1   Sep  3 14:57   (:0.0)
john1          ttyp2   Sep  3 14:57   (:0.0)
john1          ttyp3   Sep  4 17:48   (:0.0)
john1          ttyp4   Sep 18 10:48   (:0.0)
john1          ttyp5   Sep 26 18:42   (:0.0)
john1          ttyp7   Sep  9 14:10   (:0.0)
```

You see the user, terminal, and login time. User *john1* logged in seven times because he has a bunch of X terminal windows, each of which counts as a login session. Although the exact output from who varies from one version of UNIX to another, it always contains at least this much. You can also type who am i, and UNIX prints just the line for the terminal (or terminal window) in which you typed the command. (A similar UNIX command, whoami, prints only the name of the user logged in at the prompt where you typed the command.)

A considerably more informative program is finger because it produces a more useful report than who does:

```
Login   Name            Tty   Idle   Login Time  Office  Phone
johnl   John R Levine   co     23d   Sep  3 14:57  NY      387
johnl   John R Levine   p1    6:10   Sep  3 14:57  NY      387
johnl   John R Levine   p2      1d   Sep  3 14:57  NY      387
johnl   John R Levine   p3     22d   Sep  4 17:48  NY      387
johnl   John R Levine   p4    1:53   Sep 18 10:48  NY      387
johnl   John R Levine   *p5          Sep 26 18:42  NY      387
johnl   John R Levine   p7    1:14   Sep  9 14:10  NY      387
```

Although finger reports the same stuff as who does, it also looks up the user's real name (if it's in the user password file) and tells you how long the terminal has been idle (how long it has been since the user last typed something). If the system administrator entered the information, finger also usually shows an office phone number, room number, or other handy info about where the user works.

You can also use finger to ask about a specific user, and UNIX looks up some extra info about that user. In this example, we used it to look up one of the authors of this book:

```
finger johnl
```

UNIX returned this information:

```
Login: johnl                     Name: John R Levine
Directory: /home/johnl           Shell: /bin/bash
Office: Trumansburg, 607 387 6874
On since Wed Sep  3 14:57 (EDT) on console, idle 23 days 10:34

Last login Sat Sep 27 01:31 (EDT) on ttyp0 from bebel.iecc.com
Project: Working on "UNIX for Dummies, 5th Ed."
Plan:
Write many books, become famous.
```

The Project and Plan lines are merely the contents of files called .project and .plan in the login directory. (Yes, the filenames start with periods.) It has become customary to put a clever remark in your .plan file, but please don't overdo it. If the user is logged in on more than one terminal or terminal window, finger gives a full report for each terminal. The finger johnl command we gave reported all the logins — but we edited it to save paper.

The w command provides yet another version of the same info:

```
 1:24AM  up 23 days, 9:50, 7 users, load averages: 2.16, 1.72, 1.44
USER     TTY FROM       LOGIN@  IDLE WHAT
johnl    co  -          03Sep03 23days xinit /home/johnl/.xinitrc
johnl    p1  :0.0       03Sep03 6:06 tail -f current
johnl    p2  :0.0       03Sep03 27:34 -bash (bash)
johnl    p3  :0.0       04Sep03 22days ./dnetc
johnl    p4  :0.0       18Sep03 1:49 -bash (bash)
johnl    p5  :0.0       Fri06PM 1:13 (pine)
johnl    p7  :0.0       09Sep03 1:10 -bash (bash)
```

Finding Out Who's on Other Computers

If your machine is on a network, you can use rwho to find out about other machines. We can check nearby systems, by typing this command:

```
rwho
```

The computer responds with this output:

```
abuse     xuxa:ttyp4    Sep 22 15:19  6:30
johnl     bebel:ttyv0   Sep 22 14:08 99:59
johnl     tom:console   Sep  3 14:57 99:59
johnl     tom:ttyp1     Sep  3 14:57  6:15
johnl     tom:ttyp2     Sep  3 14:57 27:42
johnl     tom:ttyp3     Sep  4 17:48 99:59
johnl     tom:ttyp4     Sep 18 10:48  1:57
johnl     tom:ttyp5     Sep 26 18:42  1:21
johnl     tom:ttyp7     Sep  9 14:10  1:19
johnl     xuxa:console  Sep 22 09:29 27:54
johnl     xuxa:ttyp0    Sep 22 01:54  2:32
johnl     xuxa:ttyp6    Sep 24 14:23  1:32
```

The finger command is set up to work over the net, and if you're on the Internet, you can — in principle — finger any machine on the Internet. Because no rule says that machines must answer when you call, however, in most cases you get a "connection refused" response or even no response.

Some systems, particularly main network machines at universities, have set up finger to return user-directory information. Suppose that you ask who's at MIT:

```
finger @mit.edu
```

You get an introduction to the MIT online directory:

```
[mit.edu]
Student data loaded as of Dec 15, Staff data loaded as of Dec
        19. Notify the Registrar or Personnel as
        appropriate to change your information.
Our on-line help system describes
How to change data, how the directory works, where to get
        more info.
For a listing of help topics, enter finger help@mit.edu. Try
        finger help_about@mit.edu to read about how the
        directory works. Please see help_url@mit.edu for
        questions about the new URL field.
```

You can try to finger a particular individual at MIT, too:

```
finger chomsky@mit.edu
```

Now you can see the public data about that individual:

```
[mit.edu]
... There was 1 match to your request.  name: Chomsky, Noam A
email: CHOMSKY@MIT.EDU
phone: (617) 555-7819
address: ZZZ-219
department: Linguistics & Philos
title: Linguistics, Institute Professor
alias: N-chomsky
```

Chatting with Other People on Your Computer

After you figure out who is on your computer, you may want to send them a message. Message sending has two general schools. The first is the real-time school, in which the message appears on the other user's screen while you wait, presumably because it's an extremely urgent message. The write and talk commands enable you to do that. Excessive use of real-time messages is a good way to make enemies quickly, however, because you interrupt people's work all over the place. Be sparing in your blather.

The second school is electronic mail, or e-mail, in which you send a message the other user looks at when it's convenient. E-mail is a large topic in its own right, so we save that for Chapter 17.

Real-time terminal communication has been likened to talking to someone on the moon because it's so slow: It's limited by the speed at which people type. Here on Earth, because most of us have telephones, the most sensible thing to do is to send a one-line message asking the other user to call you on the phone.

The simpler real-time communications command is `write`. If someone writes to you, you see something like this on your screen:

```
Message from johnl on iecc (ttyp1) [ Wed Jan 6 20:28:42 ] ...
Time for pizza. Please call me at extension 8649
<EOT>
```

Usually the message appears in the middle of an editor session and scrambles the file on your screen. You will be relieved to know that the scrambling is limited to the screen — the editor has no idea that someone is writing to you. The file is okay.

In either `vi` or `emacs`, you can tell the editor to redraw what's supposed to be on-screen by pressing Ctrl+L (if you're in input mode in `vi`, press Esc first).

To write to a user, use the `write` command and give the name of the user to whom you want to talk:

```
write dguertin
```

After you press Enter, `write` tells you absolutely nothing, which means that it is waiting for your message. Type the message, which can be as many lines long as you want. When you finish, press Ctrl+D (the general end-of-input character) or the interrupt character, usually Ctrl+C or Delete. Because the `write` command copies every line to the other user's screen as you press Enter, reading a long message sent by way of the `write` command is sort of like reading a poem on old Burma-Shave signs as you drive by each one.

You want to send an important message, for example, to your friend Dave, so you type these lines:

```
write dguertin
Yo, Dave, turn on your radio. WBUR is rebroadcasting
Terry Gross's interview with Nancy Reagan!
```

You press Enter at the end of each line. After the last line, you press Ctrl+D.

I'm talking — where are you?

Sometimes `write` tells you that the user is logged in on several logical terminals:

```
dguertin is logged on more than one place.
You are connected to "vt01".
Other locations are:
ttyp1
ttyp0
ttyp2
```

The `write` command is pretty dumb. If the person you are writing to is logged in on more than one terminal — or, more typically, is using many windows in X — `write` picks one of them at random and writes there. You can be virtually certain that the window or terminal `write` chooses is not the one the user is viewing at the time. To maximize the chances of the user's seeing your message, use the `finger` command to figure out which terminal is most active (the one with the lowest idle time) and write to that window. Remember the results of the `finger` command, for example, from a few pages back:

```
Login         Name            TTY  Idle  When  Office
root       0000-Admin(0000)   co   1:11  Tue   20:16
dguertin  David S. Guertin    vt   1:11  Mon   15:19
dguertin  David S. Guertin    vt   1:35  Tue   16:47
dguertin  David S. Guertin    p2   1:11  Wed   16:36
dguertin  David S. Guertin    p1         Wed   17:20
dguertin  David S. Guertin    p0         Wed   16:36
```

The best candidates to send a message to are `ttyp1` and `ttyp0`. (The `finger` command cuts the `tty` from terminal names.)

To write to a specific terminal, give `write` the terminal name after the username:

```
write dguertin ttyp1
```

If you are writing back to a user who just wrote to you, you should use the terminal name that was sent in his `write` message (in this case, it was also `ttyp1`).

Can we talk?

You can have a somewhat spiffier conversation with the `talk` command, which allows simultaneous two-way typing. You use it the same way you use `write`: by giving a username and, optionally, a terminal name:

```
talk margy
```

The other user sees something like this:

```
Message from Talk_Daemon@iecc at 20:47 ...
talk: connection requested by johnl@IECC
talk: respond with: talk johnl@IECC
```

If someone tries to talk to you and you're interested in responding, type the `talk` command it suggests. If you're in the middle of a text editor or other program, you must exit to the shell first.

While `talk` is running, it splits your screen and arranges things so that what you type appears in the top half and what the other user types appears in the bottom half. Unlike `write`, `talk` immediately passes what you type — without waiting for you to press Enter — which means that you can see all the other user's typing mistakes and vice versa. When you get tired of `talk`, exit by pressing Ctrl+D.

Chatting with faraway folks

The `talk` command is designed to "talk" to users on other computers. If the other computer is a long way away, typing rather than talking over the telephone can make sense. As the Internet stretches around the world, you may find yourself exchanging messages with someone for whom English is not a native language. In that case, typing can be faster than trying to understand someone with a strong accent across a noisy phone connection.

Computers have names, too, which are usually called *machine names* (more about this in Chapter 16). To talk to someone on another computer, give `talk` the username and machine name:

```
talk zac@greattapes.com
```

After you're connected, `talk` works just like talking to a local user, except that sometimes several seconds can pass for characters to get from one machine to another on an intercontinental link.

If you want to talk to a number of other people, maybe thousands and thousands of them, you can use a system called Internet Relay Chat (IRC). We don't have room to describe it in this book, but you can read about it at our Web site:

```
http://net.gurus.com/irc
```

If you don't know how to find this Web site, see Chapter 18.

Reading the writing on the wall

For the truly megalo-maniacal among you, a program called `wall` blats what you type to every single terminal and window on your entire computer. You use it much like `write`:

```
wall
Free pizza in the upstairs conference room in 5 minutes!
```

As with `write`, you tell `wall` that you're finished by pressing Ctrl+D. Be sparing in your use of `wall` unless you want a bunch of new enemies. Note that `wall` affects only the people who use your computer, not everyone on your network (or on the whole Internet).

Getting On the Net

If you have a home UNIX or Linux system, you'd probably like to connect to the Internet. The good news is that it's possible, the bad news is that it can be, ah, a little tricky.

The easiest way to get on the Net is with a connection that looks, to your UNIX system, like you're on an office LAN, because UNIX systems generally are all set up for LANs right out of the box. If you have a broadband connection, and the connection uses a setup scheme called DHCP, you win. Plug your UNIX box's Ethernet adapter into the broadband box, and the connection starts right up. This happy state of affairs most often occurs with cable modems.

The other broadband connection scheme is known as PPPoE and requires that you or your computer send a username and a password to your ISP so it can be sure you're actually the person plugging into its service and not one of the hundreds of other people who might live in your house. (What? Nobody lives in your house but you? Well, how's the phone company supposed to know that?) Although setting up a PPPoE connection on your UNIX box is possible, it's way more complex than we can describe here. Unless you have a geeky friend who can set it up for you, the path of least resistance is to run out and get a $30 router, plug that into your PPPoE connection, plug your UNIX box into the router that does nice simple DHCP, and configure the necessary passwords into the router using its handy Web page.

Setting up a dialup connection isn't as bad as PPPoE but is still more complex, and varies too much from one flavor of UNIX to another. Some versions of Linux have a nice Window-ish setup system, but failing that, you still need that geeky friend or a router with a dial-out modem.

Chapter 16

Across a Crowded Network

*1*f your computer is on a network, sooner or later you have to use computers other than your own. Although you can do lots and lots of things over a network, the two most widespread activities are remote login and file transfer. If your computer is on a LAN (Local Area Network), you can probably use files directly that are located on other computers.

On a Computer Far, Far Away

Most UNIX systems are attached to the Big Mazooma of networks, the Internet, which hooks together several million computers around the world. Because most of the UNIX network software descends from stuff originally written at Berkeley specifically for use on the Internet, all the commands discussed in this chapter work just fine on the Internet. The only difference you may notice is that although you can refer to computers on your own network with simple names, such as `pumpkin`, in order to talk to computers on the Internet, you have to give their true names, which can be long and tedious, such as `iecc.cambridge.ma.us` (a name our computer used to have).

Remote login is no more than logging in to some other computer from your own. While you're logged in to the other computer, whatever you type is passed to the other computer; whatever responses the other computer makes are passed back to you. In the great UNIX tradition of never leaving well enough alone, two slightly different remote-login programs exist: `telnet` and `ssh`. You can also use `ssh` to give commands one at a time on other computers.

A *file transfer* copies files from one system to another. You can copy files from other systems to your system and from your system to others. Two different file-transfer programs exist (how did you know that?): `ftp` and `scp`. We talk about `ftp` in Chapter 18.

How do I get networked, anyway?

If your UNIX system is in an office with an Ethernet LAN or you have a home network with a router, you can usually put your system on the net with little effort. When most UNIX software is first installed, it asks whether you have a LAN connection. Make sure a network cable is plugged from your computer to the LAN hub or router and tell the installation software that yes,

there's a LAN. (Um, well, yeah, that's kind of obvious.) If it asks whether you want to get your network address automatically, dynamically, or using DHCP, three increasingly geeky ways of saying the same thing, also say yes. Barring bad luck, your computer automatically connects to the local network each time it starts up.

Telnet It Like It Is

Telnetting (in English, you can "verb" any word you want) involves no more than typing **telnet** and the name of the computer you want to log in to:

```
telnet pumpkin
```

UNIX tells you that it is making the connection and then gives the usual login prompt:

```
Trying...
Connected to pumpkin.bigcorp.com.
Escape character is '^]'.
FreeBSD 4.8 (pumpkin.bigcorp.com)
login:
```

At the login prompt, you type your username and then your password. After the other computer connects, you log in exactly as though you are sitting at the other computer. In the following example, we typed **john1** as our username and then gave our secret password:

```
login: john1
Password:
Last login: Thu Oct 3:03:58 from squash
FreeBSD 4.8-RELEASE (PUMPKIN) #0: Thu Jul 24 14:49:39 EDT
        2003
Please confirm (or change) your terminal type.
TERM = (xterm
```

Terminal type tedium

If you use a full-screen program, such as the UNIX text editors emacs and vi or the mail programs elm and Pine, you have to set your *terminal type*. This problem shouldn't exist in the first place, but it does, so you have to deal with it.

The problem is that about a dozen different conventions exist for screen controls such as *clear screen* and *move to position (x,y)*. The program you're using on the remote host has to use the same convention your local terminal program does.

If the conventions are not the same, you get *garbage* (funky-looking characters) on-screen when you try to use a full-screen program. In most cases, the remote system asks you which terminal type to use. The trick is knowing the right answer. Here are a few hints to help you find out:

✔ If you're using the X Window system, with or without Motif, the answer is more likely to be *VT-100,* a popular terminal from the

1970s that became a de facto standard. You may also try *xterm,* the name of the standard X program that does terminal emulation.

✔ If you're using a PC and an emulation program, the best answer is usually ANSI because most PC terminal programs use ANSI terminal conventions. (*ANSI* stands for the American National Standards Institute. One of its several thousand standards defines a set of terminal-control conventions that MS-DOS PCs — which otherwise wouldn't know an ANSI standard if they tripped over one — invariably use.)

✔ In places where a great deal of IBM equipment is used, the terminal type may be *3101,* an early IBM terminal that was also popular.

The ANSI and VT-100 conventions are not much different from each other, so if you use one and your screen is only somewhat screwed up, try the other.

If the other computer asks you what type of terminal you're using, give the answer appropriate to the terminal you're using. (If you're using an X terminal window, it's xterm. Try VT-100, ANSI, or TTY if you're using a dumb terminal or PC.)

The normal way to leave telnet is to log out from the other computer:

```
logout
```

UNIX gives you the following message to tell you that the other computer has hung up the phone, so to speak:

```
Bye Bye
Connection closed by foreign host.
```

Sometimes the other computer is recalcitrant and doesn't want to let you go. Remember that you're in control. To force your way out, you first must get the attention of the `telnet` program by pressing Ctrl+] (that's a right square bracket). A few versions of `telnet` use a different escape character to get `telnet`'s attention. (It tells you which character when you first connect to the other system.) After you get `telnet`'s attention, type **quit** to tell `telnet` to wrap things up and return to the shell:

```
Ctrl-]
telnet> quit
```

3270: The Attack of the IBM Terminals

All the terminals discussed earlier in this chapter that are handled by `telnet` are basically souped-up Teletypes, with data passed character by character between the terminal and the host. This kind of terminal interaction can be called *Teletype-ish.*

IBM developed an entirely different model for its 3270-series display terminals. The principle is that the computer's in charge. The model works more like filling in paper forms. The computer draws what it wants on-screen, marks which parts of the screen you can type on, and then unlocks the keyboard so that you can fill in whichever blanks they want. Whenever you press Enter, the terminal locks the keyboard, transmits the changed parts of the screen to the computer, and awaits additional instructions from headquarters.

To be fair, this method is a perfectly reasonable way to build terminals intended for dedicated data-entry and data-retrieval applications. The terminal on the desks at your bank or the electric company are probably 3270s — or more likely these days, cheap PCs *emulating* 3270s. Because the 3270 terminal protocol squeezes a great deal more on a phone line than Teletype-ish, having all the 3270s in an office sharing the same single phone line, with reasonable performance is quite common.

The Internet is a big place, and plenty of IBM mainframes run applications on the Internet. Some of them are quite useful. Some large library catalogs that haven't moved to the Web yet speak 3270-ish. Usually, if you `telnet` to a system that wants a 3270, it converts from the Teletype-ish that `telnet` speaks to 3270-ish so that you can use it anyway. Some 3270 systems speak only 3270-ish, however, and if you `telnet` to them, they connect and disconnect without saying anything in between.

A variant of telnet that speaks 3270-ish is called *tn3270*. If a system keeps disconnecting, try typing the command tn3270 instead. (Large amounts of UPPERCASE LETTERS and references to the IBM operating systems VM or OS/390 or z/OS are also tip-offs that you're talking to a 3270.) Even if a 3270 system allows regular telnet, you get a snappier response if you use tn3270 instead.

ssh: The Lazy Man's Remote Login

The telnet command has been around since the 1970s, but is now considered largely obsolete and dreadfully insecure. (If you use a computer in the kind of place where people can plug into your network and watch the bits go by, they can read your entire telnet session, passwords and all.) These days the ssh, short for *secure shell,* command is both more secure and more convenient because it automates more of the process. You can use ssh in much the same way you use telnet:

```
ssh pumpkin
```

UNIX responds:

```
Last login: Thu Oct 3:03:58 from squash
FreeBSD 4.8-RELEASE (PUMPKIN) #0: Thu Jul 24 14:49:39 EDT
        2003
```

Hey! It didn't ask for the username or password. What happened? Often you have accounts on a bunch of machines in a group, and if you log in to one of them, you use the same username to log in to others. When setting up *ssh,* the system manager can configure each machine with the secret *ssh* keys (a long string of digits) of the other machines in its group so when someone sshes in, it can say "oh, that machine, it's OK." If you have accounts on a variety of UNIX or Linux machines, setting up your own authorized keys files so you can log in from one host to another without passwords is possible.

The ssh command also passes along the type of terminal you're using so that even if the other system asks you to enter your terminal type, it always guesses correctly if you don't tell it explicitly.

If the remote system doesn't recognize your username, it asks you to type a username and password, just like telnet does. If it does recognize your username but not your secret ssh key, it just asks for a password.

Escaping from ssh

One place where ssh is quite different from telnet is in how you escape from a recalcitrant remote system: You type ~. (a tilde followed by a period) on a line by itself. What you have to do is press Enter (or Return), tilde, period, Enter.

Username and secret key matching for ssh

This section is pretty nerdy. If you work in an office with a bunch of workstations, you can assume that they all generally share usernames (the system manager should have arranged for all the necessary keys), and you can skip this section.

The control files for ssh are in a directory called .ssh. On each computer you need to have your own ssh key (actually a pair of keys: the private key that only stays on that computer and the *public* key that you copy to all of the other computers from which you plan to log in to this one). Assume you have two computers called squash and pumpkin, and you want to be able to log in to each from the other. The keys for each computer are in the .ssh directory and are called id_rsa and id_rsa.pub, or id_dsa and id_dsa.pub. (Either will do; rsa and dsa are two different coding schemes that ssh can use.)

To log in to each computer, follow these steps:

1. **On** pumpkin, **if the keys don't exist, create them by running** ssh-keygen -t dsa **and waiting a minute or so while it thinks up a really good secret key for you.**

    When it asks for the filename to use, press Enter to use the normal names, and it also asks for optional pass phrases to secure the keys, and press Enter again not to use them.

2. **Copy the public key** id_dsa.pub **you just created on** pumpkin **to** squash, **where you call the copy** pumpkin-key.

    Copy the file using scp or ftp, both of which are discussed later in this chapter.

3. **On** squash, **copy** pumpkin.key **to** .ssh/authorized_keys.

4. **Log in from** pumpkin **into** squash **without a password.**

    To go the other way, do the same steps, reversing the two computers. If you have more than two computers, on each computer you need to put all the keys of the other computers into authorized_keys, like this:

```
cat pumpkin.key squash.key gourd.key >>
        .ssh/authorized_keys
```

Now you see why we give each key file a different name. Putting a computer's own key into `authorized_keys` is harmless. If you have more than two computers, make all the keys, combine all the public keys into one big `authorized_keys` file, and then `scp` copy that combo file to all of the computers with `scp`.

If your login names on the various machines are different, this password-avoidance trick still works fine, but you have to tell `ssh` what login name to use. Either of these works:

```
ssh -l fred pumpkin     # old-fashioned form
ssh fred@pumpkin        # groovy new form
```

Using ssh one command at a time

Sometimes a complete login session is overkill for what you want to do — you just want to run one command at a time. In this type of situation, `ssh` can also do one command at a time:

```
ssh pumpkin lpq
ssh fred@pumpkin lpq       # if your user name is different
          there
```

You give `ssh` the name of the system you want to use and the command you want to run on that system. This example runs the `lpq` command on system `pumpkin` (remember that `lpq` asks what's waiting for the printer on `pumpkin`).

If you can use `ssh` to log in to a system and not give a username or a password, you can also use it a command at a time without a password.

scp: Blatting Files across the Network

Although `telnet` and `ssh` may be the next best thing to being there, sometimes there's no place like your home machine. If you want to use files that are on another machine, `scp` is often the easiest thing to do. (You can also use `ftp` to blat files across the network, but because that's a larger topic, we give it all of Chapter 19.)

The idea behind `scp` is that it works just like `cp` (the standard copy command) — except that it also works on remote files that you own or that you at least have access to. To refer to a file on another machine, type the machine name and a colon before the filename. To copy a file named `mydata` from the machine named `pumpkin` and call it `pumpkindata`, you type

```
scp pumpkin:mydata pumpkindata
```

To copy it the other way (from a file called `pumpkindata` on your machine to a file called `mydata` on a machine called `pumpkin`), you type this line:

```
scp pumpkindata pumpkin:mydata
```

The `scp` program uses the same username rules as does `ssh`. If your username on the other system is different from that on your own system, type the username and an @ sign before the machine name:

```
scp steph@pumpkin:mydata pumpkindata
```

If you want to copy files in another user's directory (`tracy`, for example) on the other system, place the user's name after a ~ (a tilde) before the filename. Suppose that you need one of Tracy's files:

```
scp pumpkin:~tracy/somefile tracyfile
```

To copy an entire directory at a time, you can use the `-r` (for *recursive*) flag to tell `scp` to copy the entire contents of a directory:

```
scp -r pumpkin:projectdir .
```

This command says to copy the directory `projectdir` on machine `pumpkin` into the current directory (the period is the nickname for the current directory) on the local machine.

You can combine all this notation in an illegible festival of punctuation:

```
scp -r steph@pumpkin:~tracy/projectdir tracy-project
```

Translation: "Go to machine `pumpkin`, where my username is `steph`, and get from user `tracy` a directory called `projectdir` and copy it to a directory on this machine called `tracy-project`." Whew!

If you're copying large files, `scp` gives you reassuring progress reports to tell you how it's doing and when it thinks it'll be done. `sscp` is done when you see the UNIX prompt.

If you copy stuff *to* another machine and want to see whether it worked, use `ssh` to give an `ls` command afterward to see which files are on the other machine:

```
scp -r projectdir pumpkin:squashproject
ssh pumpkin ls -l squashproject
```

Although `scp` is reliable (if it didn't complain, the copy almost certainly worked), it never hurts to be sure.

NFS: You'll Never Find Your Stuff

If your computer is on a LAN, the computer is probably set up to share files with other computers. Quite a few different schemes enable computers to use files on other machines. These schemes are named mostly with TLAs (Three Letter Acronyms) such as AFS, RFS, and NFS. This chapter talks mostly about NFS (you'll *N*ever *F*ind your *S*tuff) because that's the most commonly used scheme, even though it works, in many ways, the worst. If you didn't like the C shell or the vi editor, you won't like NFS either; it also was written by Bill, the big guy with the strong opinions.

What's NFS?

The NFS (Network File System) program enables you to treat files on another computer in more or less the same way you treat files on your own computer.

You may want to use NFS for several reasons:

✔ **Often you have a bunch of similar computers scattered around, all running more or less the same programs.** Rather than load every program on every computer, the system administrator loads one copy of everything on one computer (the server) so that all the other computers (the clients) can share the programs.

✔ **Centralizing the files on a server makes backup and administration easier.** Administering one disk of 4,000MB is easier than administering 10 disks of 400MB apiece. Backing up everything is also easier because everything is all in one place rather than spread around on a dozen machines.

✔ **Another use of NFS is to make a bunch of workstations function as a shared time-sharing system.** Setting up a bunch of workstations so that you can sit down at any one of them, log in, and use the same set of files regardless of where on the network they physically reside is reasonably straightforward. This capability is a great convenience. Also, by using programs such as ssh (discussed earlier in this chapter), you can log in to another machine on the network and work from that machine (which is handy if the other machine is faster than yours or has some special feature you want to use).

✔ **NFS works in *heterogeneous networks,* a fancy term for networks with different kinds of computers.** NFS is available for all sorts of computers, from PCs to mainframes.

TECHNICAL STUFF

Why NFS is out of state

We discuss the technical theology of remote file access here. Still reading? Geez, what a glutton for punishment.

The communication between the *server* (the machine with the files) and the *client* (the machine that wants to use them) is handled in two general ways: One approach is known as *stateless,* and the other (for lack of a better word) is called *stateful*.

The stateful approach is more straightforward: The two machines have a conversation, the gist of which runs something like this:

"I want to read a file called /usr/elvis/current-whereabouts."

"Very good, sir — an excellent choice."

"Can I have the first piece of that file I just asked about?"

"Certainly, sir. It's so-and-so."

"Thank you so much. May I have the next piece?"

"My pleasure. It's such-and-such."

The only problem in this example occurs if one or the other machine crashes during the conversation. When it comes back, the server has no recollection of what it was talking about, the conversation cannot be reestablished easily, and all sorts of special recovery schemes are necessary to get things back in sync. ("Beg pardon, old boy, I've had a spot of amnesia. Can you remind me what we were chatting about?")

Back when Bill was writing NFS, he didn't feel like writing all that recovery code (it's difficult to write and boring, to boot) so he made NFS stateless. This decision gave NFS a severe case of amnesia on the part of all the servers. Rather than keep track of which client is asking for

which file, NFS couldn't care less. The NFS servers don't have the faintest idea who their clients are, and they forget everything about a client from one request to the next. The conversation goes more like this:

"I want to read /usr/elvis/current-whereabouts."

"It's all the same to me. On my disk, it's file number 86345."

"Send me the first piece of file 86345."

"Well, okay, if you insist. It's so-and-so."

"Send me the second piece of file 86345."

"Who the heck are you? Hardly matters — I wouldn't remember, even if you told me. Anyway, the answer is such-and-such."

The advantage here is that, if the server crashes, when it comes back up, the server can pick up where it left off. Because the server didn't know anything about its clients anyway, it doesn't forget anything. The disadvantage is that determining whether a request got lost or, because of network glitchery, got handled twice is difficult. In a stateful setup, figuring out what happened is easier: Every message has a number. If messages 106 and 108 arrive without 107 between them, you know that something got lost. Because stateless messages don't have numbers (it wouldn't matter if they did, because the stateless server doesn't remember the number from one message to the next), you have no way to tell whether a message got lost. In practice, if a client doesn't get an answer to a request within a few seconds, it repeats the request because NFS requests are supposed to be *idempotent* (this 25-cent word means that it doesn't hurt if the server does them more than once).

Most requests are indeed idempotent (whether you write the same stuff to the same part of a file twice in a row doesn't matter) — but not all of them are. If the request was something like "delete the `furble` file" and the server in fact received the request but lost the response, the second time the client sends the request, the server complains that the file is not there and sends back an error (even though, from the client's point of view, the file was there when it asked to delete it). Are you confused yet? We certainly are.

More complex sequences of repeated and lost messages can cause the contents of a file to be thrown away by mistake. (No, we don't go into detail — we know that you have already stopped reading this part.) Fortunately, such sequences are rare, although they have been known to happen.

NFS doesn't handle tapes, printers, and the like because even Bill couldn't figure out how to make an idempotent printer — one in which printing a page twice was the same thing as printing it once. Perhaps he could have used transparent ink.

Ignoring NFS

Except when NFS screws up, you don't have to worry about using it. Your system administrator did all the hard work when she installed it.

Files passed over the network act almost exactly like those on the local machine; in most cases, you can treat them the same. The primary difference is that access to files through NFS is about twice as slow as access to files on the local machine. This problem usually isn't a big one because, for most of the stuff you do, the machine doesn't spend much time waiting for the disk anyway.

When you do something *really* big and slow (such as repaginate a 500-page document), seeing whether you can log in to the machine on which the files reside and run the program there may be worth the time.

Where are those files, anyway?

NFS works by mounting remote directories. *Mounting* means pretending that a directory on another disk or even on another computer is actually part of the directory system on your disk. Files stored in lots of different places can then appear to be nicely organized into one tree-structure directory.

Whenever UNIX sees the name of a directory — /stars/elvis, for example — it checks to see whether any names in the directory are *mount points,* which are directories in which one disk is logically attached to another.

Your system may have the directory /stars mounted from some other machine, for example, and then the directory elvis and all the files in it reside on the other machine.

The easiest way to tell which files are where is with the df (Disk Free space) command. It prints the amount of free space on every disk and tells you where the disks are. Here's a typical piece of df output:

```
Filesystem  kbytes   used    avail capacity Mounted on
/dev/sd0a   30383    6587    20758  24%   /
/dev/sd0g   157658   124254  17639  88%   /usr
/dev/sd0h   364378   261795  66146  80%   /home
/dev/sd3a   15671    1030    13074  7%    /tmp
/dev/sd3g   1175742  758508  299660 72%   /mnt
srvsys:/usr/spool/mail  300481  190865  79567   71%   /var/spool/mail
srvsys:/usr/lib/news 300481  190865  79567 71% /usr/lib/news
```

In this example, the directory / resides on a local disk (a disk on your own computer) named /dev/sd0a; /usr resides on /dev/sd0g; /home resides on /dev/sd0h; and so on. (We don't go into the subject of disk names other than to say that anything in /dev is on the local machine.) The directory /var/spool/mail is really the directory /usr/spool/mail on machine server-sys, and /usr/lib/news is really /usr/lib/news on machine server-sys.

Some of the local directory names are the same as the remote machine's directory names — and some aren't. This situation can and often does cause considerable confusion; unfortunately, it's usually unavoidable. A system administrator with any sense at least mounts each directory with a consistent name wherever it's mounted so that /var/documents/bigproject is the same no matter which computer you're working on.

A database known as NIS (Network Information System) makes keeping the naming process straight easier. Don't worry about it unless your system administrator messes up.

NFS and system crashes

What happens if you're working with NFS, your files are stored on a server, and the server crashes? The answer is, you wait. Eventually, when the server comes back, you continue from where you left off. If the crash is severe, you may wait a long time. In one extreme case (so we have heard), a program on an NFS client system waited more than six months while the server crashed, was dismantled and shipped back to the manufacturer, and then was refurbished, shipped back, reloaded from tape, and rebooted — at which point the client program continued. You probably won't be so patient.

The worst practical problem is that, if a program stalls while it is waiting for a dead NFS server, you have no way to stop or kill the program, short of rebooting your UNIX computer.

Recent versions of NFS have features called *soft* and *hard mounts* (not as indecent as they sound, but close) that make stopping a program that has stalled while waiting for a dead server possible. The problem is that, if a server is merely slow and not dead (and believe us, a server loaded with hundreds of clients can be impressively slow), a client may assume that the server is dead and stop a program. Had the client been a little more patient, the server would have responded, and the program could have completed its task.

The UNIX/Windows Accords

Sometimes UNIX computers are on networks with computers running other operating systems, such as Windows 98, Me, NT, 2000, or XP. So how do you get your UNIX and Windows computers to communicate with each other?

When computers want to speak to one another, they can't just chuck data at one another indiscriminately. They have to use what's known in computer-ese as protocols. *Protocols* are sets of rules by which computers exchange data and commands. If two computers know the same protocols, they can talk turkey, even if one of those computers is running UNIX and the other is running Windows.

Computers use all kinds of protocols to communicate. On a network, clients connect to servers by using protocols, such as *TCP/IP* (Transmission Control Protocol/Internet Protocol) and *IPX* (Internetwork Packet eXchange). Computers connected by way of the Internet exchange files by using protocols such as *FTP* (File Transfer Protocol) and *HTTP* (HyperText Transfer Protocol).

Let's Samba

The particular protocol of interest here is the *Server Message Block,* or SMB, protocol. SMB has been around in one incarnation or another since 1987, when Microsoft and Intel (the chip maker) first defined it. Because they helped to invent SMB, Microsoft includes an SMB client in all its versions of Windows. Any server that can talk SMB, therefore, can do business with a Windows computer, so the Windows computers can use disks and printers on the server just like on a Windows NT server, for example.

Enter Andrew Tridgell, a UNIX hacker from Canberra, Australia, with a firm grasp of the obvious. He wrote a suite of programs collectively named Samba, which turns almost any version of UNIX you care to mention into an SMB server. Samba lets UNIX and Windows computers do snazzy, friendly stuff, such as access one another's files and share printers. In typical UNIX style, dozens of programmers from around the world have contributed to Samba over the years, and it's distributed for free under the infamous GNU public software guidelines.

SMB is a *request-response* protocol, in which a client makes requests of the server and the server responds. Because nothing is ever as easy at it seems where computers are concerned, a client has to make several requests of a server before anything useful happens. First, the client has to ask the server which *dialect* of SMB it wants to speak (yup, dialect, just like in real life). Then the client has to get down on bended knee and politely request access to the server by giving the server a username and password. If the server grants the client an audience, the client can start petitioning the server with a series of requests — for example, to locate, open, and print a particular file.

The latest version of Samba is 2.2.8 or higher. Nearly all current versions of UNIX come with Samba installed, or you can download it from one of the Samba Web sites such as `http://us1.samba.org`. (If you don't know what these curious strings of seeming gobbledygook mean, read Chapter 19.)

Listening to Windows

Samba lets a UNIX system provide file and printer service to Windows machines. Occasionally you need to go the other way, either to copy a bunch of files or to use a remote Windows disk.

Samba includes a program called *smbclient* that works sort of like FTP (see Chapter 18) to copy files to or from a Windows shared folder. Some UNIX systems also have an SMB mounter that can mount remote Windows folders on the local machine just like remote NFS disks. Check with your system manager if you need to set this up.

Chapter 17

Automating Your Office Gossip

. . . .

. . . .

*E*lectronic mail (or *e-mail*) is the high-tech way to automate interoffice chatter, gossip, and innuendo. Using e-mail, you can quickly and efficiently circulate memos and other written information to your coworkers, including directions to the beer bash this Saturday and the latest bad jokes. You can even send and receive e-mail from people outside your organization, if you and they use networked computers.

If your organization uses e-mail, you probably already have some. In fact, vitally important but unread mail may be waiting in your mailbox at this very moment. Probably not, but who knows? You can tell whether unread messages are in your mailbox because UNIX displays this message when you log in:

```
You have mail.
```

Actually, you might have mail even if it doesn't say so — the UNIX system is just telling you whether any mail is on the local hard drive. If you're using your UNIX system as a home desktop, and you dial up to an ISP, then you may have mail on its server, which you need to download. In this chapter, we discuss local e-mail and remote e-mail separately. *Local e-mail* is what you use on a typical UNIX machine that is part of a network, such as a corporate or university environment. *Remote e-mail* is what you use on a home machine running UNIX.

All the news that's fit to print

E-mail isn't the only way to gossip. There's also Usenet news. You can read Usenet news using Mozilla — one of the e-mail clients we discuss here, although you're better off with a dedicated newsreader if you read much mail. We recommend `trn`, which is incredibly flexible, but more than a little confusing at first. Some people swear by `tin` and `nn`. Newsreaders tend to have short names, and be command-line programs. A lot of newsreaders are out there; almost as many as e-mail clients.

Usenet has gradually decayed under swarms of spammers and binary newsgroups (newsgroups where people post huge files, instead of discussing anything), and a lot of people have written it off, yet pockets of Usenet are still usable. Look for moderated groups, or groups with very specialized topics.

Not sure what Usenet has to offer? The Google Groups area is an interface to Usenet; point a browser at `http://groups.google.com/` and poke around.

For general information about Usenet newsgroups, see our Usenet page at `net.gurus.com/usenet/`.

To use Usenet, you need these three Important News Skills:

✔ How to read the news that interests you

✔ How not to read the news that doesn't interest you, because much more news is sent every day than any single human can ever read

✔ How to post articles of your own (definitely optional)

If you start reading news, learn to use the kill file early. It's the only way to stay sane — or so we're told, by people who are still sane.

What You Need in Order to Use Local E-Mail

Any UNIX system handles local e-mail for users on that system. To exchange e-mail with the outside world, your computer must be on a network — or at least have a phone line and a modem. You definitely don't want to know how to set up a mail network — if your computer doesn't already have e-mail on it, it's time to talk to a UNIX wizard.

In the great tradition of UNIX standardization, UNIX has about 14 different mail-sending-and-receiving programs. (Fortunately, they all can exchange mail with each other.) To find out whether your computer can do e-mail, try using the simple `mail` program to see whether you have any mail waiting. Just type this line:

```
mail
```

UNIX mail programs

We can't list all the mail programs that exist, but this table gives you a brief summary.

Program name	Description
mail	One of many plain-text mail readers.
Mail	Another plain-text reader.
mailx	You guessed it, another plain-text reader.
elm	A fairly old plain-text mail reader, with some support for attachments.
pine	A newer plain-text mail reader, based partially on elm (PINE stands for Pine Is Not Elm).
mutt	Yet another mail reader.
mh	A particularly arcane mail reader — lots of gurus use it, everyone else thinks they're crazy.
Mozilla	It's a Web browser! It's a mail reader! It's... Mozilla!
KMail	The graphical mail reader that comes with KDE.
Evolution	The all-in-one mail reader, calendar, and personal assistant that comes with GNOME.
nail	A program evolved from mailx, but with support for MIME.
exmh	Early graphical client, providing a friendly front-end to mh.
spruce	Another graphical e-mail client, based on GNOME.
XFMail	Don't have enough graphical e-mail clients? Here's another.
balsa	Another mail program named after a tree.

We mention all these and give special attention to a few of them, throughout this chapter. But don't worry, there's more where that came from.

UNIX says No mail if no mail is waiting or blats a copy of the first unread message to your screen. In the latter case, if you don't want to read your mail right now, press **x** (for *exit*) and press Enter to get out. We talk more about reading your mail later in this chapter.

To receive mail, you need a mailbox. (Not one of those tasteful roadside mailboxes, in this case. It's an invisible mailbox made up entirely of electronic data.) Your system administrator can make (or already has made) one for you if your organization uses e-mail. The mailbox comes in the form of a file named something like /var/mail/*yourusername*. It contains your unread mail and any mail you choose to leave lying around. You may also have a directory named mail or Mail (some systems capitalize it, some don't — sigh) in your home directory that you can use to sort your mail into piles and keep it for historical reference.

To read the mail in your mailbox and send mail, you use a program such as `mail` or `elm` or Pine. If you use KDE or GNOME, you can use a fancy X Windows mail program, such as `exmh`. A whole lot of these mail programs are available — see the nearby sidebar, "UNIX mail programs."

Addressing the Mail

E-mail, like regular mail (usually referred to by e-mail advocates as *snail mail*) needs an address, usually called an *e-mail address*. To send mail to a person, you send it to his or her username (refer to Chapter 1 for information about logging in with a username). If the other user uses a different computer than the one you use, the mail system has to know which computer the other person is on — and the address becomes more complicated.

Sending mail to people nearby

For people who use the same mail server you do (roughly, you both use PCs connected to the same mail-handling computer running UNIX), the mail address is just their username. If you enter `georgew` for your username, that's your mail address, too. Make sure that you don't use uppercase letters in the mail address unless the username also does.

Sending mail to people elsewhere on your local network

You can send mail to people who use other mail servers if they're connected by a network. For people who use other computers, you send mail by telling the mail system which mail server they use.

Servers have names too, you know. They sometimes have boring names that indicate what they are used for, such as `marketing` or `corpacctg`. When you're writing to someone elsewhere on your network, include the server name in the mail address by using an at sign (@) to indicate where they are "at." If your friend Nancy, for example, has the username `nancyb` and uses a server named `ginger`, her mail address is `nancyb@ginger`.

A skillful system administrator can automatically note which computer each user in an organization uses. With luck, you can merely send mail by username, and the system automagically figures out which computer to send it to.

If you have trouble with addresses, the easiest way to send a message to someone is to wait until that someone sends a message to you and then reply to it. All mail programs have a command (usually r) that replies to the message you just read. Messages almost always have return addresses, and the r command enables you to send a message without typing an address.

Sending mail to people "out there"

If your computer network has phone connections to the outside world, you can probably also send mail to people out in the wide world of the *Internet*. Check with your system administrator or other e-mail users to find out whether your organization is "on the Net" (connected to the outside world).

To correspond with people on the outside, you need an Internet address for the person you want to send mail to. After you have the address, type it *exactly* the way she wrote it. Internet addresses tend to look like this:

```
ellenz@persimmon.greattapes.com
```

The part in front of the @ is the person's username. The rest of the address is the name of the mail server and other information about where it is, usually the name of the company. The computer name, company name, and so on are connected by periods. The last three letters frequently tell you what kind of organization it is: com is for companies, for example, and edu is for educational institutions. Sometimes the parts of the address spell out the city, state, and country where the computer is located. It's all very well organized, really.

If your computer is on the Internet, you can also exchange mail with users of commercial services, such as CompuServe and America Online (AOL). For details, see the following sidebar, "Sending mail to people who use online services."

When you are typing Internet addresses, keep these points in mind:

- ✔ **Be sure you don't type any spaces in the middle of the address.** Don't use spaces in usernames or computer names or on either side of the @ or a period.

- ✔ **Don't capitalize anything unnecessarily.** Check the capitalization of the person's username and computer name. Most addresses are composed entirely of small letters.

- ✔ **Don't forget the periods that separate the parts of an Internet address.**

Sending mail to people who use online services

You can send mail to people who don't use UNIX computers. E-mail addresses use the same format everywhere, so what the other person's computer is running doesn't matter.

To send mail to an America Online (AOL) user, try this:

✔ Find out the AOL screen name, such as Steve Case.

✔ Take out any spaces and tack @aol.com to the end of the name. Voilà! — you have the person's Internet address, as shown here:

stevecase@aol.com

Most users just give you the full e-mail address these days, so you can just use whatever string of gobbledygook they send you, as long as it's got an @ in the middle somewhere.

If your computer is on the Internet and you want to try out network mail, send a message to the authors of this book, at unix5@gurus.com, and tell us what you think of the book. Our computer sends you an automatic reply, and we read your message, too. (If you can get that address right, you're already halfway to being a mail wizard.)

It's dead, Jim

If you get an address wrong, you usually get the message back within a few minutes (for mail on your own computer or your own network) or a few days (for mail that has bounced around the Internet). The dead letter usually has all kinds of cryptic automated error messages in it, but the gist is clear: The message wasn't delivered. Check the address and try again. Generally, the safest way to address a message is to reply to someone else's message.

Sending Stuff Other Than Text

These days, e-mail is getting to be such a widespread practice that you may want to send things other than plain old, short text messages. For example, we e-mailed most of the chapters in this book as Microsoft Word documents to our long-suffering editor. Most mail programs now have commands for attaching files to e-mail messages, or at least including text files in messages.

If you want to send a text file by e-mail, just include the text file as part of your message. Note, however, that UNIX e-mail is designed for sending text, not for sending programs, graphics, or formatted word processing files. Luckily, several ways of cheating have been developed so that the e-mail system doesn't realize that e-mail messages actually contain stuff other than text. *MIME* (Multipurpose Internet Mail Extensions) is the most widely used method. MIME is built into all current mail programs, so they handle it automatically. When you hear about e-mail with attachments, that generally means MIME. When we describe mail programs, we tell you whether they work with MIME.

Before sending a file by using a MIME attachment, you may want to send a plain old, nonattached e-mail message to the intended recipient, asking whether he can handle MIME. Some mail systems reject, or discard, all e-mail with attachments. Because the e-mail worms and viruses everyone complains about are attachments, this is often a security policy. Good news! Your UNIX system is probably totally immune to most e-mail worms.

Exchanging Gossip by Using Pine

Pine was originally a cut-down version of elm intended for novice users, which makes it even easier to use than elm. Now it's become much more powerful than elm ever was. It has lots of nice menus to remind you of what to do next, and it even uses pico, a simple editor, for composing mail.

To run Pine, just type **pine**. You see a display like the one shown in Figure 17-1.

```
PINE 3.89   MAIN MENU                        Folder: INBOX  0 Messages


        ?     HELP             -  Get help using Pine

        C     COMPOSE MESSAGE  -  Compose and send a message

        I     FOLDER INDEX     -  View messages in current folder

        L     FOLDER LIST      -  Select a folder to view

        A     ADDRESS BOOK     -  Update address book

        S     SETUP            -  Configure or update Pine

        Q     QUIT             -  Exit the Pine program


       Copyright 1989-1993.  PINE is a trademark of the University of Washington.
                        [Folder "INBOX" opened with 0 messages]
? Help                           P PrevCmd                    R RelNotes
O OTHER CMDS L [ListFldrs]  N NextCmd                    K KBLock
```

Figure 17-1: Pine's menu, listing the most popular commands.

If you are using UNIX by way of a communications program, watch out for which terminal you are emulating. Pine works fine if your program emulates a VT100 terminal, but not so well if it emulates an ANSI terminal. You can usually change which terminal your program emulates.

Sign here

You can make a *signature file,* a file that contains text for Pine or elm to include at the end of every message. You must name the file .signature and be in your home directory.

Use your text editor to make a signature file. Keep it short (no more than three lines long), and include your name, your e-mail address, other address information you want everyone to know, and (if you have room) a pithy or philosophical message that characterizes you.

After you create a signature file, you don't have to type this stuff at the end of every message. To test it, send a message to yourself and see how the signature looks. The signature appears at the bottom of the message when you compose it. To omit the signature information from a message, just delete it.

Figure 17-1 shows Pine's *main menu,* with a list of its favorite commands. Pine uses one-letter commands. Note that one of the commands is highlighted — you can also choose commands by pressing the up- and down-arrow keys to move the highlight and then pressing Enter.

This list shows the commands you're most likely to use:

✔ Press c to compose (write a new message).

✔ Press i to see a list of your messages.

✔ Press q to exit from Pine.

✔ Press ? for lots of helpful online help.

Into the postbox

To use Pine to send mail, press the c key. Pine runs pico, a nice, simple editor we describe in more detail in Chapter 10. Rather than start with a blank file, you see the headers, ready for you to fill in: To, Cc, Attchmnt (for attaching files to a message — skip that one for now), and Subject. Use pico to type the header information and the text of your message. Then press Ctrl+X to leave pico. Pine sends the message and displays the main menu again.

If you decide not to send the message after all, you can press Ctrl+C to cancel it.

What's all this junk at the beginning of the message?

An e-mail message has a *header* that the mail program (mail, elm, Pine, or whatever) creates automatically. The header consists of these pieces:

- The To address (the person to receive the mail)

- The From address (the return address)

- The Cc addresses (the addresses to send copies to)

- The Bcc addresses (the addresses to send blind copies to)

- The subject

- Optional information you rarely use, such as expiration date, priority, which mailer mailed

the message, and sometimes (for incoming messages) the arcane route the message took to get to you

Don't worry if the header looks like gobbledygook — it is. On incoming mail, the header can have all sorts of extra glop that reports on which systems have passed it along, which program was used to send the mail, and lots of other useless stuff. You don't need to know, unless the mail is spam, and you want to complain; then you want to send the whole header along with the e-mail you're complaining about, so the mail wizards on the other end can decipher it and figure out who to blame.

You can specify cc addresses, the subject, and other information for messages you send.

This list shows you some cool things you can do while you're writing your message:

- For lots of helpful information about how to use Pine, you can press Ctrl+G. Pine has complete online help.

- You can even check the spelling of your message — just press Ctrl+T. Pine checks all the words in your message against its dictionary and highlights each word it can't find.

I'm pining for some mail

To read your mail, press the i key to see the index of messages, as shown in Figure 17-2. The messages are numbered, with codes (N for new messages you haven't read, D for messages you deleted, and A for messages you answered) in the left margin. One of the messages is highlighted.

To read a message, move the highlight to it, by pressing the up- and down-arrow keys or by pressing the p key (for previous) and the n key (for next). Then press the v key to view the message.

```
  PINE 3.89   FOLDER INDEX                 Folder: INBOX  Message 1 of 3 NEW
+ N 1   Apr  6 Margy Levine Young     (695) How about lunch?
+ N 2   Apr  6 To: John R Levine      (474) Trying out some software!
+ N 3   Apr  6 Margy Levine Young     (710) It's budget time again...




? Help        M Main Menu   P PrevMsg   - PrevPage    D Delete     R Reply
O OTHER CMDS  V [ViewMsg]   N NextMsg  Spc NextPage    U Undelete   F Forward
```

Figure 17-2:
A list of your messages, in Pine.

When you are looking at a message, here are some things you can do:

✓ **Forward the message to someone else, by pressing the f key.** Pine lets you start composing a message, with the text of the original message included in the text of this message.

✓ **Reply to the person who sent the message, by pressing the r key.** Pine automatically addresses the message to the person who sent the original one.

✓ **Delete the message by pressing the d key.** The message doesn't disappear right away, but it is marked with a D on the list of messages. When you exit from Pine, your deleted messages really are deleted. (If you change your mind, you can undelete a message by pressing the u key.)

✓ **Move on to the next message by pressing the n key or move back to the preceding one by pressing the p key.**

✓ **Return to Pine's main menu by pressing the m key.**

Send this file, too

Pine can handle MIME attachments with great ease and flair — nothing to it. To attach a file in Pine, move the cursor to the Attchmnts: line and press Ctrl+J while you're composing the message. When Pine prompts you for the filename, type it and press Enter. That's all it takes!

Creating your own address book

If you use Pine to send messages to Internet addresses, it can certainly be annoying to type long, complicated Internet addresses. That's a good reason to let Pine do it for you — set up an address book.

When you press the a key at the Pine menu, you switch to address book mode. (It even says ADDRESS BOOK at the top of the screen.) If you already entered some addresses, Pine lists them.

When you finish fooling with your address book, press the m key to return to Pine's main menu.

To create an entry in your address book when the program is in address book mode, follow these steps:

1. **Press the a key.**
2. **Type the person's last name, a comma, and then the first name, and then press Enter.**
3. **Type the nickname (make it short but easy to remember).**
4. **Enter the e-mail address just as you do when you address a message.**

   Pine stores the entry in your address book and lists it on the address book screen.

If you make a mistake, you can edit an entry later. Just highlight it on the list of addresses, and press the e key to edit it.

You can also create an address book entry directory from the address of a message. If you're looking at a message from someone whose address you want to save, just press the t key. Pine prompts you for the person's full name (it may even suggest it, if it's part of the message header), nickname, and e-mail address (Pine suggests the address of the sender of the current message). To use an address book entry, just type the nickname on the To: or Cc: line of a message.

Saving messages

Pine enables you to create lots of folders in which to put your messages so that you can save them in an organized manner. To save a message in a folder, press the s key when you're looking at it or when it's highlighted on the list of messages.

If you save a message to a folder that doesn't exist, Pine asks whether you want to create it. Press the y key to do so. When you move a message to a folder, Pine automatically deletes it from your inbox. Very tidy.

Looking in a folder

After you put messages in folders, you may want to look at them later. When you see Pine's main menu, you can press the l key (the lowercase letter *L*) to select which folder to look in. Pine automatically makes several for you, including these:

- ✔ **INBOX:** Your incoming messages. Messages remain there until you delete or move them.
- ✔ **Sent mail:** Messages you sent.
- ✔ **Saved messages:** A place to save messages before you send them.

Move the highlight to the folder you want, and then press Enter. Pine lists the messages in the folder.

You can make more folders by moving messages into them (as described in the preceding section).

What You Need in Order to Use Remote E-Mail

Nowadays, your e-mail is usually received and stored by another computer, for you to download at your leisure. We look at a few of the mail programs that support remote e-mail later in this chapter. Most mail programs are graphical clients, meaning you can't use them from within a terminal window. If you really need to fetch remote mail and read it in a terminal window, the program you'll probably end up using is `fetchmail`, which takes remote mail and puts it into a local mailbox.

Some common ground does exist among remote e-mail programs. They don't actually send and receive your mail, so they need to be told where your mailbox is. To configure your e-mail program, you need an *inbound mail server* and an *outbound mail server*.

A machine is somewhere out there with your mail on it. Because mail comes into that machine for you, it's called an *inbound mail server*. When you configure a mail client to talk to the mail server and get your mail, the mail client configuration probably talks about incoming mail. Most likely, you get your mail via Post Office Protocol (POP). This is also called an *incoming mail server*, or a *POP server*.

If you want a good snail mail analogy, think of this as like the mailbox where letters to you are dropped off. (To continue the analogy, the spam messages you invariably get are sort of like bills, only they're not bills for anything you actually bought.)

You have an account on an inbound mail server with a username and password, which is used to keep anyone else from reading your mail and you from reading anyone else's mail. Most often, the username is your username — the thing that goes on the left side of the @ in your e-mail address. To set up an inbound mail server, you need this name and password.

When you want to send mail out, you need to use another mail server. Sometimes, the inbound and outbound mail servers are the same; sometimes, they're different. It doesn't matter! You just go into your mail program's setup (we show you how later in this chapter for some of the common ones) and select an outbound mail server. The most common way to do this is *Simple Mail Transfer Protocol* (SMTP). This can also be called an *SMTP server.*

Mail hound

Another UNIX mail program worth mentioning is the humbly named `mutt`. Michael Elkins, a physics undergrad at California's Harvey Mudd College, wrote the original version of `mutt` in 1995 when he finally got fed up with the limitations of `elm`. (`mutt`'s motto for the ages: "All mail clients suck. This one just sucks less.")

Although written from scratch, `mutt` was originally based on `elm`, with various ideas from Pine and other UNIX mail clients thrown in to create a unique hybrid, or mongrel — in short, a `mutt`. (And you thought that `mutt` was an ultra-nerdy acronym for Mail User Transaction Terminal, didn't you?) Unlike `elm`, which is a basic text-based, one-message-at-a-time affair, `mutt` can handle colors (fancy that!) and message threads. *Threads* group messages based on their subjects so that you can tell which messages are responses to which. Threading is particularly useful if you carry on lengthy e-mail conversations with a number of different correspondents or if you subscribe to especially active mailing lists.

All in all, this `mutt` can hunt. It lets you attach files to e-mail messages by using MIME. It supports PGP (*pretty good privacy*) encoding for keeping your love letters secret. It automatically opens a Web page in your browser when you click a URL in a mail message (if you don't know what that means, try Chapter 19). It has tons of options. It's small. And in the best UNIX tradition, it's free.

You can download `mutt` from FTP sites all over the Internet, including the FTP archive at the computer science department of Michael Elkins' alma mater (it's at `ftp://ftp.cs.hmc.edu/pub/me`). It also comes along with various versions of Linux, such as Red Hat Linux and Caldera OpenLinux.

TIP

In our snail-mail analogy, this machine is like a street corner mailbox; you go to it and drop the mail off.

Netiquette

E-mail has been around long enough for an etiquette style to spring up around it, just as with real mail. Here are some tips:

Be polite. The written word tends to sound stronger and more dogmatic than speech. Sarcasm and little jokes don't always work.

Don't write anything when you are annoyed. If you get a message that you find totally obnoxious, *don't answer it right away!* You will be sorry if you do, because you will overreact and look just as obnoxious yourself. How do we know this? We used to do it, too. Everyone does at first, until they learn not to take e-mail too seriously. The exchange of needlessly obnoxious messages is so common that it has a name: *flaming.* Don't do it.

Be brief.

Be sure to sign your messages. The header shows where a message comes from, but your recipient may not remember who you are from your cryptic e-mail address.

Use normal punctuation and capitalization. That is, DON'T CAPITALIZE EVERYTHING. It looks as though you are shouting, and that's not polite (see the first tip in this list).

Watch out for acronyms. E-mail is full of them, and you had better know what the common ones mean. A list of acronyms is at the end of this sidebar.

Don't assume that e-mail is private. Any recipient of your mail can easily forward it to other people. Some mail addresses are really mailing lists that redistribute messages to many other people. Also, glitches in the mail system may send your messages to various electronic dead-letter offices. In one famous case, a mistaken mail address sent a message to tens of thousands of readers. It started "Darling, at last we have a way to send messages that is completely private. . . ."

If you need to indicate emotion, most people use *emoticons,* little pictures made up of characters to look like faces. If you see : -), for example, just look at it sideways: You see a little smiley face, which usually means that whatever you just read was a joke. (You get a sad face if you use the other parenthesis for the mouth.) Some people — particularly those who use CompuServe — type <grin> or <g> or <smile>. (An opposing viewpoint says that if you need one of those emotion things, rewriting your message to make it clearer what you mean is a better idea.)

Here's a list of the most common e-mail acronyms:

BTW	By The Way
IANMTU	I Am Not Making This Up
IMHO	In My Humble Opinion
IOW	In Other Words
PITA	Pain In The Armpit
PMFJI	Pardon Me For Jumping In
ROFL	Rolling On Floor, Laughing
RSN	Real Soon Now (ha!)
RTFM	Read the Manual (that is, you could have looked it up yourself)
TIA	Thanks In Advance
YMMV	Your Mileage May Vary (you may not have the same experiences)

As of this writing, most outbound mail servers don't need a password, but some do. Ask your ISP for local details.

Sometimes, just to try to confuse you, people refer to either or both of these as a *mail server*. In general, if you're not sure, you can stop someone and say, "wait, do you mean an inbound or an outbound mail server?" and expect to get a helpful answer. Inbound means the mail is coming in for you; outbound means you're sending it.

Mail Bonding with Mozilla

In previous versions of this book, we discussed setting up e-mail in Netscape 3.0, and also in Netscape 4.0 — they were totally different, so it was pretty exciting. Now, we just recommend that you use Mozilla. Mozilla is the open source version of Netscape, which means it's still being maintained even though no one found a way to make money off of it. If you used Mozilla for mail on a Mac or Windows system, you'll find it eerily familiar. If a version of Netscape is on your system (some flavors of Linux include it), its mail works just like Mozilla.

The part of Mozilla that does e-mail (and news!) is called Mail & Newsgroups. It's easy to start it; just select Window⇨Mail & Newsgroups.

When you first open the Mail & Newsgroups window, you'll probably be confronted with a series of windows where Mozilla tries to set up your e-mail account. Remember all that stuff we said you'd need to set up a remote mail account? Here's where you need it. Follow these steps to answer them all.

1. **Mozilla asks whether you want to set up an e-mail or a newsgroup account. Pick the e-mail account, and then click Next.**

2. **Mozilla asks for your name and your e-mail address. Enter them, and then click Next.**

3. **Mozilla asks whether you're using POP or IMAP. Choose the appropriate server and click Next.**

   If you're not sure, enter POP; if you've been told you're using IMAP, pick that.

4. **Mozilla asks for the names of your incoming and outgoing mail servers. Enter these names, and then click Next.**

   If you aren't sure, ask your ISP about them. If your ISP isn't sure either, try guessing the name `mail`, which works for a lot of ISPs.

5. **Mozilla asks for your account name. Enter it, then click Next.**

   If you aren't sure, a likely guess is the left-hand side of your e-mail address (before the @). Check with your ISP.

6. Mozilla asks you to name this account. Pick a name and click Next.

This is a friendly feature; Mozilla lets you check multiple e-mail accounts, so it wants you to give them unique names. You can give it a name like "Betty's Email", or you can use names like "Work" or "Personal". If you only have one, it doesn't matter much what you call it — just don't call it late for dinner!

7. Mozilla asks for confirmation. Reassure it, and then click Finish.

8. Mozilla asks for your e-mail password. Give it your password.

We do not recommend that you use the Password Manager feature to remember your password. It sounds really convenient, but after you go without typing your password for a few months, if you lose your Mozilla settings, you're out of luck.

After you make it through the grueling windows of preference setting, Mozilla tries to download your mail. If it's configured correctly, spam starts pouring in almost immediately.

To send a message, follow these steps:

1. Click the Compose button on the toolbar.

The Write Mail window opens, chock-full of incomprehensible icons, although you can ignore most of them.

2. Enter the name of your recipient in the To box.

At the top of the window are a couple of lines that look sort of like lined notebook paper. Near the left end of the line may be an entry that says To or Cc or Bcc. If it says anything other than To, click the little arrow to the left of the Cc or Bcc and switch it to To. Having done that, type your recipient's address in the right half of your freshly updated To: line. If you have other recipients, you can enter them on the next lines, one per line.

3. Type the subject in the Subject box.

4. Enter your message into the rest of the window.

Mozilla offers a fantasia of fantastic formatting features. *Don't use any of them.* Mail that isn't plain text is likely to show up as unintelligible gibberish in mail programs like Pine, and makes you look like a newbie. It sounds really neat to have mail that's all formatted, but lots of different programs format mail in different ways. In fact, mail sent in HTML is often used as a sign of probable spam, because so much spam uses HTML formatting.

5. Click the Send button.

If you use any of the formatting features, or sometimes even if you haven't, Mozilla pops up a window warning you that your recipient may not be able to handle the beautiful formatting and giving you some options. Pick the Send in Plain Text Only option, and click Send again. Whew!

Outlook: Partly cloudy

You may be wondering why we haven't mentioned Outlook Express, the Microsoft answer to Netscape Messenger. Simple! Outlook Express doesn't run on UNIX systems — and with all the e-mail viruses that only spread through Outlook Express, that may not be such a bad thing. There were some versions of it, but development has stopped, and references to UNIX versions of Outlook Express, or Internet Explorer, are now on an "if I told you, I'd have to kill you" basis only. Microsoft ignores UNIX, except for the annual Making of the Excuse, where they explain that it will be *this* year that Windows 200X finally replaces UNIX. We think they should have used "the dog ate my reliability."

To see your new mail, click the Get Msg button on the toolbar. (You may be prompted for your login password, depending on your mail setup.) After you have mail in your mailbox, double-click a message in the message listing to see that message in a new window. The Reply, Forward, Next, and Previous buttons do what they look like they should.

Kool! It's KMail

If the command-line mail clients aren't doing it for you, you might want to give KMail a try. It's a fairly standard e-mail client, which means that you can take a two-year degree in configuring it. Setting KMail up is a lot like setting up Mozilla, except that you have to do everything yourself; it won't prompt you. Here are the steps.

1. **Start KMail.**

   It's probably one of the icons at the bottom of the screen — look for an envelope with an E next to it.

2. **Choose Settings⇨Configure KMail.**

   The Configure KMail window appears.

3. **If an identity is in the list area in the window, select the Modify option; otherwise, select the New option.**

4. **Enter your name, organization, and e-mail address and click OK.**

   Many people put funny things in the Organization field; if you're like us, put None, or Fairly cluttered.

   You may want to come back here later and add a signature (something attached to every message you send). This is also where you specify a Reply-To header, but most people don't need one.

5. **Click the Network icon in the left side of the window.**

6. **Select the Add option on the Sending tab.**

7. **Enter the name of your outgoing mail server.**

   Just like with Mozilla, if you aren't sure, ask your ISP. You can try `smtp` and `mail`, both of which are likely guesses. Just put the host name in the Host field.

8. **Click the Receiving tab. Specify the name of the host.**

   Before you're allowed to enter settings for a host, you're asked what kind of account it is; select the POP option from the list.

   Your ISP should be able to tell you. Remember, your POP server is the same thing as your incoming mail server. It's more likely `mail`, `pop`, or `pop3`.

9. **Type your username and password.**

   Your username is whatever your ISP told you to use to get your mail. Generally, the username is the same as the part before the @ in your e-mail address.

You can check your mail, send replies, and everything else. If it didn't work, good luck — you have to call your ISP's tech support. They may not know how to use KMail, but the instructions they give you should work. Just remember that you get to all of these settings by choosing Settings⇨Configure KMail. If you're having trouble checking your mail, everything you need to do is on the Receiving tab. If you're having trouble sending mail, check the Sending tab.

Advanced e-mail magic

Some pretty cool stuff is out there, and a lot of it is too deep to go into in any depth here. Want something to sink your teeth into? Here are a few recommendations.

✔ The **MH e-mail client** (or NMH, an updated version that's more actively maintained) is what all the cool kids use. It's arcane, complicated, and completely scriptable. Instead of being a single program, it's a set of programs, which you glue together yourself. Hard to use, but it can do anything.

✔ Want to sort your mail, preprocess it, and set up autoresponders? You're looking for **procmail**. A bit tricky to figure out, but very flexible. Some good information about it is written by our friend Nancy McGough at `www.ii.com/internet/robots/procmail/`.

✔ Sick of spam? A wonderful program, called **SpamAssassin**, can identify a lot of it and throw it out for you. Most people who use SpamAssassin have it as a plug-in to procmail.

You can play with a lot of the other settings. One setting you shouldn't touch is the HTML mail setting. By default, KMail plays nice and sends plain text e-mail. We like plain text e-mail. It's got words in it. You can configure KMail to send HTML mail, with the same problems HTML mail always has. Just don't go there!

KMail's toolbar may be confusing at first. Just hover the mouse over a button, and you get an actual description of what it does. For instance, the button that looks like a dog-eared sheet of paper with an envelope in front of it is the New Message button. Using KMail is otherwise a lot like using any other mail program.

E-Mail with Evolution

Using Evolution as an e-mail client and not using any of its other features is probably silly. It's amazing. It does everything. It probably has a hidden "bring about world peace" menu item. It does calendar stuff; it does everything. But if you can't read your e-mail in it, who cares? After you have your e-mail running, you can explore the other stuff at your leisure.

Follow these steps to set up e-mail in Evolution.

1. **Select Tools⇨Settings.**

   The Settings window opens.

2. **Click the Mail Accounts button on the left side.**

3. **Click the Add button on the right side of the window.**

   A wizard starts that is somewhat similar to the one Mozilla uses to ask you all the questions it needs answers to.

4. **Click Next.**

5. **Enter your name and e-mail address, and then click Next.**

   The Reply-To and Organization fields are optional. Organization is generally the organization you're associated with — your employer, for work e-mail. Reply-To is a special e-mail header used to tell people where to send replies to your mail. You only set it if you want replies to go to an address other than the e-mail address you entered, and you probably don't have any reason to do that.

6. **Select the POP option from the pop-up list of server types.**

   New fields appear.

7. **Enter your host name and account name, and then click Next.**

   As always, the host name is the one your ISP gave you and is your inbound mail server. If your ISP requires or supports SSL connections, you can change the Use Secure Connection option, but most ISPs won't. As always, we don't recommend that you have the program remember your password. Get used to typing it. Evolution supports a number of authentication types. You probably don't need to know anything about these; password works at most ISPs. If it seems to be a problem, try clicking the Check for Supported Types button. (This button is only available after you enter the host name.)

8. **Change settings if you want, and then click Next.**

   The settings are probably best left alone. Checking automatically for mail can be very annoying. Leaving mail on the server is only useful if you use multiple e-mail clients, and you want to read the same mail several times.

9. **Enter the name of your outgoing mail server, and then click Next.**

   This is the same drill as before. Again, Evolution has tons of options. If your ISP requires POP before SMTP, this is the panel to enter it on; select the Server Requires Authentication option, and select the POP before SMTP option from the pop-up list.

10. **Name this account, make it your default, and click Next.**

    This is like the account names in Mozilla — anything you want is fine. A lot of people like creative names such as "work" or "home". If it's your only account, you may as well select the Make This My Default Account check box.

11. **Click Finish.**

    That's it! You're done.

You can close the Settings window and start checking and reading your mail. Evolution has a single button for sending outgoing mail and grabbing incoming mail. This feature allows you to compose responses and get new mail as soon as you try to send them all off. If you're trading mail with enough people, you may never have to work again!

Chapter 18

Web Surfing for UNIX Users

The World Wide Web (WWW, or just the Web) is the zoomiest, coolest Internet facility around. It contains lots of information, including pictures and other non-text stuff, in the form of *hypertext*. As you read through the information, therefore, you can click (or otherwise select) words, pictures, or buttons to zoom right to related information. These clickable words, pictures, and buttons are called *links*.

The amazing thing about all these linked pages is that a page may be stored on any Internet host computer in the world. If you're looking at a page stored on a computer in Brookline, Massachusetts, a link on that page may jump you to a page stored in Basel, Switzerland. You never even notice, unless you look carefully at the names of the Web pages.

What's a Browser?

You read the World Wide Web by using a *browser*. If you use X Windows, you can use a graphical browser such as Mozilla, Konqueror, or Opera. With a graphical browser, you get to see all the cool stuff as well as the text. (Does this type of browser make the browsing experience any more educational or enriching? In some cases, maybe, but mostly it just makes browsing more fun.) If you're familiar with a browser on Windows, you'll find browsing on UNIX quite familiar, and if you use Mozilla, Netscape, or Opera on Windows, you'll find their UNIX versions nearly identical. This chapter describes both Mozilla and Konqueror.

URL!

The World Wide Web brought us the extremely useful concept of Uniform Resource Locators, or URLs. The point of a URL is to have a simple and consistent way to name Internet resources that tells you both the type of the resource and where to find it. A URL consists of a resource type, a colon, and a location. URLs look horrendous. In most cases, the location is two slashes, the host name where the resource can be found, a slash, and a filename on that host.

Commonly used resource types are shown in this list:

- **http:** A HyperText Transfer Protocol document; that is, something in native Web format

- **ftp:** A directory or file on an FTP server

Here's a typical URL:

```
http://net.gurus.com/toc-
    u4d5.html
```

The reason that most URLs look more like run-on typos than actual locations is that they were originally designed to be read by computers rather than actual human beings. Still, their structure has an underlying order, and understanding that order helps to demystify them (a little). The sample URL is a Web document. Reading backward, the part after the last slash is the filename: `toc-u4d5.html`. The part following the two slashes is the host name of the computer: `net.gurus.com`. Finally, back at the beginning, you see `http:`, which just tells the browser to use the `http` resource type (the Web) to view this file.

Although URLs were originally intended as a way for computers to pass around resource names, they've also become widely used as a way to tell people about Internet resources, and that's how we use them in this section of the book. It's unfortunate that they're so difficult to type!

When you start your browser, you can begin with the Web page it suggests and find your way to the information you want by following the hypertext links. (Don't worry — we tell you how.) Alternatively, you can jump directly to a Web page if you know its name. These names are called *URLs* (for Uniform Resource Locators) — see the nearby sidebar, "URL!" to read about them.

Browsing with Pictures: Mozilla and Konqueror

The most common browsers for UNIX are currently Mozilla, Konqueror, and Opera. Mozilla is the open source core of Netscape (which is itself available on some UNIX flavors, but works almost exactly like Mozilla). Konqueror is the browser that comes with KDE. Mozilla and KDE are open source and available for free. Opera is from Opera Software in Norway, and shows ads, which go away if you buy an expensive license.

Because UNIX versions of Mozilla, Netscape, and Opera are nearly identical to their equivalents on other systems (you know which ones we mean), if you're already a Mozilla or Opera user, there's little reason to switch. We don't cover Opera in detail here, but it's a perfectly good browser, and if you can use any other graphical browser, it takes about two minutes for you to figure out Opera.

(Don't bother) configuring Mozilla or Konqueror

Because Mozilla is an X application, it uses dozens and dozens of X resources you can customize. Here's our advice: Forget it. The standard configuration works fine, and our sad experience is that most changes you can make only make Mozilla worse. Konqueror is even worse, being both an X and a KDE application, but the same advice applies.

Starting them up

You start your browser by typing **mozilla** or **konqueror** in your shell. (More likely you have a Mozilla or Konqueror entry on your screen's toolbar, so just click it.)

TIP

There's no place like home

You hear a great deal these days about home pages. Everyone who is anyone has a home page. So what are they?

A *home page* is a page on the World Wide Web that serves as a starting point for information about something. If, for example, you want information about our *For Dummies* books, you may want to start at the Internet Gurus Central home page, which is at `http://net.gurus.com`.

Home pages generally contain introductory information about the entity whose home page it is, along with lots of links to other pages. Many home pages for organizations have URLs such as `www.`*something*, where *something* is the Internet domain name for the organization. Guess whose home page is `www.microsoft.com`?

The browser starts up with whatever home page it's been set up with. You see a window like the one shown in Figure 18-1 (Konqueror) or Figure 18-2 (Mozilla). Konqueror is also a file browser, so rather than a Web page, you may see a page full of icons for the files in your home directory.

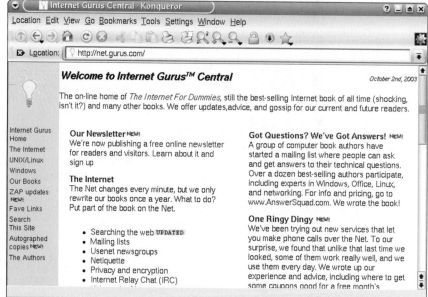

Figure 18-1:
Fine
literature in
Konqueror.

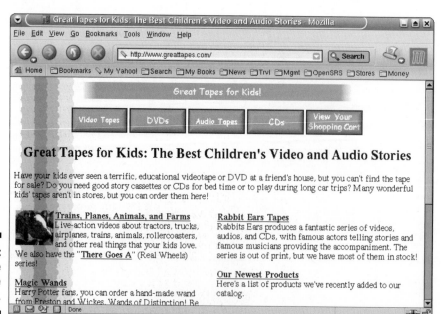

Figure 18-2:
Fine
literature
in Mozilla.

The text, the whole text, and nothing but the text

If you're stuck with a plain old, text-based terminal (for example, if you connected to a remote UNIX host with `telnet` or `ssh`), you can use a text-only browser named Lynx. `Text-only` means that you don't get to see any of the cool pictures, animations, and sounds that make the Web the phenomenally popular success that it is. On the other hand, Lynx is blindingly fast (drawing those pictures is slow) and quite adequate for a quick look at sites where you don't care about the pictures.

Lynx is entirely controlled from the keyboard, so you navigate around the screen with the up and down arrows, follow links with the right arrow, and select and change fields with Enter. After you do this for a few minutes, it's surprisingly usable, and Lynx is very good about keeping a help line at the bottom telling you where you are and what characters you might want to type now. The most important one is q for quit.

Surfing with Your Browser

At the top of the window are a bunch of buttons and the Location line, which contains the URL or filename for the current page. Remember that URLs are an important part of Web lore because they're the secret codes that name all the pages on the Web. For details, see the sidebar "URL!," earlier in this chapter.

The main part of the browser window is taken up by the Web page that you're looking it. After all, that's what the browser is *for* — displaying a Web page! The buttons, bars, and menus around the edge help you find your way around the Web and do things, such as print and save pages.

Getting around

You need two simple skills (if we can describe something as basic as a single mouse-click as a skill) to get going on the Web. One is to move from page to page on the Web, and the other is to jump directly to a page when you know its URL (see the section, "Going places," later in this chapter).

Moving from page to page is easy: Click any link that looks interesting. That's it. Underlined blue text and blue-bordered pictures are links. (Although links may be a color other than blue, depending on the look the Web page designer is going for, they're always underlined unless the page is the victim of a truly awful designer.) Anything that looks like a button is probably a link. You can tell when you're pointing to a link because the mouse pointer changes to a little hand. If you're not sure whether something is a link, click it anyway because doing so doesn't hurt anything. Clicking outside a link selects the text you click, as in most other programs.

TECHNICAL STUFF

Here's HTML in your eye!

As you may know, Web pages are written in a language called *HTML,* which includes instructions to tell the browser about text, headings, links, graphics, and anything else a Web page may contain. Each browser reads the HTML information about a page, formats it tastefully, and displays it. Different browsers use different formatting.

If you want to see the actual HTML version of a page in your browser, left-click somewhere in the page and in the menu that appears, select View Page Source or View Document Source.

```
<HTML>
<HEAD>
<TITLE>Great Tapes for Kids!
        www.greattapes.com </TITLE>
<!-- Changed by: Margy Levine Young, 11-
        Nov-2003 -->
</HEAD>

<BODY BGCOLOR="#FFFFFF"
        BACKGROUND="back.gif">
```

```
<CENTER><IMG SRC="title.gif" HEIGHT=30
        WIDTH=500></CENTER>
<H1>Great Tapes for Kids: A Catalog of
        the Best Children's Video and
        Audio Tapes</H1>
Have you ever seen a terrific,
        educational tape at a friend's
        house, a tape that your kids
        loved, and then never been able
        to find the tape for sale? Many
        of the best kids' video- and
        audiotapes aren't in your local
        video store, but you can order
        them here!
```

All those brackets surround HTML markings, which tell Web browsers how to format the text and where to put pictures and links. If you want more information about HTML, you can find about a billion Web sites and books on the topic. On the Web, a decent introduction is at www.w3.org/MarkUp/Guide. Book lovers can check out *HTML For Dummies* by Ed Tittle (published by Wiley Publishing, Inc.).

Backward, ho!

TIP

Web browsers remember the last few pages you visited, so if you click a link and decide that you're not so crazy about the new page, you can easily go back to the preceding one. To go back, click the Back or Previous button on the toolbar (its icon is an arrow pointing to the left, and it's the left-most button on the toolbar) or press Alt+←.

All over the map

Some picture links are *image maps,* such as the big picture shown in the middle of Figure 18-3. In a regular link, where you click doesn't matter; on an image map, it does. The image map in Figure 18-3 is typical and has a bunch of obvious places you click for various types of information, either on the map itself to zoom in on a point, or on the symbols at the bottom to move or zoom the whole map.

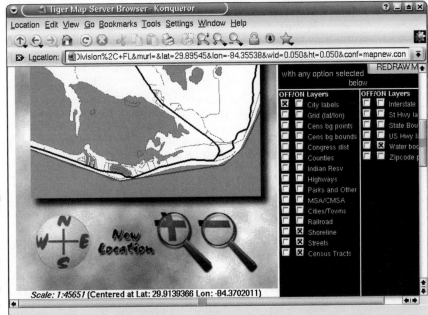

Figure 18-3:
Click the part of the image map that you want to choose.

TIP

As you move the mouse cursor around a Web page, whenever you're pointing at a link, the URL of the place it links to may appear in small type at the bottom of the screen. If the link is an image map, it shows the link followed by a question mark and two numbers that are the X and Y positions of where you are on the map. The numbers don't matter to you (it's up to the Web server to make sense of them); if you see a pair of numbers counting up and down when you move the mouse, however, you know that you're on an image map.

Going places

These days, everyone and his dog has a home page. A *home page* is the main Web page for a person or organization. When you see a URL you want to check out, here's what you do:

1. **Click in the Location near the top of the Mozilla or Konqueror window.**

2. **Type the URL in the box. Browsers let you leave off the** http:// **part.**

   The URL is something like http://net.gurus.com — you can just type **net.gurus.com**. Be sure to erase the URL that appeared before you started typing.

3. **Press Enter.**

If you receive URLs in electronic mail, instant messages, documents, Usenet newsgroup messages, or anywhere else on your computer, you can use the standard cut-and-paste techniques and avoid retyping: In KDE, if you merely highlight a URL, it opens a menu asking whether you want to open it in a browser window.

Most e-mail programs highlight URLs in e-mail messages. All you have to do is click the highlighted link, and your browser pops up and opens the Web page.

You can leave the `http://` off the front of URLs when you type them in the Location or Address box. Your browser can guess that part!

Where to start?

A good way to get started is to just explore: Go to the Yahoo! page. Type this URL in the Location or Address box and then press Enter:

```
www.yahoo.com
```

You go to the Yahoo page, in the middle of which are links to a directory of millions of Web pages by topic. Just nose around, clicking links that look interesting, and clicking the Back button on the toolbar when you make a wrong turn. We guarantee that you'll find something interesting.

For updates to the very book you are holding, go to this URL:

```
net.gurus.com
```

Follow the links to the page about our books or about the Internet, and then select the pages for readers of *UNIX For Dummies,* 5th Edition. If we have any late-breaking news about the Internet or updates and corrections to this book, you can find them there. If you find mistakes in this book or have other comments, by the way, please send e-mail to us at `unix9@gurus.com`.

This page looks funny

Sometimes a Web page gets garbled on the way in, or you interrupt it (by clicking the Stop button on the toolbar or by pressing the Esc key). You can tell your browser to get the information on the page again: Click the Reload button (the curved arrow).

Get me outta here

Sooner or later, even the most dedicated Web surfer has to stop to eat or attend to other bodily needs. You leave your browser in the same way that you leave any other program: by choosing File⇨Quit in Mozilla, Location⇨ Quit in Konqueror. You can also click the Close (X) button in the upper-right corner of the window. Or, just leave the program running and walk away from your computer.

Windows on the World

When you know how to find your way around the Web, you are ready for some comparatively advanced features so that you can start to feel like a Web pro in no time.

Konqueror and Mozilla are known in the trade as *multithreaded* programs — that is, they can display several pages at once. When we're pointing and click-ing from one place to another, we like to open a bunch of windows so that we can see where we've been and go back to a previous page just by switching to another window. You can also arrange windows side-by-side, which is a good way to, say, compare prices for *UNIX For Dummies,* 5th Edition, at various online bookstores. (The difference may be small, but when you're buying 100 copies for everyone on your Christmas list, those pennies can add up. Oh, you weren't planning to do that? Phoo.)

Wild window mania

To display a page in a new browser window, click a link with the right mouse button and select Open in New Window or Open Link in New Window from the menu that pops up. To close a window, click the Close (X) button at the top right of the window frame. Users with three-button mice can usually open a link in a new window by clicking the middle button (although sometimes browsers are set up to open a new tab instead, as we discuss in the next section).

You can also create a new window without following a link. Press Ctrl+N or choose File⇨New⇨Navigator Window (in Netscape Navigator), File⇨New Navigator Window (in Mozilla) or Location⇨New Window (in Konqueror).

Tab dancing

Konqueror and Mozilla (and Opera for that matter) have *tabs,* which are multiple pages that you can switch among in a window. Figure 18-4 shows a Mozilla window with three tabs. Just click any of the tabs near the top of the window to show its page. Click the little star-box thing at the left end of the tab line or press Ctrl+T to make a new empty tab or the X at the right end to get rid of the current tab. In Konqueror, click a link with the middle button, or right click and select Open in New Tab or Open in Background Tab, the latter meaning that it loads the new tab while leaving the existing tab visible.

Like multiple windows, tabs are multithreaded so you can have one loading in the background while you're reading another, and little rotating arrows in the tab bar show you which ones are loading and which are ready. For most purposes, we find tabs more convenient than windows. You can use both; if you open several windows in Konqueror. In Mozilla, each window can have several tabs.

Short attention span tips

If you have a slow Internet connection, use at least two browser tabs or windows at the same time. While you're waiting for the next page to arrive in one tab or window, you can read the page that arrived a while ago in the other.

If you ask your browser to begin downloading a big file, it displays, most usefully, a small window in the corner of your screen. Mozilla displays a "thermometer" showing the download progress. Although some people consider watching the thermometer grow or the pages fly enough entertainment (we do when we're tired enough), you can click back to the main browser window and continue surfing.

Doing two or three things at a time in your browser when you have a dial-up Net connection is not unlike squeezing blood from a turnip — you can squeeze only so much blood. In this case, the blood is the amount of data your computer can pump through your modem. A single download task can keep your modem close to 100 percent busy, and anything else you do shares the modem with the download process. When you do two things at a time, therefore, each one happens more slowly than it does by itself.

If one task is a big download and the other is perusing Web pages, everything usually works okay because you spend a fair amount of time looking at what the Web browser is displaying; the download can then run while you think. On the other hand, although browsers let you start two download tasks at a time (or a dozen, if you're so inclined), doing more than one at a time than one after another is no faster, and it can get confusing.

Figure 18-4:
A Mozilla window with three tabs.

My Favorite Things

The Web really does have cool places to visit. Some you will want to visit over and over again. (We've probably visited the Google Web site thousands of times by now.) All the makers of fine browsers have, fortunately, provided a handy way for you to remember those spots and not have to write down those nasty URLs just to have to type them again later.

Although the name varies, the idea is simple: Your browser lets you mark a Web page and adds its URL to a list. Later, when you want to go back, you just go to your list and pick the page you want. Konqueror and Mozilla call these saved Web addresses *bookmarks;* other browsers you may use call them *favorites.*

You can handle bookmarks in two ways. One way is to think of them as a menu so that you can choose individual bookmarks from the menu bar of your browser. The other is to think of them as a custom-built page of links so that you go to that page and then choose the link you want. Mozilla, a prime example of the "Great Expanding Blob" approach to software design, does both. Konqueror favors the menu, although it is happy to put the menu at the top, bottom, left, right, or even in a little window of its own.

Bookmarking with Mozilla and Konqueror

Mozilla and Konqueror bookmarks all lurk under the Bookmarks menu.
To bookmark a Web page — that is, to add the address of the page to
your bookmarks — choose Bookmarks➪Bookmark This Page (Mozilla) or
Bookmarks➪Add Bookmark (Konqueror).

After you create some bookmarks, your bookmarks appear as entries on the
menu that you see when you click the Bookmarks menu. To go to one of
the pages on your bookmark list, just choose its entry from the menu.

If you're like most users, your bookmark menu gets bigger and bigger and
crawls down your screen and eventually ends up flopping down on the floor,
which is both unattractive and unsanitary. Fortunately, you can smoosh
(technical term) your menu into a more tractable form. Choose Bookmarks➪
Manage Bookmarks (Mozilla) or Bookmarks➪Edit Bookmarks (Konqueror) to
display your Bookmarks window (shown in Konqueror in Figure 18-5).

Because all of these bookmarks are live links, you can go to any of them. In
Mozilla just click them, in Konqueror right-click and select Open in
Konqueror. (You can leave this window open while you move around the Web
in other browser windows.) You can also add separator lines and submenus
to organize your bookmarks and make the individual menus less unwieldy.
Submenus look like folders in the Bookmarks window.

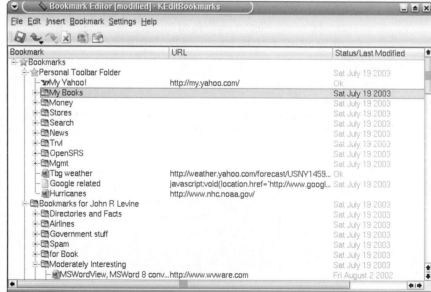

Figure 18-5:
The
Bookmarks
window
includes
commands
for moving,
editing, and
deleting
bookmarks.

In the Bookmarks window, choose File⇨New⇨Separator (Mozilla) or Insert⇨ Insert Separator (Konqueror) to add a separator line and File⇨New⇨Folder (Mozilla) or Insert⇨Create New Folder (Konqueror) to add a new submenu. (It asks you to type the name of the submenu before it creates the folder.) You can then drag bookmarks, separators, and folders up and down to where you want them in the Bookmarks window. Drag an item to a folder to put it in that folder's submenu, and double-click a folder to display or hide that submenu. Because any changes you make in the Bookmarks window reflect immediately on the Bookmarks menu, fiddling with the bookmarks until you get something you like is easy. Mozilla preloads your bookmark window with pages it likes you to look at, but feel free to delete them if your tastes are different from Mozilla's.

When you're done fooling with your bookmarks, choose File⇨Close (Mozilla) or File⇨Quit (Konqueror) to close the Bookmarks window.

The Personal or Bookmark toolbar is a row of buttons that usually appears just below the Location box. If it's not there, choose View⇨Show/Hide⇨ Personal Toolbar (Mozilla) or Settings⇨Toolbars⇨Bookmark Toolbar (Konqueror) to display it. This row of buttons gives you one-button access to a bunch of the browser author's favorite Web sites. Wouldn't it be nice if your favorite Web sites appeared there instead? No problem! In Mozilla, stick your top favorite sites in the Personal Toolbar Folder — any sites in this folder automagically appear on the Personal toolbar. In the Konqueror bookmark window, right-click the folder you want to use as your toolbar folder and select Set as Toolbar Folder. You can even add folders with bookmarks in them. Folders appear as folder icons, and bookmarks appear as blue ribbons. We love this feature.

Where do we start?

In Mozilla: Mozilla has an informative home page that it shows each time it starts up. After one or two times, beautiful though the page is, you will probably find that you can do without it. You can tell Mozilla not to load any Web page, or a different page, when you start the program:

1. **Choose Edit⇨Preferences.**

   You see the Preferences dialog box.

2. **Click Navigator in the Category box down the left side of the window.**

   This category may already be selected, and its settings appear in the Preferences window. The first Navigator setting is called Navigator Starts With (or When Navigator Starts Up Display) — the Web page that Netscape displays on startup.

3. **To start with no Web page, click Blank Page. To choose a page to start with, click Home Page, click in the box below it, and type the URL of a page you would rather see (how about** http://net.gurus.com, **which is our page?). To make the last page visited your home page, select that option.**

The home page is (surprise!) the page that Mozilla displays when you click the Home button on the toolbar. To set the home page to the page you're looking at right now, click Use Current Page. To display a page stored on your own computer, click Browse or Choose File and choose a file.

You also have the option of starting where you left off last time by clicking Last Page Visited.

4. **Click OK.**

You can set your Mozilla home page to your own list of bookmarks — handy! Choose Edit⇨Preferences, click the Navigator category if it's not already selected, click the Browse or Choose File button in the Home Page section, and go to the Bookmarks.html file that stores your bookmarks. It's usually in a sub-sub-sub-folder of the .mozilla directory in your home directory.

In Konqueror: Konqueror usually displays your home directory, which is a pretty boring start page. Follow these steps to change your start page:

1. **Choose Settings⇨Configure Konqueror from the menu.**

You see the KDE Control module window.

2. **Click the Behavior tab at the top left.**

Actually, it's probably already selected, but we say this in case you've been looking around at what's on the other tabs.

3. **In the Home URL box, type or paste the URL you want.**

If the URL is long and complex, open it in a browser window, highlight the location box, and copy the text with Ctrl+C, and then paste it here with Ctrl+V.

4. **Click OK.**

Filling In Forms

Back in the Dark Ages of the Web (that is, in 1993), Web pages were just pages to look at. Because that wasn't anywhere near enough fun or complicated enough, Web forms were invented. A *form* is sort of like a paper form, with fields you can fill out and then send in. Figure 18-6 shows a typical form.

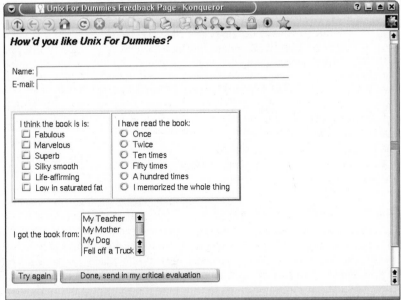

Figure 18-6:
Just fill out
a few forms.

White boxes in a form are fill-in text boxes in which you type, in this case, your name and e-mail address. Little square boxes are *check boxes,* in which you check whichever ones apply (all of them, we hope, in this case). Little round buttons are *radio buttons,* which are similar to check boxes except that you can choose only one of them from each set. In Figure 18-6, you also see a *list box,* in which you can choose one of the possibilities in the box. In most cases, you see more entries than can fit in the box, so you scroll them up and down. Although you can usually choose only one entry, some list boxes let you choose more.

Forms also include buttons. Most forms have two: one that clears the form fields to their initial state and sends nothing, and one, usually known as the Submit button, that sends the filled-out form back to the Web server for processing.

After the data is sent from the form back to the Web server, it's entirely up to the server how to interpret it.

Some Web pages have *search items,* which are one-line forms that let you type some text for which to search. Depending on the browser, a Submit button may display to the right of the text area, or you may just press Enter to send the search words to the server. For example, the Google search page at `google.com` has a box into which you type a word or phrase; when you press Enter or click the Google Search button, the search begins.

Pop off, buddy

One of the worst innovations in recent decades is *pop-up* windows that appear on your screen unbidden (by you), when you visit some Web sites. Some pop-ups appear immediately, some are *pop-unders* that are hidden under your main window until you close the main window. The pop-ups you're most likely to see are ads for spy cameras, airline tickets, and mortgage refinancing (no, we're not going to give their names here; they have plenty of publicity already).

Mozilla and Netscape shocked us all by giving users something they actually want, a way to get rid of pop-ups. On the menu for either, open the Preferences window via Edit⇨Preferences, double-click Privacy & Security to expand it if it's not already, and then Popup Windows. Click the Block Unrequested Popup Windows box,

and your pop-ups, for the most part, disappear. In older versions of Mozilla that don't have a Popup Windows panel, click Advanced to expand its list, and then Scripts & Plugins, and in that window uncheck the Open Unrequested Windows check box.

In Konqueror, open the KDE Control module via Settings⇨Configure Konqueror, click Java & Javascript at the left, and then in the window that appears click the Javascript tab at the top and (at last!) two-thirds of the way down you find JavaScript Web Popups Policy. The four options are Allow (not recommended), Ask (pop up a window asking if you want a popup, not much of an improvement), Deny, or Smart. Try Smart, to let it guess which pop-ups are useful, or Deny to get rid of all of them.

What Should I Look At?

Now that you know all about how to use your browser, here's a few suggestions of places to start if you don't already have your own list of favorites:

- ✔ www.google.com: Everyone's favorite search engine, this year at least. Type in some terms of interest and see what pages it finds. Also click the News tab in the Google window to see a summary of news from the world's newspapers, updated automatically and continuously.

- ✔ net.gurus.com: Yup, it's our site (we never said we weren't vain). Click the Zap Updates and Fave Links at the left for our updated thoughts on interesting stuff on the Net.

Also see our book *The Internet For Dummies,* 9th Edition, for lots more advice on browsing, Web sites, and the Net in general.

Chapter 19

Grabbing Files from the Net

In This Chapter

▶ Getting files from all over the Internet

▶ Stashing files all over the Internet

▶ Lotsa swell stuff for FTP

▶ Navigating in anonymous land

▶ Finding files by name

In Chapter 18, we explain how to use your Web browser to grab files stored on the Internet. Web browsers are definitely the easiest way to download files to your computer; just find a Web page with a link to the file and click the link.

If you want to copy to or from a non-UNIX machine, however, or if you want to retrieve files from a public file archive on a machine on which you don't have a personal account, you need an industrial-strength file-copying program. Your Web browser just can't cut the mustard (whatever that means). Instead, you can use the File Transfer Protocol (FTP) system, which is widely used on computers all over the Internet.

You can use FTP to transfer files to or from computers on which you have accounts. You can also use FTP to *download* (transfer to your computer) files from any of a bunch of publicly available FTP servers out there on the Internet. Thousands of public FTP servers are on the Internet, each with hundreds of files that may be of use, including text, pictures, and programs. It's just a matter of locating them and downloading them!

You're a Copying Machine

Copying a file from one place to another is simple (but don't forget — computers are involved). Here's how it works: Log in to the other computer for FTP, and tell it what you want to copy and where you want it copied.

Getting connected

To run the `ftp` program, you type **ftp** and the name of the host computer where the FTP server you want is:

```
ftp ftp.iecc.com
```

(That's John's computer. It has files, but perhaps not all that many in which you're interested, unless you care deeply about techniques for translating one programming language to another.) Substitute the FTP server's name for `ftp.iecc.com`.

Assuming that the FTP server is not too busy to let you connect, it greets you with a message like this:

```
Connected to ftp.iecc.com.
20 tom.iecc.com FTP server (BSDI Version 7.00LS) ready.
```

The computer asks for your username and password on the host computer. If you don't have an account on the computer, don't panic. See the section "No Names, Please," later in this chapter. (On this particular computer, unless you happen to be one of the authors of this book, it's extremely unlikely that you have an account. We're using it as an example.)

If the FTP server likes you, it says something like this:

```
230 User johnl logged in.
ftp>
```

The `ftp>` is the FTP prompt, telling you that it's ready for you to type a command.

Getting your file

To copy a file from the FTP server (the host computer) to your own computer, use the `get` command:

```
get README
```

Substitute the name of the file in place of *README* in this command. FTP says something like this:

```
150 Opening ASCII mode data connection for README (12686
          bytes).
226 Transfer complete.
local: README remote: README
12979 bytes received in 28 seconds (0.44 Kbytes/s)
```

FTP always tells you much more than you want to know about the transfer. When it says that the transfer is complete, you have the file.

You have to type the filename by using the syntax the server uses. In particular, if the server is a UNIX system (as most are), upper- and lowercase are different, so README, Readme, and readme are different filenames.

Getting out

When you finish transferring files, type the command **quit**. FTP responds with this heartfelt message:

```
221 Goodbye.
```

Files with Finesse

That's basically how FTP works, although you need to know, of course, about 400 other odds and ends to use FTP effectively.

When is a file not a file?

When it's a text file. The FTP definition specifies six different kinds of files, of which only two types are useful: ASCII and binary. An *ASCII file* is a text file. A *binary file* is anything else. FTP has two modes, ASCII and binary (also called *image* mode), to transfer the two kinds of files. When you transfer an ASCII file between different kinds of computers that store files differently, ASCII mode automatically adjusts the file during the transfer so that the file is a valid text file when it's stored on the receiving end. A binary file is left alone and transferred verbatim.

Patience is a virtue

The Internet is pretty fast, but not infinitely so. When you're copying stuff between two computers on the same local network, information can move at about 200,000 characters per second. When the two machines are separated by a great deal of intervening Internet, the speed drops — often to a few thousand characters per second or fewer. If you're copying a file that's 500,000 characters long, it takes only a few seconds over a local network, but it can take several minutes over a long-haul connection.

You tell FTP which mode to use with the `binary` and `ascii` commands:

```
ftp> binary
200 Type set to I.
ftp> ascii
200 Type set to A.
```

In the preceding example, the *I* is for binary or image mode (after 25 years, the Internet protocol czars still can't make up their minds what to call it), and the *A* is for ASCII mode. Like most FTP commands, `binary` and `ascii` can be abbreviated by lazy typists to the first three letters — so `bin` and `asc` suffice.

How to foul up your files in FTP

The most common FTP error that inexperienced Internet users (and experienced users, for that matter) make is transferring a file in the wrong mode. If you transfer a text file in binary mode from a UNIX system to a DOS, Windows, or Macintosh system, the file looks something like this (on a DOS or Windows machine):

```
This file
        should have been
                        copied in
                                ASCII mode.
```

On a Mac, the entire file looks like it's on one line. When you look at the file with a text editor on a UNIX system, you see strange ^M symbols at the end of each line. You don't necessarily have to retransfer the file. Many networking packages come with programs that do ex post facto conversion from one format to the other.

If, on the other hand, you copy something that isn't a text file in ASCII mode, it gets scrambled. Compressed files don't decompress; executable files don't execute (or they crash or hang the machine); images look unimaginably bad. When a file is corrupted, the first thing you should suspect is the wrong mode in FTP.

If you are FTP-ing (Is that a verb? It is now) files between two computers of the same type, such as from one UNIX system to another, you can and should do all your transfers in binary mode. Whether you're transferring a text file or a non-text file, it doesn't require any conversion, so binary mode does the right thing.

Getting a directory listing before issuing a `get` or `put` command is often comforting, so that you can have an idea of how long the copy will take.

The directory thicket

Every machine you can contact for FTP stores its files in many different directories, which means that to find what you want, you have to learn the rudiments of directory navigation. Fortunately, you wander around directories in FTP in pretty much the same way as you do on your own system. The command you use to list the files in the current directory is dir, and to change to another directory you use the command cd, as in this example:

```
ftp> dir
200 PORT command successful.
150 Opening ASCII mode data connection for /bin/ls.
total 23
drwxrwxr-x  19 root     archive      512 Jun 24 12:09 doc
drwxrwxr-x   5 root     archive      512 May 18 08:14 edu
drwxr-xr-x  31 root     wheel        512 Jul 12 10:37 systems
drwxr-xr-x   3 root     archive      512 Jun 25 1992 vendorware
... lots of other stuff ...
226 Transfer complete.
1341 bytes received in 0.77 seconds (1.7 Kbytes/s)
ftp> cd edu
250 CWD command successful.
ftp> dir
200 PORT command successful.
150 Opening ASCII mode data connection for /bin/ls.
total 3
-rw-rw-r--   1 root     archive   87019 Dec 13 2003 R
-rw-rw-r--   1 root     archive   41062 Dec 13 2003 RS
-rw-rw-r--   1 root     archive  554833 Dec 13 2003 Rings
drwxr-xr-x   2 root     archive     512 May 18 09:31
             administrative
drwxr-xr-x   3 root     archive     512 May 11 06:44 ee
drwxrwxr-x   8 root     234         512 Jun 28 06:00 math
226 Transfer complete.
200 bytes received in 63 seconds (0.0031 Kbytes/s)
ftp> quit
221 Goodbye.
```

In a standard UNIX directory listing, the first letter on the line tells you whether something is a file or a directory. d means that it's a directory — anything else is a file. In the directory edu in the preceding example, the first three entries are files and the last three are other directories. Generally, you FTP to a host, get a directory listing, change to another directory, get a listing there, and so on until you find the files you want. Then you use the get command to retrieve them.

You often find that the directory on your machine in which you start the FTP program is not the one in which you want to store the files you retrieve. In that case, use the lcd command to change the directory on the local machine.

TECHNICAL STUFF

What's with all these three-digit numbers?

You may notice that whenever you give a command to FTP, the response from the remote host begins with a three-digit number. (Or you may not notice; in which case, never mind.)

The three-digit number is there so that the FTP program, which doesn't know any English, can figure out what's going on. Each digit means something to the program.

Here's what the first digit means:

1: The program has begun to process your request but hasn't finished it.

2: It has finished.

3: It needs more input from you, such as when it needs a password after you enter your username.

4: It didn't work but may if you try again.

5: You lose.

The second digit is a *message subtype*.

The third digit distinguishes messages that would otherwise have the same number (something that in the computer world would be unspeakably awful).

If a message goes on for multiple lines, all the lines except the last one have a dash rather than a space after the number.

Note: Most FTP users have no idea what the numbers mean, by the way, so now that you're one of the few who does know, you're an expert.

To review: `cd` changes directories on the other host; `lcd` changes directories on your own machine. (You may expect `cd` to change directories correspondingly on both machines, but it doesn't.)

What's that name again?

Sometimes on your machine, you have to give a file a name that's different from the name it has on a remote machine. (This statement is particularly true on DOS machines, on which many UNIX names are just plain illegal, as well as when you're retrieving Macintosh or Windows files, which can contain spaces and special characters.) Also, if you need to get a bunch of files, typing all the `get` commands can be tedious. Fortunately, FTP has work-arounds for both those problems. Suppose that you find a file named `rose` and you want to download it as `rose.gif` because it contains a GIF-format image. First, make sure that you're in binary mode, and then retrieve the file with the `get` command. This time, however, you give two names to `get` — the name of the file on the remote host and the local name — so that it renames the file as the file arrives. You do this as shown in this interaction:

```
ftp> bin
200 Type set to I.
ftp> get rose2 rose2.gif
200 PORT command successful.
150 Opening BINARY mode data connection for rose2 (47935
          bytes).
226 Transfer complete.
local: rose2.gif remote: rose2
47935 bytes received in 39 seconds (1.2 Kbytes/s)
```

Next, suppose that you want to get a bunch of files that begin with ru. In that case, you use the mget (which stands for *m*ultiple *GET*) command to retrieve them. The names you type after mget can be either plain filenames or wildcard patterns that match a bunch of filenames. For each matching name, FTP asks whether you want to retrieve that file:

```
ftp> mget ru*
mget ruby? n
mget ruby2? n
mget ruger_pistol? n
mget rugfur01? n
mget rush? y
200 PORT command successful.
150 Opening BINARY mode data connection for rush (18257
          bytes).
226 Transfer complete.
local: rush remote: rush
18257 bytes received in 16 seconds (1.1 Kbytes/s)
mget rush01? y
200 PORT command successful.
150 Opening BINARY mode data connection for rush01 (205738
          bytes).
local: rush01 remote: rush01
205738 bytes received in 200.7 seconds (1.2 Kbytes/s)
mget rush02?
```

If you find that mget matches more files than you expected, you can stop it with the usual interrupt character for your system — typically Ctrl+C or Delete:

```
^C
Continue with mget? n
ftp> quit
221 Goodbye.
```

You can even interrupt in the middle of a transfer if a file takes longer to transfer than you want to wait.

You also can do an *express* mget, which doesn't ask any questions and enables you to find exactly the files you want. To tell FTP not to ask you about each file, use the prompt command before you give the mget command, as this example shows:

```
ftp> prompt
Interactive mode off.
ftp> mget 02-1*
200 PORT command successful.
150 Opening BINARY mode data connection for 02-10.gz (123728
        bytes).
226 Transfer complete.
local: 02-10.gz remote: 02-10.gz 123728 bytes received in 2.8
        seconds (43 Kbytes/s)
200 PORT command successful.
150 Opening BINARY mode data connection for 02-11.gz (113523
        bytes).
226 Transfer complete.
local: 02-11.gz remote: 02-11.gz 113523 bytes received in 3.3
        seconds (34 Kbytes/s)
200 PORT command successful.
150 Opening BINARY mode data connection for 02-12.gz (106290
        bytes).
226 Transfer complete.
local: 02-12.gz remote: 02-12.gz 106290 bytes received in 2.2
        seconds (47 Kbytes/s)
```

Here's a file in your eye

Okay, now you know how to retrieve files from other computers. How about copying the other way? It's just about the same procedure, except that you use put rather than get. The following example shows how to copy a local file called rnr to a remote file called rnr.new:

```
ftp> put rnr rnr.new
200 PORT command successful.
150 Opening ASCII mode data connection for rnr.new.
226 Transfer complete.
local: rnr remote: rnr.new
168 bytes sent in 0.014 seconds (12 Kbytes/s)
```

(As with get, if you want to use the same name when you make the copy, leave out the second name.)

The mput command works just like the mget command does, only in the other direction. If you have a bunch of files whose names begin with uu and you want to copy most of them, issue the mput command, as shown in this example (boldface indicates the user's input):

```
ftp> mput uu*
mput uupick? y
200 PORT command successful.
150 Opening ASCII mode data connection for uupick.
226 Transfer complete.
local: uupick remote: uupick
156 bytes sent in 0.023 seconds (6.6 Kbytes/s)
mput uupoll? y
200 PORT command successful.
150 Opening ASCII mode data connection for uupoll.
226 Transfer complete.
local: uupoll remote: uupoll
200 bytes sent in 0.013 seconds (15 Kbytes/s)
mput uurn? n
```

(As with mget, you can use the prompt command to tell it to go ahead and not to ask any questions.)

Most systems have protections on their files and directories that limit where you can copy files. Generally, you can use FTP only to put a file anywhere that you could create a file if you were logged in directly. If you're using anonymous FTP (see the section "No Names, Please," later in this chapter), you usually can't put any files to the other host.

A bunch of other file-manipulation commands are sometimes useful, as in this example of the delete command:

```
delete somefile
```

(Replace *somefile* with the name of the file you want to delete.) This command deletes the file on the remote computer, assuming that the file permissions enable you to do so. The mdelete command deletes multiple files and works like mget and mput do. The mkdir command makes a new directory on the remote system (again assuming that you have permissions to do so):

```
mkdir newdir
```

(Replace *newdir* with the name of the directory you want to make.) After you create a directory, you still have to use cd to change to that directory before you use put or mput to store files in it.

If you plan to do much file deleting, directory creation, and the like, logging in to the other system by using ssh or telnet is usually much quicker (discussed in gory detail in Chapter 16) to do your work and using the usual local commands.

No Names, Please

The first part of this chapter shows you how to FTP to systems where you already have an account. What about the other 99.9 percent of the hosts on the Internet, where no one has ever heard of you?

You're in luck. On thousands of systems, you can log in with the username anonymous. For the password, enter your e-mail address. (This arrangement is strictly on the honor system — if you lie, they still let you log in.) When you log in for *anonymous FTP,* most hosts restrict your access to only certain directories that are allowed to anonymous users. You can hardly complain, though, because anonymous FTP is provided free, out of sheer generosity.

Hello, anonymous!

When you log in, you frequently get a friendly message, like this one:

```
230-   If your FTP client crashes or hangs shortly after login
           please try
230-   using a dash (-) as the first character of your
           password.  This will
230-   turn off the informational messages that may be
           confusing your FTP
230-   client.
230-
230-   This system may be used 24 hours a day, 7 days a week.
           The local
230-   time is Fri Aug 15 12:15:10 2003.
230-
230-   You are user number 204 out of a possible total of 250.
230-
230-   All transfers to and from wuarchive are logged.  If you
           don't like
230-   this then disconnect now!
230-
230-   Wuarchive is currently a DEC Alpha AXP 3000, Model 400.
           Thanks to
230-   Digital Equipment Corporation for their generous
           support of wuarchive.
230-
230-Please read the file README
230-   it was last modified on Sat May 17 15:02:13 2001 - 452
           days ago
230 Guest login ok, access restrictions apply.
```

When you're logged in, you use the same commands to move around and retrieve files as you always do.

An FTP cheat sheet

Command	Description
get *old new*	Copies remote file *old* to local file *new*; can omit *new* if same name as *old*
put *old new*	Copies local file *old* to remote file *new*; can omit *new* if same name as *old*
del *xxx*	Deletes file *xxx* on remote system
cd *newdir*	Changes to directory *newdir* on the remote machine
cdup	Changes to next higher directory
lcd *newdir*	Changes to directory *newdir* on the local machine
asc	Transfers files in ASCII mode (use for text files)
bin	Transfers files in binary or image mode (all other files)
quit	Leaves FTP
dir *pat*	Lists files whose names match pattern *pat*; if no *pat*, lists all files
mget *pat*	Gets files whose names match pattern *pat*
mput *pat*	Puts files whose names match pattern *pat*
mdel *pat*	Deletes remote files whose names match pattern *pat*
prompt	Turn name prompting on or off in mget and mput

A few anonymous FTP tips

Here are a few items to remember when you're FTP-ing:

- ✔ **Some hosts limit the number of anonymous users or the times of day that anonymous FTP is allowed.** Please respect these limits because no law says that the owner of the system can't turn off anonymous access.

- ✔ **Don't store files in the other computer unless the owner invites you to do so.** Usually a directory called incoming or something similar is available where you can put stuff.

- ✔ **Some hosts allow anonymous FTP only from hosts that have names.** That is, if you try to FTP anonymously from a host that has a number but no name, these hosts don't let you in. This problem occurs most often with personal computers, which, because they generally offer no services that are useful to other people, don't always have names assigned. If you have that problem, check with your local administrator to see whether assigning a name to your PC is possible and to set up the reverse lookup database the remote host uses to figure out what your name is.

URLs for FTP-ing

URLs? Yikes! It's that three-letter acronym from Chapter 18. More than just a way to denote hypertext Web pages, URLs are ways of naming general Internet resources, including FTP sites. Here's the way you describe a file you can get over the Internet by using the `ftp` program:

```
ftp://hostname/pathname
```

Suppose that you see this URL:

```
ftp://rtfm.mit.edu/pub/net/inte
    rnet.txt
```

That means to FTP to `rtfm.mit.edu`, move to the `/pub/net` directory, and get the `internet.txt` file.

Mouse-Centric Approaches to FTP

If all these commands look like way more trouble than they're worth, you have alternatives. The most popular FTP program these days is undoubtedly our old Web-browsing friends Mozilla and Konqueror. By entering the FTP site as a URL, you can download files with the simple click of a mouse. (You can't download multiple files at one time, as you can with `xftp` or `xdir` or even with the `mget` command from plain FTP, but everything has its drawbacks.)

Great Stuff on FTP

Hundreds of gigabytes of stuff are available for FTP, if you know where to find them. Before you start cruising FTP sites, however, here are a few words about strategy.

A word from those etiquette ladies again

Please recall that all *anonymous FTP* servers (hosts that enable you to log in for FTP without requiring that you have an account there) exist purely because someone feels generous. Any or all can go away if the provider feels taken advantage of, so remember these rules:

✔ **Pay attention to restrictions on access times noted in the welcome message.** Remember that servers are in time zones all over the world. If the server says to use it only between 6 p.m. and 8 a.m., but it's in Germany, and you're in Seattle, you can use it between 9 a.m. and 11 p.m. your time.

✔ **Do not upload material unless you're invited to.** (And don't upload material inappropriate to a particular archive — we hope that this advice would be obvious, but experience suggests otherwise.)

Mirror, mirror, on the Net, where's the file 1 want to get?

Many archives are *mirrored,* which means that the contents of an archive are copied mechanically from the home server to other servers. Usually, the mirroring systems are larger and faster than the home server, so getting material from the mirror is easier than from the home system. Mirrors are usually updated daily, so everything on the home system is also at the mirrors.

When you have a choice of mirrors, use the one that's closest to you. You want the one that's closest in terms of the number of network links between you and it. Because the number of hops is practically impossible to figure out, however, use the mirror that's physically closest. In particular, use one in your own country if at all possible, because international network links are relatively slow and congested.

A few words about navigation

All the FTP servers discussed in this chapter require you to log in using the username anonymous. For the password, use your e-mail address.

Many servers have a small file called readme that you should retrieve the first time you use the server. This file usually contains a description of the material that's available and the rules for using the server.

If you log in to an FTP server and don't see any interesting files, look for a directory called pub (for public). For reasons lost in the mists of history, UNIX systems by tradition put all the good stuff there.

Chapter 20

Now Serving the Internet

In This Chapter

▶ Getting yourself an Internet presence

▶ What domains are

▶ Choosing Web server software

▶ What you need to serve e-mail, FTP, and other cool Internet resources

▶ A few words about Webmastering

*I*n the preceding few chapters, we tell you everything you ever wanted to know (more, probably) about how to use your UNIX computer to take advantage of popular Internet resources such as ssh, telnet, e-mail, newsgroups, FTP, and the World Wide Web. Well, you have something to offer the world yourself, dadgum it! You're wondering how all those *other* people got their stuff on the Internet, and whether you can do it, too.

Of *course* you can do it, too. With UNIX, in fact, you have ways to get yourself on the Internet rather inexpensively, assuming that your ambitions are modest. No matter what approach you end up taking, getting on the Internet is a matter of setting up, or at least getting access to, some kind of Internet *server*. To be more specific, you have to set up (or get someone else to set up for you) server programs for each kind of Internet resource you want to provide. If you want to serve your own e-mail, you need POP (Post Office Protocol) and SMTP (Simple Mail Transfer Protocol) servers. If you want your computer to act as a telnet site, you need a telnet server. If you want to make interesting files available for people to download to their own computers, you need an FTP server. If you want people to read your exquisite, erudite, and potentially moneymaking Web pages, you need a Web server.

In this chapter, we talk mostly about Web servers, not because we think that e-mail, ssh, FTP, and other non-Web resources are unimportant, but because full-featured Web servers such as the ones we tell you about in this chapter usually come with all the software you need in order to set up those other Internet resources.

The Internet, at Your Service

What you do on the Internet is a function of who you are and what you want to accomplish. An Internet presence can be as simple as a set of Web pages that trumpet to the world your personal tastes in music and literature. It can be as complex as a full-fledged online catalog sales company, replete with shopping carts, virtual cashiers, automatic e-mail notification, password-protected customer accounts, and encryption capabilities to ensure secure transactions.

If you're interested in doing something as foolhardy, er, complex as setting up your own online catalog sales company, you need much more information than we have space to provide in this book about UNIX. *Starting an Online Business For Dummies,* 3rd Edition, by Greg Holden (Wiley Publishing, Inc.), gives you some hints of where to start.

To make things as simple as possible, you have only two realistic approaches to getting yourself an Internet presence. The approach that's right for you depends on what you want to do, how much time and money you're willing to spend, and the height of your technical pain threshold:

- **Host your own site.** To host your own site, you need at least one dedicated computer, permanently connected to the Internet and running some brand of Web server software. Hosting your own site requires you to act as your own system administrator and Webmaster (the author and manager of your Web site). Although administering and maintaining your own Web site is not for the technically faint of heart, it's well within the powers of a mere mortal such as yourself. In exchange for the money you spend to buy the stuff you need and the time you spend to set everything up and keep it running, you get complete freedom and total control over whatever it is you want to do on the Internet. Because a permanent Net connection good enough to run servers (home cable modems and DSL won't do) costs at least several hundred dollars per month, you probably don't want to choose this approach until you're sure that you're serious about your Web site.

- **Get someone to host your site for you.** In practice, that "someone" usually turns out to be an Internet service provider, or ISP. *ISPs* are the people who sell you basic Internet services, such as e-mail and Web access. Many ISPs also offer Web-hosting services: For a monthly fee, they do all the technical heavy lifting for you. If you don't need your own dedicated server, you can usually buy a few megabytes of space on one of your ISP's servers for about $20 a month (less, in some cases) and upload your Web pages via FTP.

Domainia

If your Web site supports a business or other official organization, you may want to consider applying and paying for your own domain name. *A domain name* is a unique name that identifies a computer or group of computers on the Internet. For example, we registered the domain name gurus.com, so our Web site is named www.gurus.com, and our FTP site is named ftp.gurus.com. Registering a domain name costs about $15 per year, and on top of that you need at least two separate servers — a main server and a backup server — with permanent Internet connections to qualify for a domain name. Your server has to have DNS (domain name system) software running on it so that it can respond to requests for a name in your domain. If you don't want to deal with the gory technical details, you can pay an Internet service provider to act as your domain server. (Most ISPs are only too happy to find a reason to take your money, and in this case it's probably money well spent.)

The part of a domain name to the right of the last dot is called the *zone.* A number of so-called generic domains also exist: com for profit-making enterprises, org for nonprofit outfits, gov for the U.S. government, and edu for educational institutions are some examples. Two-letter country domains also exist — fr for France, mx for Mexico, and us for United States, for example.

Dozens of companies register generic domains, but whoever hosts your Web site can probably do it for you.

A complete discussion of setting up your own Web site is well beyond the scope of this book. It's a book in its own right, in fact. Nonetheless, in the following sections, we try to give you some pointers to get you started on the right foot.

For a discussion of Webmastering that doesn't shy away from the gory details, see *Building a Web Site For Dummies,* by David and Crowder Rhonda Crowder (Wiley Publishing, Inc.).

Serving Yourself

If you're hosting your own Web site, you have to have a computer with a permanent, dedicated connection to the Internet. The speed, or bandwidth, of your connection depends on such factors as how much traffic you expect your Web site to get and how much money you have to spend. For example, a full-time business DSL connection offering standard speeds of about 400 kilobits per second (a kilobit is a thousand bits of datas) costs somewhere in the neighborhood of $100 a month. A T1 line, at 1.5 Mbps per second, is four times as fast and four times as expensive. If you're serving a modest little Web site, DSL works just fine, thank you. If you're running your business online, you have to bite the bullet and get a T1 if you expect more than a few customers at any one time. (A T3 line gives you a speed of 45 Mbps per second. These babies cost at least $10,000 a month, so we figure that you're not planning to run one to your home computer any time soon.)

After you have your connection squared away, you have to install the software that turns your computer into a Web server. A *Web server* is simply a computer that hosts Web pages. The Web server computer runs a program that fulfills requests from other computers for Web pages stored on the Web server's hard drive. A UNIX machine makes a great Web server because the Web was designed using UNIX programs.

For example, John has computer named `net.gurus.com` on the Internet. It runs Apache (an excellent choice on John's part because Apache is fast, reliable, and — most important — free). When you view the author team's Web site, at `http://net.gurus.com`, your computer sends a request for a Web page to the Apache program on `net.gurus.com`, and Apache sends the page back to your computer so that you can see it on your screen. We talk more about UNIX Web servers later in this chapter.

After you install a Web server on your UNIX system, you tell the Web server the directory where the Web pages will be stored (the Web directory). You can store Web pages in that directory and its subdirectories. To make a Web page accessible to the world, you create the page with a Web-authoring program (or with any text editor), test it on your own system to avoid embarrassing typos, and move or copy the page to your Web directory. After the page is in the Web directory, anyone can see the page if they know its URL (Web address).

If you're learning about UNIX to be a Webmaster, you need to know how to

✔ Install, configure, and maintain your Web server program

✔ Create and modify Web pages

If other people will be working on the Web site, too, you have to know how to give them permissions to create and modify the files in the Web directory and its subdirectories. If you want active Web pages with forms and other interaction, you'll also dabble in the mysteries of server-side includes and CGI scripts. Finally, if you want to add more Internet resources to your Web site, such as e-mail and FTP, you have to learn how to configure your Web server program to provide them. If your Web server program doesn't offer what you need, you have to cast about for the right software, install it, and configure it.

Getting Served

Suppose that you decided to forego the expense and hassle of hosting your own site. You opted to pay your Internet service provider a reasonable monthly fee (probably around $20) to give you some space on one of its Web servers. On your own computer, you create and store the Web pages you want to put out, or *post,* on the Internet. You can see them by using your own Web browser, although no one else can see them until you upload them to your ISP's server.

Usually, you upload your Web pages to a Web server by using FTP (see Chapter 19 to find out how to transfer files). Ask your Internet service provider (or whoever runs the Web server you are using) where to put your Web page files. Also ask whether you need to give any special commands to tell the Web server about your files.

Here are some tips for uploading Web pages:

- ✔ Because Web pages are text, you upload your Web pages as ASCII (not binary) files. Graphics files are not text, so upload them as binary files.

- ✔ UNIX cares about capitalization in filenames. If you create Web pages on a PC or Mac and upload them to a UNIX-based Web server, check the capitalization of your filenames.

- ✔ Name your main Web page with the name index.html, which is the default Web page name. If you omit the filename from a URL when you're retrieving a Web page, your Web browser usually gets the page index. html. For example, if someone types the URL http://www.greattapes. com/, the Web browser displays the index.html file on that computer.

Web Servers Galore

If you're hosting your own Web site, you have to get a Web server, install it, configure it, and keep it running. Choosing the UNIX Web server package that's best for you is a question of finding the right set of features at the right price. (In the case of Apache, the right price happens to be free.)

Most UNIX and Linux distributions include, for free, Web servers along with server software for other Internet resources, such as databases, e-mail, news, and FTP. Lots of Web servers are available, but the one most people use is Apache.

Not too patchy

Turn the wayback machine to 1994 — the Pleistocene era in the computer world. A fellow named Rob McCool is about to leave the hallowed halls of the National Center for Supercomputing Applications (NCSA) at the University of Illinois. His legacy: The most popular Web server software in the world, the HTTP daemon, or HTTPd.

After Rob leaves the NCSA, work on HTTPd pretty much stops. Webmasters hooked on HTTPd, however, keep on using it. Because they're resourceful UNIX hackers, many of them add new stuff and fix broken stuff. A year later, so many of these additions and fixes (called *patches* in computer lingo) exist that intrepid Bay Area hackers Brian Behlendorf and Cliff Skolnick decide to recruit a few stalwarts like themselves to pull together, test, and publish all these patches in a new release of HTTPd. The result is the first official version of the Apache server, which sees the light of day in April 1995.

Why Apache? Because it's "a patchy server," based on some existing code and a slew of patches. Well, you asked.

Over the years, the original team of eight contributors grows to about 20, with hundreds of users weighing in with ideas, new code, and documentation. This team of about 20 volunteers from around the world makes up the Apache Group. The Apache Group uses "the Internet and the Web to communicate, plan, and develop the server and its related documentation."

For the Apache server, 1998 was a banner year. As of June 1998, Apache ran on more than 48 percent of all Web sites (an estimated 1,100,000 sites). Running a distant second were Microsoft (non-UNIX) servers, at about 22 percent of all Web sites. Netscape servers accounted for less than 10 percent of all Web sites.

Turn the clock ahead to 2003, and Apache continues its dominance, despite Microsoft's best efforts to push its Windows-based servers. Surveys consistently show upwards of 60 percent of all Web sites run Apache, with Microsoft's IIS a distant second at about 25 percent.

Apache and PHP are king

The Apache Web server is free and fast and popular. It runs on every UNIX you can think of, including Linux. (Versions for Windows are also available, but much less popular.) In fact, it's the most popular Web server of any kind in use today (see the sidebar "Not too patchy" for details). If you're on the Web, surf to the home page of the Apache HTTP Server Project, at www.apache.org, for information and downloads.

PHP is a programming language designed to be built into Web pages. Although it's developed separately from Apache, PHP is designed to be easy to integrate with Apache, and most pre-configured versions of Apache include PHP. By putting little bits of PHP into a Web page, you can make minor customizations on the fly. For example, in our home page at `http://net.gurus.com`, the Reader Quote of the Day section uses some PHP code to insert the current day's comment from a daily file so we don't have to edit the Web page every night. Using a lot of PHP, you can write large, beautiful Web applications, as you see in the next section.

The other popular language people use for Web work is Perl, often described as the duct tape of the Internet. Although building bits of Perl into Web pages is possible, more commonly it's used in *CGI scripts,* programs that run in a response to a request from a browser and build a Web page from scratch. As programming languages go, Perl is relatively easy to learn and use, although it's still definitely a programming language. *Perl For Dummies,* 4th Edition, by our friend Paul Hoffman, tells you more.

Most sophisticated Web applications also need a database to hold the dynamic data for the site. Fortunately, UNIX has plenty of those available, too. The two most popular free ones are MySQL and PostgreSQL, both of which are packaged with most UNIX and Linux systems. They both work well; MySQL is faster while PostgreSQL has more complete data management abilities. If you need a really serious database, Oracle or IBM is happy to sell you all the database you need to run on your UNIX or Linux system.

Building a Web site with almost no work

Use someone else's work, of course. A remarkably large amount of PHP and Perl code is available for free on the Internet, some of which is quite good. Drop by our sister site `http://privacyfordummies.com`, for example. We put in the beautiful graphics and sparkling and witty contents (well, one of our co-authors did), but all of the technical code that manages the articles, counts votes in polls, handles user registrations, and all of the other flashy features of the site come from a package with the odd name of Postnuke, an extremely powerful and flexible content management system written in PHP and MySQL and available for free at `www.postnuke.com`. You need to download Postnuke, or at least the parts of it you need, install it as a Web site on your server, and then start it up and configure it. A fair amount of work is involved, but it's about 0.1 percent of the work of writing something like that from scratch.

If you look around, you can find everything from online calendars to blogging packages to shopping carts to online photo albums available for free in PHP or Perl. A good place to start looking is `http://dmoz.org/Computers/Programming/Internet/Server_Side_Scripting`.

We're from AOL, and we're here to give you a really good Web server for free

Hey, stop laughing. Believe it or not, it's true. AOL has one of the world's busiest Web sites, and it all runs on an open source server called AOLserver, available for free download at `http://aolserver.com`. It's the only plausible alternative to Apache for busy Web sites.

AOLserver is definitely intended for serious Web developers. The documentation is practically non-existent, the Web page programming is in an arcane language called TCL (sort of like PHP, but not very), and you have to know enough about programming to download the source code, configure it including setting up a connection to whatever database you're using, build a running version on your system, install it, and start it up. We did it in an afternoon, but it took a fair amount of geeky skill.

Once you have it running, AOLserver is really fast. The best-known AOLserver site other than AOL is `http://photo.net`, which reports that using a largish Sun database server running Oracle and a handful of PC Web servers running AOLserver on Linux and Solaris, it handles 6 million hits a day serving about 56GB, peaking at 520,000 hits an hour. That's a lot of pictures.

Daemons Run Amok

Providing most Internet services is a matter of installing, configuring, and running daemons. A *daemon* is simply a program you configure, start up, and then forget about. It runs in the background, where you can't see it. The only time you have to deal with it is when something goes wrong with it (a mercifully rare occurrence) or when you want to change the way it behaves. We introduce daemons in Chapter 9, where we talk about the daemon that handles UNIX print jobs.

Some Internet resource servers, such as `telnet` and FTP, are standard parts of all UNIX distributions. Some UNIX (and Linux) distributions also include Internet servers for other resources, such as e-mail and news. In some cases, these servers are included with your Web server. If neither your UNIX nor Web server package includes the servers you need, you have to find or purchase them separately. Fortunately, free versions abound on Web sites and FTP sites on the Internet.

Here are a few tips about what you may need to help get you started:

✓ **E-mail:** If you want to serve your own e-mail, you need an SMTP server and a POP or IMAP server. *SMTP* (Simple Mail Transfer Protocol) defines the way computers pass a mail message to each other until it gets delivered to a user's mailbox. *POP* (Post Office Protocol) and *IMAP* (Internet

Mail Access Protocol) define how the user who got the message retrieves it from the mailbox. Some mail clients require POP; others, such as Pine, require IMAP instead. The most popular, although not the best, SMTP server is called `sendmail`, and large books are devoted to its care and feeding.

✔ **Telnet, `ssh`, and FTP:** Use the `telnet`, `ssh` and FTP daemons included in your UNIX or Linux distribution. Because security issues are always a major concern when you give unknown computers access to your computer, be vigilant about potential security breaches and be sure to install new versions if security holes are reported.

Other resources you may consider providing are the highly addictive Internet Relay Chat, equally addictive games such as MUDs (Multi-User Dungeons) and MUSHes (Multi-User Shared Hallucinations), Gopher, and streaming video and audio. As with the basic services, you have to determine whether your OS or Web server package includes the server software you need.

A Few Tips for Webmasters

Now you've done it: You've gone ahead and decided to host your own Web site. You registered a domain name, shelled out big bucks for computers and Internet connections, installed and configured server software, and even posted your first home page on the World Wide Web. Your job here is finished, right?

Not on your life. Your job is just beginning. For Web surfers, the beauty of the Internet is that it's available 24 hours a day, seven days a week. For Webmasters, the round-the-clock nature of the Internet can become a maintenance nightmare. If your site is down for a few hours or longer or if it goes down for short periods on a regular basis, you quickly lose your audience. If you're trying to run a business online, these types of outages can be disastrous.

The Apache server is extremely reliable, which, along with being free, is a good reason to use it. Problems do occur, however, and you have to know how to recover from them quickly. Make sure that your backup server is an accurate copy, or *mirror*, of your main server so that you can cut over to it in case your main server fails. You should also make sure that you can log on to your computer from a remote location so that you can do server administration (troubleshooting, shutdowns, restarts) without having to be in the same room with your computer. Your vacation in Fiji will be ruined if the server running your catalog sales company quits working and you have to fly home to deal with it.

Often, problems with a Web site occur because of gremlins running around in your Web pages. *HTML,* the language you use to define your Web pages, is extremely literal and unforgiving. Make sure that you have a good HTML reference and a way to test your pages before casting them on the waters of the Web. Mozilla has a graphical Web page program called Composer, which has an HTML editor that novice Web page designers may find easy to use. We recommend that you use a text editor with at least syntax highlighting to make your coding job easier (see Chapter 10 for some suggestions).

Web surfers think of Web sites as *places* rather than *pages.* The only way you can keep people coming back to your place on the Web is to change it and update it constantly. Really big sites employ really big teams of writers, designers, and developers who do nothing other than work on the site. Some sites are updated two or three times a *day.* For a lone Webmaster, updating a modest site once a *week* is a big job. When you're planning your site, think about how often you need to update it. Then design your site to make updating it as quick and painless as possible.

Our last tip is perhaps our most important: Whatever you do, keep it simple. Updating and maintaining your site's content is a big job. If you're going it alone, you have to become a graphics designer, writer, software developer, and system administrator all rolled into one — not an easy task for anyone. If you run into trouble, ask for help. Many people in situations similar to yours are only too happy to share with you their horror stories and hard-earned wisdom. A good place to look for help is Usenet, the Net's distributed bulletin board, where you can find and communicate with UNIX Webmasters in newsgroups such as `comp.infosystems.www.servers.unix`. (See `net.gurus.com/usenet` for more information on Usenet, and Chapter 26 for a listing of UNIX-related newsgroups.)

Part V
Help!

In this part . . .

The point of this book is to help you when things go wrong. That's what makes it different from "good news" books that talk only about how everything *should* work in a perfect world. As you've seen if you read the book up to this point, "good news" and UNIX rarely appear in the same sentence. This part of the book lists things that go wrong, error messages you may see, and what you can do about them.

Chapter 21

Disaster Relief

. . . .

In This Chapter

▶ "My computer won't turn on"

▶ "My mouse is acting glitchy"

▶ "The network is gone"

▶ "These aren't my files!"

▶ "It's not listening!"

▶ Wrecked X

▶ "I give up"

. . . .

*T*he tiny, infinitesimal chance that you may run into some kind of problem with your computer always exists. The problem can be something major (such as losing the funniest interoffice memo you have seen in years) or minor (perhaps accidentally deleting the analysis you have spent two months creating).

Some computer problems you can fix — some you can't. The situation is similar to cars: You can pump gas yourself and maybe change the oil, but when it's time to rebuild the engine, call for help. (We do, anyway.)

This chapter describes some problems you may run into, with suggestions for what to do.

"My Computer Won't Turn On"

You come in to the office one morning, flip the switch on your computer, and nothing happens. No friendly whir, nothing on-screen. Uh-oh. Lots of things could have happened, so check these possibilities:

> ✔ **Is your computer plugged in?** It sounds stupid, but we have had computer problems when the people who clean the office bumped their vacuum cleaners into the outlet all our equipment was plugged in to. If you're using a terminal or X terminal, this check applies to both the terminal and the computer.

✔ **Is the power-strip on?** If the computer is plugged in to a power strip that has its own on-off switch, check that switch's position. People have been known to turn off the switch inadvertently with their toes.

✔ **Is the computer still attached?** Are the cables that connect the computer, keyboard, screen, and whatever else still connected? If your terminal is connected to a network, is the network cable firmly attached to the computer? Try wiggling it a little, even if it looks okay.

✔ **Does the rest of the office have power?** Plug a lamp into the same outlet as the computer and make sure that the lamp turns on. (True story: "Hello, help desk? My computer won't turn on." "Is it plugged in correctly?" "I can't tell. The power failed, and none of the lights work.")

✔ **Is the picture on the screen turned off?** The computer can be turned on, and the screen can even be on, but the picture on the screen can be dimmed. Fool with the brightness knob (remember where the knob was positioned when you started fiddling with it).

✔ **Does your computer have a screen-blanker program?** Press a key to make sure that a screen-blanker program hasn't blacked out your screen as a favor to you. (We like to press the Shift key because it has no other effect on the computer.) Moving the mouse a little also unblanks the screen.

If the problem isn't the power, it's probably not something you can fix yourself. Call your system administrator for help. Some component may have burned out. Stay calm — it does *not* mean that the files stored on your hard drive are gone. They are probably fine: Disks remember data perfectly well with the power off.

"My Mouse Is Acting Glitchy"

If you have a computer with a male mouse (a mouse with a ball underneath), dust or crumbs inside it can prevent the ball from rolling smoothly. Most mice with balls have a way to remove the ball for cleaning, usually by turning a plastic ring that surrounds the opening for the ball or by sliding the ring to the front or side. (We don't begin to suggest appropriate names for that ring.) Turn the mouse over so that the ball falls into your hand and not on the floor, gently wipe off the grit, carefully pick the lint off the little rollers inside, and snap it all back together. Female mice (optical mice, with no balls) appreciate it if you occasionally wipe off the mouse pad with a tissue. Also, look at the bottom of your female mouse: If it's turned on and working, you see a little red LED through one of the openings.

"The Network Is Gone"

You can't print on the printer down the hall, and you can't run certain programs. The problem may be that your computer is not communicating properly with the network to which it is normally attached.

Trying to solve most network problems is not for the faint of heart. One thing you can try is to check the cables in the back of your computer. Is the network cable firmly attached to the computer? Try wiggling it a little, even if it looks okay. Otherwise, it's time to call in the experts.

"These Aren't My Files!"

Normally, when you log in, you start working in your home directory. If you type the following line, you return to the home directory from whichever directory you may have roamed to:

```
cd
```

If cd doesn't get you back home, you may not be who you think you are. Try typing whoami or who am i. If someone else's username appears, your computer thinks that that's who you are! A coworker may have logged in to your computer to do some work for a moment.

You then have several options:

✔ Send some malicious e-mail, which will arrive looking as though your coworker sent it. Delete all her files that look important, and then log out and pretend that nothing happened.

✔ Log out without fouling anything up, and then log in as yourself. Type this line:

```
logout
```

Maybe you have to type **exit** or just press Ctrl+D. At any rate, when you see the login screen, log in as yourself.

Most courses in business ethics tell you that the second option is preferred by all except the slimiest of bottom-feeding MBAs, but the urge to send goofy e-mail is sometimes irresistible. *Remember:* You may be caught.

Wrecked X

If you use Motif or another X Window variant, now and then you may find your screen in a most peculiar state, one in which you can move the mouse pointer around, but none of the windows changes, and you can't type anything in any windows. Often you can fix this problem by restarting the window manager, which is the program that controls which window gets what.

Move the mouse pointer outside any window and click and hold the left or right mouse button (which one depends on which window manager you're using) to display the window manager menu. That menu should have a Restart mwm or Restart fvwm item. Choose that option. The borders around all your windows disappear (the window manager handles the borders), and after a few seconds, they reappear. With luck, everything is fixed. If there's no way to restart the window manager, see if you can log out from the window system and log back in.

"It's Not Listening!"

The computer is on, you are working away, and suddenly it doesn't respond to anything you type. It's the Abominable Frozen Computer.

The computer is probably fine — it's a program that has frozen up. Try these things to try to get the program's attention:

- Press Esc a bunch of times.
- Press Ctrl+C a bunch of times.
- Press Ctrl+D a bunch of times.
- Press Ctrl+S and then Ctrl+Q a bunch of times. (You never know what works.)
- If you are running KDE, GNOME, or another X Windows-based system, see whether you can use the mouse to select another window or whether you can type a command or two in a shell window. If you can, you can probably arrange to murder the frozen program and start it up again (see the following section).
- If your window system is completely stuck, you can usually murder the window system and start it over again without having to restart your computer (refer to Chapter 4).

If your computer is on a network or has more than one terminal, you can ask a computer guru to kill the program. If you're feeling brave, you can kill the program yourself. When you kill a program, you lose any work you were doing in that program since the last time you saved data to the hard drive.

Tell the wizard what happened (in order), which programs were running, and what you did. She will probably kill the process, as described in Chapter 23. If you have a number of processes running, she may kill one after another until your computer feels better.

"I Give Up"

Sometimes discretion is the better part of valor (whatever that means). If you need to call for help, be sure to do the following:

- ✓ **Don't turn off the computer.** Unless flames are coming from the screen and threatening to engulf your entire office, this option is not a good idea. Even then, you may be better off waiting for it to trip the circuit breaker than facing your wizard, who will surely ask, "Did you turn it off?"

- ✓ **Know the symptoms.** Be ready to tell someone what happened and which actions you took to fix the problem.

- ✓ **Know what has changed recently.** Did you install new software? Did you run something you have not run before? New things are always suspicious. A claim of "I didn't change anything" does not endear you to your wizard. Something, somewhere, *must* have changed.

- ✓ **If you call for help by phone, call from within reach of your computer.** Your savior may want you to try a few maneuvers at the keyboard.

Chapter 22

The Case of the Missing Files

In This Chapter

▶ Four easy ways to lose files

▶ Some ways to get files back

▶ Three almost-as-easy ways not to lose files

Sooner or later, you will delete a file by mistake. Scratch that "later": Sooner than you think, you will delete a file by mistake. In far too many cases, you are out of luck, although you can do a few things to avoid disaster.

How You Clobber Files

Contrary to the usual image of UNIX users being radically technical and without a creative bone in their bodies, we submit that typical UNIX users are immensely creative: They can come up with a zillion inventive ways to avoid the computer altogether and, when forced to sit down to stare the computer in the face, they can come up with a dozen more inventive reasons for why things went wrong. UNIX programmers have written thousands of useful freeware and shareware programs, when they should have been getting some work done. You can make files disappear in lots of ways (either intentionally or accidentally). This section lists the four main ways you can trash files — although you can probably come up with a dozen new and creative ways to do the vanishing act with your files.

Clobbering files with rm

Because hard drives are not infinitely large, sooner or later you have to get rid of some files. (Some wag once commented that the only thing that's standard among UNIX systems is the message-of-the-day reminding users to delete unneeded files.)

The normal way to get rid of files is the rm (for *remove*) command. Until (notice that we didn't say *unless*) you screw up, rm removes only what you want it to. Recall that you tell rm the names of the files you want to remove:

```
rm thisfile thatfile somedir/anotherfile
```

You can remove more than one file at a time, and you can specify files in other directories (rm removes just the file and not the directory).

This method is usually pretty safe. The tricky part comes when you use wild-cards. If you use a word processor that leaves backup files with names ending in .bak, for example, you can get rid of all of them with this command:

```
rm *.bak
```

That's no problem — unless you put in an extra space *(Do not type this line!)*:

```
rm * .bak
```

Note the little, tiny space between the asterisk and the dot. In response to this command, UNIX says

```
rm: .bak non-existent
```

Uh-oh. UNIX decided that you wanted to delete two things: * and .bak. Because the asterisk wildcard matches every single filename in the working directory, every single filename in the working directory is deleted. Then UNIX tries to delete a file named .bak, which isn't there. Bad move.

At this point, we recommend that you panic, gnash your teeth, and throw Nerf balls at the computer. After you calm down a little, read the rest of this chapter for some possible ways to get your files back.

You can also make slightly less destructive but still aggravating mistakes when you forget just which files you have. Suppose that you have files named section01, section02, and so on, up to section19. You want to get rid of all of them, so you type this line:

```
rm sec*
```

Now suppose that you forgot that you also have a file named second.version, which you want to keep. Oops. Bye-bye, second.version.

The obvious solution is to delete things one at a time. Unless you are an extremely fast and steady typist, however, that's not practical. In the following sections, we make some suggestions about that, too.

Clobbering files with cp, mv, and ln

Are you feeling paranoid yet, as though every time you press the R and M keys you're going to blow away a year's worth of work? Wait — it gets worse.

The cp, mv, and ln commands can also clobber files by mistake: If you use one of these programs to copy, rename, or link a file (respectively) and a file already has the new name, the existing file gets clobbered. Suppose that you type this command:

```
mv elbow armpit
```

If you already had a file named armpit — *bam!* It's gone! The same thing happens if you copy or link. (Copying is a *little* different: If you care, see the nearby sidebar, "Links, copies, moves, truncations, and other details about file destruction.") Here's an example of the most annoying case of blasting away good files with trash when you use the copy command:

```
cp important.file.save important.file
```

As a responsible and paranoid computer user, you want to save a copy of an important file before you make some changes. But your fingers work a little faster than your brain and you get the two names switched (left-handed users are particularly prone to getting names sdrawkcab) — and *bam!* (again) you just copied an obsolete saved version over the current version. Fortunately, you can arrange your file-saving habits to make this kind of mistake harmless, or at least mostly harmless.

Creaming files by using redirection

A third popular way to blow away valuable files is by using redirection. If you *redirect* the output of a command to a file that already exists, whammo! UNIX blows away the existing file and replaces it with your redirected output.

For example, if you type this command:

```
ls -al > dirlist
```

and you already have a file named dirlist, it's gone now, replaced by the new listing.

Links, copies, moves, truncations, and other details about file destruction

Clobber-wise, copying files works a little differently from moving and linking files. More often than not, the practical difference is unimportant, although, in a few cases, it can be worth knowing about.

The cp command does one thing as it clobbers a file; mv and ln do another. The difference is noticeable only if additional names or links were created for that file with ln. (Refer to Chapter 8 to find out how to create *links,* or additional names, for files using the ln command.)

Clobbering a file with cp: Suppose that you have two files: first and second. You give second an additional name by using this ln command:

    ln second extra.name

Now suppose that you accidentally (who knows why?) type **cp first second** (remember that you already have a file named second). What happens to the file named second? The cp command replaces the current contents of second with a copy of first. That is, it replaces the text (or whatever) that second contains with whatever the file first contains. This change also affects the file named extra.name because it's another name for the file second. If you use cat or a text editor to look at either second or extra.name, you see a copy of first. The original contents of second and extra.name are gone with the wind.

Clobbering a file with mv or ln: "So what?" you ask, to cut to the heart of the matter. Here's the interesting part (interesting to us, anyway). If you used mv or ln rather than cp, the second file would not be gone. The mv and ln commands don't fool with the contents of the file —

they just change which filename is connected with which contents. Suppose that you type this command:

    mv first second

The mv command disconnects the name second from its current contents. Because the contents are still linked to the name extra.name, that file is still safe and sound. The mv command then connects the name second to the contents of first and, finally, disconnects the name first from the file. Now no file is named first.

As a result, the contents of the second file are not clobbered (to see them, you can use the other name for the file). The ln command works the same way as mv to disconnect filenames and not touch the contents of files.

The message here is that if you have just fouled up an mv or ln command, you may still have the hope of retrieving the old file (if it had other links).

Clobbering files with soft links: To add more confusion, the story is a little different if you use soft links rather than regular hard links. (Refer to Chapter 8 to learn how soft links can link files from different file systems.) Because soft links are just aliases for the true filename, if you do something to the original file, all the links refer to the changed file because it has the same name. On the other hand, if you use cp to change one of the links, the cp command replaces the contents of the original file. The mv and ln commands affect just the link.

Confused? The moral is the same with soft links: After a botched instance of mv or ln, you may still be able to find the original file, if it had another name. It can't hurt to look.

If you use the BASH shell, you can give this command:

```
noclobber=1
```

If you use the C shell, you can give this incantation:

```
set noclobber
```

Better yet, get a UNIX wizard to help you include this command in your .cshrc or .profile file so that the command is given automatically every time you start the shell. This command tells the shell to *ask* you before using redirection to clobber files.

When you redirect output to a file, you can tell UNIX to add the output to the end of an existing file. Rather than type one >, you type two:

```
ls -al >> dirlist
```

You have little reason not to use >> every time you think of using >.

Wrecking files with text editors

The fourth way you're likely to smash files is in a botched editor session. The problem usually comes up after you have been editing a file for a while and realize that you have screwed up: The changes you made are not what you want, so you decide to leave the editor. On the way out, however, you write the botched changes to the disk and wreck the original file. A similar problem occurs when you use an editor to look at a file: Although you may not intend to change anything, you may make some inadvertent changes anyway. (This can easily happen in emacs, where pretty much anything you type goes straight into the file.) If you're not careful, you can write the changes to the disk by mistake.

If you use vi, you can avoid the accidental-clobber problem by typing **view** rather than **vi**. The view editor is the same as the vi editor (vi and view are links to the same program). The view editor works the same as vi except that it doesn't let you write changes to the file. Keep it in mind.

Although some versions of emacs can mark files as read-only so that you can't make changes to the files, the methods of doing so aren't entirely standardized. In GNU Emacs, you press Ctrl+X, Ctrl+Q in a file window, and Emacs puts an inscrutable %% on the status line at the bottom of the screen. To be even more careful, you can press Ctrl+X and then Ctrl+R to open a file as read-only in the first place.

Ways to Try to Get Files Back

Now you've done it: You clobbered something important, and you really, *really* want it back.

If you're used to other systems, such as Windows, in which you can magically get deleted stuff back from the Recycle Bin, we're sorry to tell you that UNIX doesn't let you do that (unless you're lucky enough to be using a UNIX desktop with a Trash tool; see the section in Chapter 4 about talkin' trash). If it's gone, it's gone.

Copies, copies, everywhere

Maybe you have stashed away in a different directory other copies of the file you deleted. For our important files, we stick copies in a directory named save (or something similar). Also, sometimes you can reconstruct the information from a different form. If you clobber a word processor file, for example, you may have a backup version (the .bak files mentioned earlier in this chapter) that's close to the current version. You may have printed the deleted file to a file (rather than directly to the printer) and can edit the print file back into document form.

If you share your computer with other people or use a network, see whether someone else has a copy. It's a rare file that exists in only one place.

Call in the backup squad

It's really gone, huh? Now it's time for the final line of defense: backups. You *do* have backups, don't you?

We interrupt this chapter for a stern lecture: *Always make backups.* If your system administrator is on the ball, tape backups are made automatically every night. All you have to do is go to the administrator, with chocolate-chip cookies in hand, and ask politely for some help in getting your valuable file back from the previous night's backups. If no backups exist, it's fair to jump up and down and scream that someone had better get on the ball.

Seriously, backups are a standard part of any administrator's job, by either making the backups personally or overseeing operators who do the backing up. (After the procedures are set up, making backup tapes is so simple that you can practically train your dog to do it. One reason that it sometimes doesn't get done is that backing up is boring.)

Why you need backups

Making backups is a pain. The question isn't *whether* you will lose data — it's *when*. Here are some events that have sent us heading for the backup tapes:

✔ The obvious one: We deleted a file by mistake.

✔ Just as we were saving a file, the power failed and scrambled both the old and new versions of the file. Yikes!

✔ One day, while working on the insides of the computer (one of us is a closet nerd), we accidentally dropped a screwdriver on the disk controller. Exciting sparks came out and fried the controller card that attaches the disk to the rest of the computer. We got a new controller card and found that, although the disk was physically fine, the new controller wasn't quite compatible with the old one, and we had to reformat the disk and restore everything from tape.

✔ We remembered hearing that we should absolutely, positively run a "disk-head parking" program before moving our hard drive, so we ran one. Unfortunately, it was a version that was incompatible with the hard drive, so it parked the disk head right off the edge of the disk, way out past what you may call the Long-Term Parking Area. We could hear the disk head banging on the side of the hard drive as it tried to get back on. Rats! (Modern disks park themselves, but we've had a few that became permanently unable to unpark.)

✔ Back in the good old days, computers weighed about 15,000 pounds, and you needed a forklift to move one. Now they weigh about 25 pounds, which means that if the cleaning people bump into one with a vacuum cleaner, they can knock it over with a clunk that can put an unreadable ding into the disk. Oops — sorry, lady.

Although you probably have horror stories of your own, they all have the same moral: Make those backups.

If your system administrator doesn't make backups, you had better learn how to do it yourself. If you have a tape unit on your machine, the procedure is usually as follows:

1. **Put a tape in the tape unit and flip the latch to seat the tape firmly. Wait for the tape to load itself into the tape unit.**

2. **Give a command to copy files to the tape, usually the** tar **(***t*ape *a*rchive**) or** pax **(***p*ortable *a*rchive *ex*change**) program.**

   On Sun workstations, the program is bar (*b*ackup *ar*chive). The exact things you have to say to the tar program vary from one system to another, mostly because of the peculiarities of different kinds of tape units. You can't use the regular cp command because tapes aren't logically organized the same way disks are. This process can take awhile — as long as overnight to dump a largish disk.

3. **Take the tape out of the tape unit.**

4. **Write the current date on the label so that you know that it's a current backup.**

   (The sensibly paranoid alternate several tapes, in case one of them goes bad. We describe this subject in more detail in the "Backup strategies" sidebar, later in this chapter.)

5. **Put the tape back in its box, and put the box back on the shelf.**

6. **Once a week (or some other frequency), take the backup tape and store it off-site, such as in another office or at someone's house or, if you're really serious, in your safe-deposit box. (We do that.)**

The usual way to back up stuff on Linux is to use tar. To back up to tape, type this fabulously memorable command:

```
tar cvf /dev/rft0 *
```

The cvf means Create, Verbose Report, to File, and /dev/rft0 is the name of the tape unit. The * means to back up all the files in your directory; if you have a large number of them, you can list specific files and directories instead.

If you have a large number of files, copying everything to tape can take awhile (perhaps an hour or so). You may want to do the backup over lunch. Or do what we do, and have your administrator arrange to run the tar program automatically every morning at about 3 a.m. We leave a tape in the tape unit every night. When we come back the next morning, the backup has been done, and we take the tape out and put it away. The tar command creates a report that is e-mailed to us so that we can check to see whether the tape was written correctly.

Disks, floppy and otherwise

Some systems don't have tapes; they have removable disks, either diskettes or larger removable disks, such as ZIP disks or CD-R discs. Diskettes are a major pain for backup use for two reasons: You need a stack of them because each one holds only a little over a megabyte, and you must format them first.

Before you can use a diskette, you must format it, which means that the computer writes some bookkeeping junk on it to mark where to put the data and in the process checks to be sure that no bad spots are on the disk. Fortunately, you have to do this only one time per disk. Formatting disks is easy but tedious and (sing along with us as we say this) varies, of course, from one system to another. You stick the blank disk in the computer, type the formatting command, something like fdformat, and UNIX formats it. If you're stuck with diskette backups, ask your administrator for help in setting up the procedure, and while you're feeding all the disks into the drive, consider getting a tape drive.

If you back up to diskettes, type this line in Linux:

```
tar cvMf /dev/fd0 *
```

The M means *m*ultiple disks because you can't put much stuff on one disk. Linux tells you when to swap disks. Be sure to write the backup date and the disk number on each disk so that they don't get out of order.

UNIX systems can also use ZIP disks, CD-R and CD-RW discs. ZIP disks are the easiest because (most likely with an expert's help to set up) you can mount the disk as a part of the UNIX file system called something like /z, at which point you use cp to copy files to /z just like you do any other disk. When done, you tell UNIX to unmount the disk, and then you physically take it out and put it on the shelf. Writing CDs is harder because if you want to read your CD on other computers, it has to be in a format called ISO 9660, which UNIX systems can only write to with special programs. This is a good application for chocolate chip cookies, to bribe a nearby UNIX expert to set up a script to automate the process of collecting your files, making an ISO 9660 version of them, and writing it to a CD.

Thank goodness it's backed up!

Getting stuff back from a tape or diskettes also involves the use of tar but is somewhat trickier because you want to restore just the files you clobbered. Ask for help — at least the first time. Generally speaking, you put the tape in the drive in the same way you did to make the backup, and then you type a tar or pax command similar to one of these:

```
tar xvf /dev/tape somedir/clobberedfile
pax -rv -f /dev/tape somedir/clobberedfile
```

In the tar command, xvf stands for *ex*tract *v*erbosely *f*rom. In the pax command, -rv -f similarly means *r*ead *v*erbosely *f*rom. Either way, the command is followed by the name of your tape drive (it's often /dev/tape, except on Linux, where it's usually /dev/rft0) and the name of the file to look for. The tape spins as tar or pax runs down the tape looking for the file you want. When it finds the file, it reads the file to the disk, reports that it did so, and stops. If you clobbered a bunch of files, you can use wildcards:

```
tar xvf /dev/tape "somedir/*"
pax -rv -f /dev/tape "somedir/*"
```

You have to use quotation marks around the wildcards because the files to match are on the tape, where tar or pax can find them, not on the disk where the shell (which normally handles wildcards) can find them.

To restore files on Linux from a tape, type

```
tar xvf /dev/rft0 "somedir/*"
```

To restore from diskettes, type

```
tar xvMf /dev/fd0 "somedir/*"
```

If you want to see which files are on the tape and not restore any of them just now, use one of these commands:

```
tar tvf /dev/tape
pax -v -f /dev/tape
```

You should try to run the restore command from the same directory where the program that made the backup tape ran. If it's a system backup, that's probably the root directory (/).

To restore from ZIP disks or CD, put the disk in the drive, tell UNIX to mount the disk (mounting CDs to read them works just fine), and then copy the backed up files from /z or /cdrom or wherever the disk is mounted. Then tell UNIX to unmount it and put the disk back on the shelf.

Backup strategies

The obvious way to do tape backups is to copy the entire contents of the disk to a tape every night. Here are a couple reasons, however, that it may not be the best approach:

- The disk may contain too much stuff to fit on a tape. Tape and disk manufacturers continually battle to see which one can outstrip the other. The battle has see-sawed back and forth — as we write, disks are pulling ahead because you can buy a 160GB disk drive for about $200, but a 160GB tape drive costs about $1,000, and the tapes are $90 apiece.

- Because you may not notice for a day or two that you clobbered something important, a scheme that gives you a few days' grace to get your data back would be nice.

- Murphy's Law says that the system will fail as it's writing a backup tape, so you had better not depend on one tape.

The best scheme is a combination of rotating and incremental backups. With *rotating backups,* a set of tapes is used in rotation; five tapes, for example, one written every Monday, one every Tuesday, and so on. Because each tape is written only once a week, if you delete a file by mistake on Tuesday, for example, the file is still on the Monday tape until the following Monday. You then have nearly a week to realize that it's gone and get it back. The number of tapes you use depends on your budget and your paranoia. Some people use as few as two, some as many as seven. (We use eight, one for each day of the week and an extra to rotate off-site.)

With *incremental backups,* you back up only what has changed. Generally, you do a full backup of everything on the disk at infrequent intervals — once a month, for example. This process may take five or six tapes, but because you do it only once a month, it's not that bad of a job. For the daily incremental backup, you back up only what has changed since the last full backup (it should fit on a single tape). Any given file then is either on the full backup (if it hasn't changed in a long time) or on the current backup, so you have only two places to look.

If you have a large tape budget, you may want to have two sets of tapes you use alternately for full backups, in case your system fails while it is writing the full backups. Sometimes full backups are stored off-site in a bank vault or other safe place, but a trade-off exists: the security of the vault versus the inconvenience of going to the bank when you need to recover a file. If you're really careful, you can have two full backups: one off-site and one on-site.

Your system administrator should handle all this, of course. It's useful to understand at least the rudiments of backup theory, however, so that when the administrator hands you several different tapes that may contain your file, you understand why.

Three Ways Not to Lose Files

Now you're probably quaking in your boots (or sandals, depending on where you live). You figure that, if you so much as touch the keyboard, you will do horrible, irreparable damage and spend the next week spinning tapes. It's not that bad. This section tells you some tricks to avoid deleting files by mistake in the first place.

Are you sure you wanna clobber this one?

When you delete files with rm, use the -i (for *interactive*) switch:

```
rm -i s*
```

This line tells rm to ask you before it deletes each file, prompting you with the filename and a question mark. You press the y key if you want to delete it, and anything else to tell UNIX not to delete. (Remember that the question UNIX asks is, "Should I delete this?" and not "Do you want to keep this?")

The main problem with -i is that it can become tedious when you want to delete a large number of files. When you do that, you probably use wildcards. To be safe, check that the wildcards refer to the files you think they do. To make that check, use the ls command with the same wildcard. If you want to delete all the files that start with *section,* for example, and you think that you can get away with typing only *sec* and an asterisk, you had better check what *sec** refers to. First give this command:

```
ls sec*
```

UNIX responds with an appropriate list:

```
second.version   section04   section08   section12   section16
section01        section05   section09   section13   section17
section02        section06   section10   section14   section18
section03        section07   section11   section15   section19
```

Hey, look! There's that file second.version. You don't want to delete it, so it looks like you have to type **section*** to get the correct files in this case.

Idiot-proofing save files

The best way to make temporary backup copies of files is to make a directory named save and put all saved copies of files there, as shown in this example:

```
mkdir save
cp important.file save
```

These commands tell UNIX to make a directory named save and then to make a copy of important.file to save/important.file. If you reverse the order of the names, nothing happens. Suppose that you type this line instead:

```
cp save important.file
```

UNIX makes this observation:

```
cp : <save> directory
```

UNIX is saying that you can copy a file to a directory but that you can't copy a directory to a file. As a result, UNIX doesn't copy anything. To copy a file back from the save directory, you have to use its full name: save/important.file.

A variation of this process is a two-step delete. Suppose that you have a bunch of files you want to get rid of but some good files are mixed in the same directory. Make a directory named trash, and then use mv to move the files you plan to delete to the trash directory:

```
mkdir trash
mv thisfile thatfile these* trash
mv otherfile somefile trash
```

Then use the ls command to check the contents of trash. If something is in that directory you want, move it back to the current directory by using this command:

```
mv trash/these.are.still.good .
```

(The dot at the end means to put the file back in the current directory.) After you're sure that nothing other than trash is in trash, you can use rm with the -r option:

```
rm -r trash
```

This line tells rm to get rid of trash and everything in it.

Don't write on that!

Another thing you can do to avoid damage to important files is to make them read-only. When you make files read-only, you prevent cp and text editors from changing them. You can still delete them, although rm, mv, and ln ask you before doing so. The chmod command changes the mode of a file (as explained in Chapter 5). Here's how to use chmod to make a file read-only:

```
chmod -w crucial-file
```

The -w means *not writable*. To make changes to the file later, do another chmod but use +w instead. (This stuff doesn't involve inspired command syntax, but the old syntax was even worse and used octal digits.) After a file is made not writable, editors can't change it. The vi program and some versions of emacs even display a note on-screen that the file is read-only. If you try to delete it, rm, mv, or ln asks you in a uniquely user-hostile way whether that's really what you had in mind. Suppose that you type the following line and crucial-file is a read-only file:

```
rm crucial-file
```

UNIX responds with this line:

```
crucial-file: 444 mode ?
```

The number may not be 444: It may be 440 or 400 (depending on whether your system administrator has set things up so that people can normally see the contents of other people's files). As with rm -i, you press the y key if you want to delete the file, or anything else to say that you don't want to delete this valuable data.

Chapter 23

Some Programs Just Won't Die

. . . .

In This Chapter

▶ Killing a process with a keystroke or two

▶ Killing a process by using the ps command

▶ Bringing dead terminals to life

. . . .

You can almost always get rid of recalcitrant programs without rebooting. In this chapter, we talk about how to figure out which processes you have and how to make unwanted ones go away. Before reading this chapter, be sure that you've read Chapter 13, where we talk about how you can juggle processes and do neat tricks, such as stop one program, run another one, go back to the first one, and pick up exactly where you left off.

Why Killing Is Sometimes Justified

Why kill a process? Don't even the smallest processes deserve to live?

In a word, no. Sometimes a program hangs, and your computer just sits there, inert. Or sometimes a program gets stuck in some kind of loop and never ends. Or sometimes you give the wrong command and realize that you don't want to run that program after all. To stop the process in which the program is running, you kill the process.

Suppose that you're running along, minding your own business, and you find that you have a program that just won't stop. Vell, ve haff vays to make eet stop. First, we discuss the normal ways to kill a process, and then we get into some serious artillery.

What Process? (Reprise)

In Chapter 13 we tell you how to use the ps command to see which processes you have running. In case you're too weak from struggling with UNIX to turn back to Chapter 13, just type the ps command to see a list of your processes. Note the *PID* (process ID) of the process you want to kill. You can identify which process is the one that needs to be offed, because ps shows you the command line that started each process.

Fifty Ways to Kill Your Process

The usual way to get rid of a process you started from the shell is to press the *interrupt character,* which is usually Ctrl+C, although sometimes it's Delete. In most cases, the rogue program gives up peaceably, and you end up back in the shell. Sometimes, though, the program arranges to handle Ctrl+C itself. If you use the ed editor (if you're a masochist) and you press Ctrl+C, for example, ed returns to command mode rather than give up and throw away any work you have done. To exit ed, you have to use the q command.

If the interrupt character doesn't work, you can up the ante and use the *quit character,* generally Ctrl+\ (a reverse slash or backslash — not the regular forward slash). The quit character not only kills the program but also saves the dead body of the process (this description is awfully morbid, but we didn't invent these terms) in a file named, for arcane historical reasons, core (or maybe *programname*.core). The shell then gives this requiem:

```
Quit (core dumped)
```

This message tells you that the process is dead and that its body has been put on ice with the filename core.

Most programs that catch Ctrl+C give up under the greater onslaught of Ctrl+\. If the program you were running is one written locally, your system administrator may appreciate your saving the core file, because it includes clues about what was going wrong when you killed the program. Otherwise, delete any core files with rm because they're a waste of space.

Because a program can immunize itself to Ctrl+\ (ed, for example, just ignores it), the next possibility is the *stop character* (always Ctrl+Z). The stop character doesn't kill the program; it just puts it to sleep and returns you to the shell. (See Chapter 13 for more information about what Ctrl+Z really does and how it can be useful even with programs you like.) After you're back in the shell, you can apply the stronger medicine described in the following section.

For Ctrl+Z to work, your shell must do some of the work. Old versions of the Bourne shell aren't up to it and ignore Ctrl+Z. The C, BASH, and Korn shells are Ctrl+Z-aware.

Dirty Deeds, Done Dirt Cheap

No more Mister Nice Guy: It's time for merciless slaughter. If you were successful in the preceding section at putting the process to sleep with Ctrl+Z, go ahead and kill it with the procedure in this section.

All the following techniques require that you have a terminal or window in which you can type some commands to do the dirty deeds. If Ctrl+Z didn't work to put the process to sleep, you may not have a shell prompt at which to type the requisite commands. Here are other places you can use to type the commands to kill the process:

- ✔ If you're running X Windows, any window other than the one with the stuck program works.

- ✔ Otherwise, you may have to go to another computer on the network and use telnet or ssh to get into your computer.

- ✔ If no other window is available and you have no other way into the machine, you're out of luck and probably have to reboot. Before you reboot, check with your system administrator, who may know some other tricks.

This simple two-step procedure murders a rogue process:

1. **Find out the rogue process's true name.**

2. **Utter the true name in an appropriate spell to murder it.**

The true name of a process is its PID, one of the things ps reports. First do a ps command to find out the PID of your victim. To find out the PID, follow these steps:

1. **If you pressed Ctrl+Z to put the rogue process to sleep and you're using the same terminal to kill it utterly, type a plain** ps.

   Otherwise, you may have to use a different terminal to kill the process because the amok process has taken over your own terminal.

2. **In this case, you have to tell** ps **which user's processes you want to see.**

If you use Linux, type this command:

```
ps -u username
```

Replace *username* with your own login name so that you see the processes you're running.

If you use System V, type this command:

```
ps -fu username
```

If you use BSD, type

```
ps -a
```

Suppose that you see the following listing after typing ps -fu john1, which lists all the processes for user john1 (the listing is shortened to save space):

```
UID    PID   PPID  C   STIME   TTY   TIME COMMAND
john1  24806 24799 0   Jan 18  ?     0:39 xclock
```

The PID of the process you want to kill is 24806. You kill it by typing the kill command:

```
kill 24806
```

TIP

Resuscitating a terminal

If you blow away a program that reads a character at a time from your terminal, such as vi or emacs, the dead process leaves your terminal in a rather peculiar state that makes getting any work done hard. The following three-step method usually brings the terminal back:

1. **Press Ctrl+J.**

   The shell may complain about strangely named nonexistent commands. Ignore its whining.

2. **Type** stty, **a space, and** sane **(as opposed to the insane state your terminal is in). Press Enter.**

   You may not see anything on-screen. Remain calm.

3. **Press Ctrl+J again.**

   This step puts your terminal back into a usable state.

The normal type of kill sends a request to a process: "Please, nice Mr. Process, would you be so kind as to croak?" Although this method usually works, occasionally a program doesn't take the hint. Another kind of kill, the ominously named Number-Nine kill, offers the victim no choice. Type this command:

```
kill -9 24806
```

If you stop a particularly uncooperative program with Ctrl+Z, a regular kill may provoke it to retaliate by trying to take over your terminal (something the shell, fortunately, prevents). The following example shows a true-life transcript of our attempts to murder our old text editor pal, ed. First, we pressed Ctrl+Z, which put it to sleep. Then we tried a regular kill. When ed tried to strike back, we did a Number Nine. Sayonara, Bud.

```
% ed badfile
?badfile
Ctrl-Z
Stopped
% ps
   PID TTY      TIME COMMAND
 12746 ttyp1    0:00 ed
 12747 ttyp1    0:00 ps
 11643 ttyp1    0:02 -csh
% kill 12746
?
[1]  + Stopped (tty input)    ed badfile
% kill -9 12746
[1]    Killed               ed badfile
```

When X Goes Bad

If you're using X Windows in any of its multiple guises (particularly Motif) on a workstation or PC running UNIX and are especially unlucky, X itself may freeze the entire screen. If you can get into your computer through the network, you can get rid of X Windows. Doing so makes all the programs using X go away so that you have to log in all over again. The trick is to figure out which program is X Windows. Here's an edited ps report from a System V system:

```
UID    PID    PPID   C  STIME   TTY    TIME   COMMAND
johnl  24788  19593  0  Jan 18  vt01   0:00   /usr/bin/X11/xinit
johnl  24789  24788  5  Jan 18  ptmx   38:10  Xgp :0
```

In this case, X is called Xgp because the particular computer happened to have a graphics processor running the screen.

Here's the equivalent from a Sun workstation:

```
PID TT STAT TIME   COMMAND
224 co IW   0:00   /bin/sh /usr/openwin/bin/openwin
228 co IW   0:00   /usr/openwin/bin/xinit --
           /usr/openwin/bin/xnews :0
229 co S  149:23   /usr/openwin/bin/xnews :0 -auth
           /usr/johnl/.xnews
```

You can find out which process is X in two easy ways:

✔ The command line has the strange code :0, which turns out to be X-ese for "the screen right there on the computer."

✔ The amount of computer time used (in the STAT column) is large because X is, computationally speaking, a pig.

After you figure out which process is X, you can give it the old Number-Nine kill and probably be able to log back in.

Chapter 24

"My Computer Hates Me"

In This Chapter

▶ Lots of error messages

▶ What they mean

▶ What to do about them

Question: You type a command. UNIX says something incomprehensible. What does it mean? What should you do?

Answer: Look in this chapter for the error message. We tell you what the message means and what you can do to fix the problem.

Most error messages start with the name of the command you tried to use. If you want to use the cp command to copy a file, for example, but you spell the name of the file incorrectly, cp can't find a file with the name you typed, so it says something like this:

```
cp: No such file or directory
```

At the beginning of the line is the name of the command that failed to work. After the colon comes the UNIX error message — UNIX's attempt to explain the problem.

This chapter contains the most common error messages, in alphabetical order. In some of our explanations, we refer to things called *arguments,* not because we are feeling argumentative but because that's the technical name for the information you type on the command line after the command. Suppose that you type this line:

```
cp proof.that.elvis.lives save
```

cp is the command, proof.that.elvis.lives is the first argument, and save is the second argument. You can have lots of arguments on the line: The number you need depends on the command you use (cp requires two). Type a space between arguments.

UNIX also has things called *options*, which tell the command how you want it to work. Options always start with a hyphen (-). Suppose that you type this line:

```
ls -l
```

The -*l* tells the ls command how you want it to display the files. Options don't count as arguments. If you type this line:

```
ls -l *
```

the -*l* is an option, and * is the first (not the second) argument.

This stuff is nit-picky, but, if UNIX complains about a particular argument or option, knowing exactly which item it doesn't like comes in handy.

And now (drum roll, please), the error messages!

Arg list too long

Meaning: The list of *arguments* (stuff on the command line after the name of the command) is too long.

Probable cause: When you type a wildcard character as part of a filename or pathname, UNIX replaces it with the list of filenames and then calls the command. If you go wild with the asterisks, the result is a very long list. The list can be more than 5,000 characters long, so it's unlikely that you typed too long a list of filenames, unless you're an unusually fast typist.

Example: You are in the root directory (/) and type this line:

```
ls */*
```

If a large number of files is in the root directory and its subdirectories, */* turns into a really long list.

Solution: Check the wildcards you used in the command, and use fewer of them.

Newer versions of UNIX allow much longer argument lists than older ones did. If you're using a modern system, such as Linux or FreeBSD, and get this message, something strange is probably going on.

Broken pipe

Meaning: You are running two programs connected by a pipe, and the program at the receiving end of the pipe exited before it received all its data (refer to Chapter 7).

Probable cause: You get this error occasionally when you use a pipe (|) to redirect the output of a program into the `more` program and then press the q key to cancel the `more` program before you see all the output. The program has no place to put its output because you canceled the `more` program, so you get this error. In this case, it's harmless.

Example: You type this line:

```
man furgle | more
```

The `man` program (which displays frequently incomprehensible UNIX manual pages) shows you screen after screen of boring information. You press the q key to cancel the `more` program, but the `man` program gives you the error message.

Solution: Nothing to do — it's not really an error!

Cannot access

See the section "No such file or directory," later in this chapter.

Cross-device link

See the section "Different file system," later in this chapter.

Device or resource busy

Meaning: A device, such as a terminal or printer, is in use by another program.

Probable cause: Sometimes you see this message when you try to use `cu` or `tip` to access a terminal that's already in use by another program or user.

Example: You type this line:

```
cu somesystem
```

Solution: Wait until the other user finishes.

Different file system

Meaning: You're using the `ln` command to create a link to a file in a different file system (a different hard drive or a different computer).

Probable cause: You can't create a hard link from one file system to another. The file you want to link to is probably in a different file system from the directory in which you want to make the link (usually the working directory).

Solution: Use the `df` command to find out which disks your computer has and which directories are on which disk. If the two directories are indeed on different disks, use `ln -s` to make a soft link.

File exists

Meaning: A file by that name already exists.

Probable cause: When UNIX expected the name of the file you want to create, you typed the name of a file that already exists.

Solution: You rarely see this message, because most UNIX commands blow away an existing file when they want to create a new one by the same name (which is not always what you want).

File table overflow

Meaning: The system is way too busy and can't juggle as many files simultaneously as all the users have asked it to.

Probable cause: The system isn't configured correctly, or someone is doing way too much work.

Solution: Complain to the system administrator.

File too large

Meaning: You are trying to make a file that is too big.

Probable cause: The maximum file size is set by your system administrator. A maximum file size prevents a messed-up program from making a file that uses up the entire disk by mistake. You're not likely to really want to make a file this big. It usually happens when you use >> to add a copy of a file to itself, so you end up copying the file over and over until it passes the preset size limit.

Example: You type the line shown here:

```
pr myfile >> myfile
```

Solution: Check the command and make sure that you're saying what you mean. If you're sure that you want to make a really big file, talk your system administrator into upping your file-size limit.

Illegal option

Meaning: You typed an option that doesn't work with this command. (*Options* tell the command how you want it to work. They begin with a hyphen.)

Probable cause: You typed a hyphen in front of a filename, or you typed the wrong option.

Example: You type this line:

```
ls -j
```

Because the ls command has no -j option, you get an error message. Frequently, after the illegal option message, UNIX also prints a line about usage, which is its cryptic way of reminding you about which options *do* work with the command. (See the "Usage" section, later in this chapter.)

Solution: Check your typing. Look up the command in this book to make sure that you know which option you want. Alternatively, use the man command to display an exhaustive and exhausting list of every option the command may possibly understand.

Insufficient arguments

Meaning: You left out some information.

Probable cause: The command you are using needs more arguments than the ones you typed. UNIX may also print a usage message in its attempt to tell you which arguments you should have typed. (See the "Usage" section, later in this chapter.)

Example: The cp command needs two arguments: The first one tells it what to copy from, and the second one tells it what to copy to. You can't leave out either one.

Solution: Check your typing. If the command is one you don't use often, check to make sure that you used the correct arguments and options.

I/O error

Meaning: *I/O* is computerese for *i*nput and *o*utput. Some physical problem has occurred during the reading or writing of information on a disk, tape, screen, or wherever your information lives.

Probable cause: Broken disk drive.

Solution: Tell your system administrator. You may have big trouble ahead.

Is a directory

Meaning: You typed the name of a directory when UNIX wanted a filename.

Probable cause: The command you typed is trying to do something to a directory rather than to a file. You can look at a directory by using a text editor, but it looks like binary junk with filenames mixed in. You can't change a directory by editing it.

Note that emacs has a special mode (called dired mode) for "editing" directories. But emacs has its own special way to create, rename, and delete files, too.

Solution: Make sure that you type a filename and not the name of a directory.

Login incorrect

Meaning: You are trying to log in and didn't enter a correct username or corresponding password.

Probable cause: Two possibilities exist: One is that you typed your password incorrectly, and the other is that you typed your username incorrectly.

Solution: Type slowly and deliberately, especially when you type your password and can't see what you are doing. If you have trouble remembering your password, use the passwd command to change it to something more memorable, as described in Chapter 2.

No process can be found

See the section "No such process," later in this chapter.

No such file or directory

Meaning: UNIX can't find a file or directory with the name you typed.

Probable cause: You spelled a filename or pathname wrong. This problem happens to most of us ten times a day. If you typed a pathname, you may have misspelled any of the directory names it contains. You may also have capitalized something incorrectly.

Example: You typed this line:

```
cp june.bugdet save
```

The file isn't named `june.bugdet`, however — it's `june.budget`.

Solution: Check your spelling and capitalization. Use the `ls` command to see how the file and directory names are spelled and whether they have any uppercase letters. For the pathname, check to see whether it begins with a slash (which means that it is an absolute pathname that describes the path from the root directory) or not (which means that it is a relative pathname that describes the path from the working directory). See Chapter 6 for more information about pathnames.

No such process

Meaning: UNIX can't find the process you are referring to.

Probable cause: You have given a command that talks about processes, probably a `kill` command to stop a runaway process. (Chapter 23 describes what a process is and why you may want to kill the poor thing.)

Solution: The process may already have gone away, in which case no problem exists. You may have mistyped the PID that specifies which process to do in. Check your typing and use the `ps` command to check the PID.

No more processes

Meaning: Your system can't create any more new processes.

Probable cause: This message appears when you tell UNIX to create a new process, and UNIX can't do it. Refer to Chapter 23 for information about processes.

Possible reasons for this message are that the system doesn't have any more space for this kind of thing. Occasionally you get this message on very busy systems when you try to run something or if you start dozens of background processes (refer to Chapter 13).

Solution: Wait a minute and try the command again. If you have lots of background processes, get rid of some of them. If you see this message often, complain to your system administrator.

No space left on device

Meaning: The disk is full.

Probable cause: Either your files take up too much space or someone else's do.

Solution: Delete something to make space. If you don't think that you can or you don't have any large files, talk to your system administrator. She probably already has gotten the same message and is checking to see who is taking up all the space.

Not a directory

Meaning: UNIX needed the name of a directory, but you typed a filename or the name of something else.

Probable cause: Either you spelled a directory name incorrectly or you forgot to create a new directory.

Example: You type this line:

```
cd /gillian
```

but no directory is named /gillian.

Solution: If you are referring to a new directory you planned to create, make it first by using the mkdir command. If you are referring to an existing directory, get the spelling right. Use the ls command to see how it's spelled.

Permission denied

Meaning: You don't have permission to do whatever the last command you issued tried to do.

Probable cause: You are trying to change, move, or delete a file you don't own.

Example: You type this line:

```
rm /usr/bill/resignation.letter
```

But you are not Bill. Because you don't have permission to delete this file, UNIX doesn't let you.

Solution: Use the ls -l command to find out who owns the file and what its permissions are (refer to Chapter 5 for information about permissions). If you think that you ought to be able to mess with the file, make your own copy of it or talk to the owner of the file or your system administrator.

RE error

Meaning: You are using the grep program, and it doesn't understand what you are searching for. (RE stands for *regular expression*, the name for the patterns that grep uses.)

Probable cause: You probably have to use backslashes in front of a character that is a wildcard in grep.

Example: You type this line:

```
grep '[x' myfile
```

Solution: Put a backslash in front of any character that has a special wildcard meaning in grep (grep wildcards include periods, asterisks, square brackets, dollar signs, and carets). If you are searching for text that contains special characters, put single quotation marks around the text to match.

Read-only file system

Meaning: You are trying to change a file that UNIX is not allowed to change.

Probable cause: Some disks, particularly NFS remote disks and CD-ROMs, are marked read-only so that you can't create, delete, or change files on them. It doesn't matter what the permissions are for the individual files: The entire file system can't be changed.

Solution: Talk to your system administrator. Alternatively, make a copy of the file you want to change and change the copy.

Too many links

Meaning: You are trying to make so many links to a file that you have exceeded the maximum number of links to a file.

Probable cause: The maximum number of links to a file is 1,000. You must be a heck of a typist to get this message, or more likely you were running a script that linked a little more enthusiastically than you had intended. Because the parent directory is linked to each of its subdirectories, you also get this message if you try to make more than 1,000 subdirectories in one directory.

Solution: Stop making links.

Usage

Meaning: UNIX doesn't like the number or types of arguments you typed after the command. It is telling you (in its own cryptic way) the correct way to use the command.

Probable cause: UNIX usually displays this message with another, more specific message. Check out the other message to see what the real problem was. The usage message is the UNIX reminder about how to use the command. After usage, you see the command, followed by the options and arguments you can use with the command. Unfortunately, you get no clue about what the options do.

Example: You type this line:

```
kill abc
```

UNIX responds with this message:

```
usage: kill [signo ] pid
```

This line means that the correct way to use the kill command is to type **kill**, a space, (optionally) the type of signal you want to send to the process, another space, and then the process ID. Don't type the [ ] — we stuck them in to let you know which part of the command is optional — not that it's entirely clear from the message!

Solution: Check your typing, as always. Make sure that spaces are between things on the line (between filenames or between a filename and an option, for example). If you don't use this command often, check to make sure that you have the correct arguments (filenames and so on) and options (things that begin with a dash, such as the *-l* in ls -l). Look up the command in this book or consult the UNIX manual page about it (see Chapter 26 for instructions on how to display manual pages).

444 mode? (or some other three-digit number) or override r-- r-- r-- johnl/staff for foo?

Meaning: You don't have permission to change this file, but you have told UNIX to delete it.

Probable cause: You are using rm, mv, or ln to remove or replace a read-only protected file or a file that belongs to someone else. (See Chapter 5 for information about permissions.) Rather than refuse outright to do what you asked, UNIX asks whether you really want to do execute the command.

Example: You used the chmod command to make an important file read-only. Then you decide to delete it by typing this line:

```
rm important.file
```

UNIX asks whether you really want to delete it, even though the file is read-only.

Solution: The question mark at the end of this message indicates that UNIX is asking you a question. By divine intuition, you are supposed to guess that UNIX is asking whether you want to complete the command anyway. (On most modern UNIX systems, someone took pity on the poor users and changed the message to the slightly more comprehensible "override" version.) Press the y key if you want to go ahead and do the command. Press anything else if you want to cancel it (for this file, anyway).

If you own the file, you can change its permissions by typing this line:

```
chmod 644 filename
```

Rather than type filename, type the real filename. This command has the result of allowing anyone to read or write to the file.

Part VI
The Part of Tens

"I'm sure there will be a good job market when I graduate. I created a virus that will go off that year."

In this part . . .

*U*NIX uses many commands, programs, options, and other stuff — much more than we can pack into this book. The real, official manuals for a UNIX system, back when computers came with printed manuals, took up about three feet of shelf space. (For cost savings, all the pages of these manuals were blank because no one ever read them, but if you don't tell, neither will we.)

In this part of the book, we organize facts into neat lists of ten (actually, two lists) so that they're easier to remember. Astute readers may claim that neither of these lists contains exactly ten items. Well, we use mixed radix arithmetic (survivors of New Math in school may remember some of this subject from fourth grade), so a chapter with eight items has ten items counting in base 12, and a chapter — what? You say that we can't bamboozle you with such nonsense? Truth is, we can't count.

Read on — good stuff is in this part, regardless of the numbers.

Chapter 25

Ten Common Mistakes

*H*ere are ten (or so) of the most common user mistakes we have run into. Although you will probably invent some new ones yourself, at least avoid the ones on this list.

Believing That It Will Be Easy

UNIX was designed a long, long time ago in computer time (computer years are similar to dog years, except that 50 computer years equal a human year). Software design has made a great deal of progress since 1972, and UNIX has not. If you are used to a Macintosh or a PC with Windows, UNIX won't be easy to use.

On the other hand, UNIX has a certain cachet and glamour; it takes a macho person (of either gender) to face it. You should give yourself major kudos, and maybe even one or two of those cookies you made to bribe your UNIX wizard, every time you get UNIX to do something useful.

Mistyping Commands

If you type a command the UNIX shell doesn't understand, it says that it can't find the command. The reason is that it looks high and low for a file with the name you just typed, hoping to find the program you want to run. And then it says

```
eatmylunch: Command not found.
```

Or perhaps it says

```
eatmylunch: not found
```

The exact wording varies from shell to shell (we bet that you already guessed that). To make sure that you type a command properly:

- **Check your spelling (as always).** You may have typed a correctly spelled English word rather than the garbled set of letters that comprise the name of the program.

- **Check your capitalization and spacing.** Capital and small letters count as completely different things in filenames and, therefore, in commands. Nearly every command uses only small letters. Spaces matter, too, and if a command really is called `eatmylunch`, the more English-looking `eat my lunch` won't do.

- **Change directories (maybe).** You may have given the right command, but UNIX may not know where to look for the file containing the program. If you know where the program file is, move to that directory and give the command again. If you don't know where the file is, either look for it (as described in Chapter 22) or give up and ask your system administrator or local wizard.

To Press Enter, or Not to Press Enter

Depending on which program you are using, sometimes you must press Enter (or Return) after a command, and sometimes you don't. In the UNIX shell, you *always* have to press Enter or Return before UNIX performs the command. If you don't, UNIX waits forever for you to do so.

In other programs, particularly in text editors like `emacs` and `vi`, as soon as you press the command (Ctrl+K to delete a line in `emacs`, for example), the program does it right away. If you press Enter or Return after the command, `emacs` sticks a new line in your file, and `vi` moves down to the next line.

When you use a program you're not familiar with, hesitate a moment before pressing Enter or Return to see whether the computer may already be performing the command. If nothing is happening, press Enter or Return.

Working in the Wrong Directory

If you use separate directories to organize your files, make sure that you are in the proper directory when you begin working. Otherwise, UNIX won't find the files you want to work on.

To find out which directory you're in, type **pwd**. *Remember:* This command stands for *p*rint *w*orking *d*irectory.

If you're really lost, you can type **whoami**. This command tells you your username.

To move back to your home directory, type **cd**.

Not Keeping Backup Copies

Sooner or later, it happens. You give an `rm` command to delete a file, and UNIX deletes the wrong file or deletes everything in the directory. Chances are you typed an extra space or spelled a filename wrong, but the point is — what now?

See Chapter 22 to find out how to proceed if you delete something important. The best approach is to keep extra copies of important files: in another directory, on a CD-R or CD-RW disc, or on a backup tape that either you or your system administrator makes. If you haven't talked to your system administrator about backups, now is a good time to find out whether your files back up automatically; you can also tell him which of your directories contain files you want to have backed up.

Not Keeping Files Organized

Unless you do all your work on one or two files, you run into trouble if you don't do the following:

✔ **Make directories for the groups of files you use (refer to Chapter 6 to find out how).** Directories help you separate your files into groups of files you use together.

✔ **Use filenames that mean something.** UNIX lets you name your files with nice long names, so take advantage of it (up to a point, anyway). Filenames should tell you what's inside the file rather than make you guess.

Turning Off Your Computer

Leaving your computer on all the time is better than turning it off at the wrong time. Chapter 1 talks about this subject in detail. UNIX can get messed up if you turn off your computer (if you kick the plug out by mistake, for example) without warning it that you are going to do so.

If you use UNIX from a remote PC rather than directly with a workstation, turning off the PC (not the UNIX computer) at night may make sense. Check with your system administrator.

Writing Your Password on a Sticky Note

Okay, maybe this one doesn't apply if you work at home, live alone, and don't have any friends, cleaning people, or burglars. Otherwise, you should keep your password to yourself. Not that anyone has malicious intent — let's not get paranoid — but people can get curious around computers. And you never know when an inquisitive 14-year-old who knows more about UNIX than you do will appear on the scene. If you can't remember your password, choose a new one that is more memorable. (Refer to Chapter 1 for hints.)

Sending Angry Electronic Mail (Flaming)

Electronic mail can bring out your insidious side. There you are, sitting alone in your cubicle with your computer, and you get ticked off at something, usually some stupid message sent by a coworker. Before you know it, you have composed and sent a tactless, not to say downright rude, response.

Saying things in e-mail that you would never say in person or even write in a memo is easy. But e-mail has an off-the-cuff, spontaneous style in most organizations, and it can get you into trouble.

Sarcasm seldom works in e-mail — instead, you just sound mean. Gentle suggestions can turn into strident demands just because they appear in ugly computer type on a computer screen. Rude mouthing off via e-mail even has a special name: *flaming*. A message full of tactless, pointless complaints is referred to as a *flame*. A series of flames between two or more people is called a *flame war*. You get the idea.

Recipients of your mail can easily forward copies of it to anyone else, so imagine that everyone in the office may read your missives. Think twice before sending e-mail containing negative remarks! Then don't send it. Remember that the best way to end an unpleasant exchange is to let the other person have the last word.

Chapter 26

Ten Times More Information Than You Want about UNIX

*W*e wish that this book contained every single thing you may ever want to know about UNIX. We considered writing the book that way, but our publisher frowned on printing a book with 25,000 pages. (Books like that are hard to bind, not to mention hard to pick up off the floor.) So, we tried to include just the information that new UNIX users really need to know. If you read this entire book, however, you'll be well on your way to becoming a seasoned UNIX veteran. For additional seasoning, this chapter points you in the direction of more advanced facts about UNIX.

Let's Hear It from the man

You thought that UNIX was completely unhelpful. For the most part, you're absolutely right. A standard UNIX command called man (for *man*ual), however, can give you online help.

Sound good? Well, yes and no. The information is there, all right, but it's written in a rather nerdy style and can be difficult to decipher. Each part of the online manual is written, of course, on the assumption that you have read all the other parts and know what all the commands are called. The man command is definitely worth knowing about, though, when you just can't remember the options for a command or what to type where on the command line after the command name.

The man's online manual contains *manual pages* for every UNIX command, and other pages about internal functions that programmers use, formats for various system file types, descriptions of some of the hardware that you can attach to your UNIX system, and other odds and ends. When you type the man command, you indicate which page or pages you want.

All manual pages have a standard format. Listing 26-1 shows part of the manual page for the chmod command. (If you get the idea that chmod has a lot of arcane options that we didn't bother to mention in Chapter 5, you're right.)

Listing 26-1:   Part of the man **Page for the** chmod **Command**

```
CHMOD(1)                    FreeBSD General Commands Manual                    CHMOD(1)

NAME
     chmod - change file modes

SYNOPSIS
     chmod [-fhv] [-R [-H | -L | -P]] mode file ...

DESCRIPTION
     The chmod utility modifies the file mode bits of the listed files as
     specified by the mode operand.

     The options are as follows:

     -f        Do not display a diagnostic message if chmod could not modify the
               mode for file, nor modify the exit status to reflect such fail-
               ures.

     -H        If the -R option is specified, symbolic links on the command line
               are followed.  (Symbolic links encountered in the tree traversal
               are not followed by default.)

     -h        If the file is a symbolic link, change the mode of the link
               itself rather than the file that the link points to.

     -L        If the -R option is specified, all symbolic links are followed.

     -P        If the -R option is specified, no symbolic links are followed.
               This is the default.
```

The parts of the manual page include

✔ **The title (the first line):** It includes the name and page number of the manual page on the left and right ends of the line. Centered on the line may be the name of the system the command is a part of. In Listing 26-1, the chmod command is one of the standard commands that comes with FreeBSD, as it does with every version of UNIX.

✔ NAME: The one-line name of the manual page. The name is usually the command or commands the page talks about, as well as a brief description.

- ✔ SYNOPSIS: What you type when you give the command, with a terse and cryptic example of every option available. This part often makes no sense until you read the description that follows. Sometimes it still makes no sense.

- ✔ DESCRIPTION: A few paragraphs about the command. For commands with a large number of options, the description can run for a few pages. A list of options usually is included, with an explanation of every one. Sometimes you see examples, although not often enough.

- ✔ SEE ALSO: Lists names of related manual pages, if any.

- ✔ WARNINGS and BUGS: May list a command's known bugs or common problems. Then again, it may not.

- ✔ FILES: A list of the files this command uses. The `pine` and `mail` commands, for example, use your `Mail` directory, the central list of mailboxes, and other files. (Your system administrator usually sets up these files — they're rarely something you want to fool with yourself.) The manual pages for `pine` and `mail` mention these files.

Reading manual pages

To see a manual page, type this line:

```
man unixcommand
```

Except, of course, you substitute for *unixcommand* the name of the UNIX command you're interested in. Most versions of `man` present the manual page a screen at a time. Other versions just whip the page by at maximum speed, assuming that you can read 150,000 words per minute. If that happens (and you can't read that fast), you can use the usual `more` command to display the manual page a screen at a time by typing this command:

```
man unixcommand | more
```

Printing manual pages

You can also print the manual pages for later perusal. To print the manual pages, type this line:

```
man unixcommand | lpr
```

Remember to use `lp`, if that is the command you use to print. A better technique may be to put the manual pages in a file first, remove the information you don't want, and print the result. You can type the following line, for example (remember to substitute for *filename* the name of the file you want the information in):

```
man unixcommand > filename
```

Then edit the file with a text editor (see Chapter 10) and print it (see Chapter 9). Before you print the file, however, keep in mind that the online manual pages are generally identical to the printed manual pages in the dusty UNIX manuals on the shelf, except that the printed manual pages are typeset so that they're easier to read. Rather than print the online page, looking it up in the paper manual is often better. (Bet you didn't think we would *ever* tell you to do that!)

If you have a PostScript laser printer, you can often print the manual pages with nice fonts and italics and such rather than the typewriter-like version you see on-screen. Ask your local guru for advice. On many versions of UNIX, this command works, using the -t for typeset option:

```
man -t command | lpr
```

Finding the manual page you want

If you use the man command, you have no good way to find out which manual pages are available. Sometimes, finding the one you want is difficult. Suppose that you type this line:

```
man ln
```

UNIX shows you this message:

```
man: ln not found
```

The ln command has no separate manual page. Instead, it shares a set of pages with cp and mv. You get information about ln by typing this line:

```
man cp
```

(Typical UNIX ease of use!) If man doesn't display anything about the command you want, try some similar commands. BSD UNIX systems have an apropos command that suggests manual pages relevant to a particular topic, so you can type **apropos ln** to see what it has to say.

In addition to manual pages about commands, you can find lots of pages about other topics. You can type this line, for example:

```
man ascii
```

This command shows you a table of the ASCII-character codes for all the characters text files can contain. Although you probably aren't interested in them, it does look impressively technoid.

It's a bird, it's a plane, it's xman!

If you use KDE, GNOME, or other X Window-based software, you can use the xman command to look at manual pages. The nice thing about xman is that it displays a list of the available manual pages. When you run xman, it pops up a little box with three buttons, one of which is labeled Manual Page. If you click that button, a larger window then displays a manual page describing xman. Choose Display Directory from the Options menu on that page, or press Ctrl+D as a shortcut, to see a screen of all the manual pages it has — probably more than 100 of them. Click the one you want to see, and xman switches to that page. Press Ctrl+D again to return to the directory of manual pages. Read the initial description of xman for other tricks you can get xman to do, such as show you two or three different pages at a time or search for keywords in manual-page titles.

Scanning the Networks

If your system is connected to the Internet or if you have dial-up access to an Internet provider, you can connect to *Usenet,* a gigantic distributed online bulletin board system described at http://net.gurus.com/usenet, and also available on the Web at http://groups.google.com/. Because many systems on Usenet are running on UNIX systems, Usenet has a great deal of discussion of UNIX issues and questions.

Your basic UNIX news

Usenet discussions are loosely organized into about 10,000 topic areas, or *newsgroups.* Table 26-1 lists some newsgroups that discuss UNIX topics.

Table 26-1	UNIX-Related Newsgroups
Group	*Description*
comp.unix.admin	UNIX system administration.
comp.unix.advocacy	Arguments about how wonderful UNIX is.
comp.unix.aix	AIX, the IBM version of UNIX.
comp.unix.bsd.freebsd.announce	Announcements about the FreeBSD version of UNIX.

(continued)

Table 26-1 *(continued)*

Group	Description
`comp.unix.bsd.freebsd.misc`	Discussions of FreeBSD.
`comp.unix.bsd.misc`	Various BSD versions of UNIX.
`comp.unix.bsd.netbsd.announce`	Announcements about the NetBSD version of UNIX.
`comp.unix.bsd.netbsd.misc`	Discussions of NetBSD.
`comp.unix.bsd.openbsd.announce`	Announcements about the OpenBSD version of UNIX.
`comp.unix.bsd.openbsd.misc`	Discussions of OpenBSD.
`comp.unix.cde`	Discussions of the Common Desktop Environment.
`comp.unix.dos-under-unix`	Running MS-DOS programs under UNIX.
`comp.unix.internals`	The technical internals of UNIX.
`comp.unix.large`	UNIX on large systems.
`comp.unix.misc`	Random UNIX discussions.
`comp.unix.programmer`	Programming on UNIX.
`comp.unix.questions`	Questions about UNIX. The best place to ask questions. Look at articles first to see whether someone has just asked the same question.
`comp.unix.shell`	UNIX shells.
`comp.unix.solaris`	The Sun Solaris version of UNIX.
`comp.unix.wizards`	Technical discussions among UNIX wizards.
`comp.security.unix`	UNIX security issues.

Just for Linux

Because Linux is so popular, Table 26-2 lists a bunch of discussion groups of its own.

Table 26-2	Linux-Related Newsgroups
Group	*Description*
`comp.os.linux.advocacy`	Discussions of how great Linux is
`comp.os.linux.announce`	Announcements of new versions of Linux
`comp.os.linux.answers`	Answers to frequently asked questions; a good place to look
`comp.os.linux.development.apps`	Development of application programs
`comp.os.linux.development.system`	Development of the underlying Linux system
`comp.os.linux.hardware`	Making Linux work with various kinds of hardware
`comp.os.linux.misc`	Linux discussions that don't fit anywhere else
`comp.os.linux.networking`	Networking issues
`comp.os.linux.portable`	Linux OS on portable PCs
`comp.os.linux.setup`	Setting up Linux
`comp.os.linux.x`	X Windows on Linux
`linux.redhat.install`	Help on (or at least a great deal of complaining about) installing Red Hat Linux

On the Web

Sites with information about UNIX and Linux have been proliferating on the World Wide Web at an astonishing rate. Point your Web browser at any of the useful, colorful, frequently updated sites in this section.

UNIX OS

- **FreeBSD:** All about FreeBSD at `www.freeebsd.org`.
- **NetBSD:** All about NetBSD at `www.netbsd.org`.
- **BSDNet:** Maintained by a nonprofit group of BSD enthusiasts, BSDNet has tons of information about all flavors of BSD (at `www.bsdnet.org/`).
- **Sun Microsystems:** The maker of Solaris, it has a Web site at the oddly named `wwws.sun.com/software/solaris/`.

Linux

- **Linux Online!:** This site, at `http://www.linux.org/`, is *the* source for Linux information on the Web, maintained by a nonprofit organization of Linux users.
- **Slackware:** The home of the Slackware distribution of Linux at `www.slackware.org/`.
- **Mandrake:** The home of the Mandrake distribution of Linux at `www.mandrakelinux.com`.
- **The Linux Documentation Project:** The project (at `www.ibiblio.org/mdw/`) has tons of Linux documentation, news, links, and downloads.
- **Red Hat:** Red Hat maintains a site (at `www.redhat.com/`) that serves as a clearinghouse for all kinds of information about Linux.
- **The Debian GNU/Linux site:** This site (at `www.debian.org/`) is also worth checking out.
- **The LinuxMall.com:** Lots of Linux and open source stuff at `www.thelinuxmall.com/`.

X Windows and such

- **The Motif Zone:** The Motif Zone has everything you ever wanted to know about Motif (at `www.motifzone.com/`).
- **KDE:** Everything about KDE, the K Desktop Environment, is at `www.kde.org/`.
- **The GNOME Project:** The theory (of which there's a surprising amount) and practice of the GNOME desktop is at `www.gnome.org/`.
- **The XFree86 Project:** Its home is at `www.xfree86.org/`.

Web browsers

- **The Lynx Users' Guide:** Maintained by the Academic Computing Services group at the University of Kansas, the guide is yours for the viewing, at `kuhttp.cc.ukans.edu/about_lynx/about_lynx.html`.
- **Mozilla:** The latest version of Mozilla and other Mozilla news are at `www.mozilla.org`.
- **Opera Software:** The fast, small Opera browser is available for many versions of UNIX at `www.opera.com`.

Other stuff

- **The Apache Project:** It's the official Web site (`www.apache.org/`) of the most popular Web server in the world. Get documentation, FAQs, the latest news, and free downloads.

> ✔ **Samba:** Check out the worldwide home of the package that lets your
> UNIX system provide networked logical disks to Windows PCs (at
> `www.samba.org`; on the home page, click a link to your country or one
> nearby), with documentation, FAQs, how-to's, news, and downloads.

Other Sources of Information

Your system administrator or nearby UNIX users probably have copies of
UNIX manuals lying around. The pages of some of these manuals usually look
much like the manual pages you get with `man`.

The advantage of the printed manual is that an index is in the front (or the
back). It is usually a permuted or KWIC index (an overly clever abbreviation
for *key word in context*), which means that you can find an entry by looking
under any of the words in the title except for boring ones, such as *the*. To find
the page for the `cp` command (the title of the manual page is *cp, ln, mv —
copy, link, or move files*), for example, you can look in the permuted index
under *cp, ln, mv, copy, link, move,* or *files*.

Then again, typing **help** is not a bad idea, just to see what happens. Someone
may have installed some kind of help system — you never know.

UNIX is used widely enough that a growing industry of UNIX books, magazines, user groups, and conferences has sprung up. Any of them can provide
additional help and information.

Read a magazine

Several weekly or monthly magazines cover UNIX. Most of them include in
their titles either the name UNIX or the code phrase Open Systems (for systems that act like UNIX but haven't licensed the UNIX trademark). Because
you probably have already thrown away mail inviting you to subscribe to
most of them, we don't belabor the point. The major brands of workstations
(Sun, Hewlett-Packard, and IBM) also have magazines that specifically cover
those product lines. Although some of these magazines tend to be awfully
technical, they can be interesting for product reviews and announcements
about new UNIX hardware and software packages.

If you use Linux, take a look at the *Linux Journal,* the magazine for and about
Linux. (Subscription info is at `www.linuxjournal.com`.) The technical level
varies from totally introductory to fairly technical. Also see its online Linux
Gazette at `www.linuxgazette.com/`.

Read a book

Yeah, we know: You may have (or not) just read this book. We mean read *another* book. Here are a few you may like:

- Levine and Young, *UNIX For Dummies Quick Reference,* 4th Edition; Wiley Publishing, Inc. (Big surprise.) The Quick Reference has essential information from the book you're reading and a detailed command reference, squashed down into a smaller, less expensive, pocket-size form.

- *UNIX in a Nutshell;* O'Reilly. A complete UNIX reference, the one we turn to when memory fails. It comes in various editions for different versions of UNIX and is intended for more advanced users than our *UNIX For Dummies Quick Reference.*

- LeBlanc, *Linux For Dummies,* 5th Edition; Wiley Publishing, Inc. This one tells how to survive installing, using, administering, and networking Linux, for beginners with some technical tolerance.

- Welsh and Kaufman, *Running LINUX,* 4th Edition; O'Reilly. All about installing and using Linux, it's medium technical but quite informative.

- Naba Barkakati, *Red Hat Linux Secrets;* Wiley Publishing, Inc. This one covers a wide range of topics, from hardware debugging to using Linux in your business.

Join a user group

The major UNIX user group is called Usenix, and dates back to about 1976; it is traditionally for technical users. It sponsors annual conferences and publishes a newsletter. Visit www.usenix.org/ to see what it's up to. You can also find local and regional UNIX user groups; you tend to find out about these groups from notes posted on physical or electronic bulletin boards. User groups can be great sources of help because chances are good that someone already has run into many of the same problems you have and has some ideas that may help.

Index

FOR DUMMIES®

The easy way to get more done and have more fun

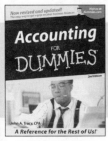

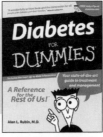

FOR DUMMIES®

A world of resources to help you grow

HOME, GARDEN & HOBBIES

0-7645-5295-3

0-7645-5130-2

0-7645-5106-X

Also available:

Auto Repair For Dummies
(0-7645-5089-6)

Chess For Dummies
(0-7645-5003-9)

Home Maintenance For Dummies
(0-7645-5215-5)

Organizing For Dummies
(0-7645-5300-3)

Piano For Dummies
(0-7645-5105-1)

Poker For Dummies
(0-7645-5232-5)

Quilting For Dummies
(0-7645-5118-3)

Rock Guitar For Dummies
(0-7645-5356-9)

Roses For Dummies
(0-7645-5202-3)

Sewing For Dummies
(0-7645-5137-X)

FOOD & WINE

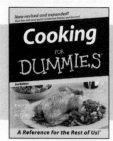

0-7645-5250-3

0-7645-5390-9

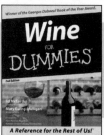

0-7645-5114-0

Also available:

Bartending For Dummies
(0-7645-5051-9)

Chinese Cooking For Dummies
(0-7645-5247-3)

Christmas Cooking For Dummies
(0-7645-5407-7)

Diabetes Cookbook For Dummies
(0-7645-5230-9)

Grilling For Dummies
(0-7645-5076-4)

Low-Fat Cooking For Dummies
(0-7645-5035-7)

Slow Cookers For Dummies
(0-7645-5240-6)

TRAVEL

0-7645-5453-0

0-7645-5438-7

0-7645-5448-4

Also available:

America's National Parks For Dummies
(0-7645-6204-5)

Caribbean For Dummies
(0-7645-5445-X)

Cruise Vacations For Dummies 2003
(0-7645-5459-X)

Europe For Dummies
(0-7645-5456-5)

Ireland For Dummies
(0-7645-6199-5)

France For Dummies
(0-7645-6292-4)

London For Dummies
(0-7645-5416-6)

Mexico's Beach Resorts For Dummies
(0-7645-6262-2)

Paris For Dummies
(0-7645-5494-8)

RV Vacations For Dummies
(0-7645-5443-3)

Walt Disney World & Orlando For Dummies
(0-7645-5444-1)

Available wherever books are sold. Go to www.dummies.com or call 1-877-762-2974 to order direct.

FOR DUMMIES®

Plain-English solutions for everyday challenges

COMPUTER BASICS

0-7645-0838-5

0-7645-1663-9

0-7645-1548-9

Also available:

PCs All-in-One Desk Reference For Dummies (0-7645-0791-5)

Pocket PC For Dummies (0-7645-1640-X)

Treo and Visor For Dummies (0-7645-1673-6)

Troubleshooting Your PC For Dummies (0-7645-1669-8)

Upgrading & Fixing PCs For Dummies (0-7645-1665-5)

Windows XP For Dummies (0-7645-0893-8)

Windows XP For Dummies Quick Reference (0-7645-0897-0)

BUSINESS SOFTWARE

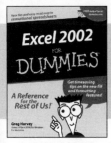

0-7645-0822-9

0-7645-0839-3

0-7645-0819-9

Also available:

Excel Data Analysis For Dummies (0-7645-1661-2)

Excel 2002 All-in-One Desk Reference For Dummies (0-7645-1794-5)

Excel 2002 For Dummies Quick Reference (0-7645-0829-6)

GoldMine "X" For Dummies (0-7645-0845-8)

Microsoft CRM For Dummies (0-7645-1698-1)

Microsoft Project 2002 For Dummies (0-7645-1628-0)

Office XP For Dummies (0-7645-0830-X)

Outlook 2002 For Dummies (0-7645-0828-8)

Get smart! Visit www.dummies.com

- **Find listings of even more *For Dummies* titles**

- **Browse online articles**

- **Sign up for Dummies eTips™**

- **Check out *For Dummies* fitness videos and other products**

- **Order from our online bookstore**

Available wherever books are sold. Go to www.dummies.com or call 1-877-762-2974 to order direct.

FOR DUMMIES®

Helping you expand your horizons and realize your potential

INTERNET

0-7645-0894-6

0-7645-1659-0

0-7645-1642-6

Also available:

America Online 7.0 For Dummies
(0-7645-1624-8)

Genealogy Online For Dummies
(0-7645-0807-5)

The Internet All-in-One Desk Reference For Dummies
(0-7645-1659-0)

Internet Explorer 6 For Dummies
(0-7645-1344-3)

The Internet For Dummies Quick Reference
(0-7645-1645-0)

Internet Privacy For Dummies
(0-7645-0846-6)

Researching Online For Dummies
(0-7645-0546-7)

Starting an Online Business For Dummies
(0-7645-1655-8)

DIGITAL MEDIA

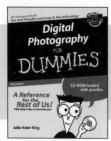

0-7645-1664-7

0-7645-1675-2

0-7645-0806-7

Also available:

CD and DVD Recording For Dummies
(0-7645-1627-2)

Digital Photography All-in-One Desk Reference For Dummies
(0-7645-1800-3)

Digital Photography For Dummies Quick Reference
(0-7645-0750-8)

Home Recording for Musicians For Dummies
(0-7645-1634-5)

MP3 For Dummies
(0-7645-0858-X)

Paint Shop Pro "X" For Dummies
(0-7645-2440-2)

Photo Retouching & Restoration For Dummies
(0-7645-1662-0)

Scanners For Dummies
(0-7645-0783-4)

GRAPHICS

0-7645-0817-2

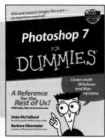

0-7645-1651-5

0-7645-0895-4

Also available:

Adobe Acrobat 5 PDF For Dummies
(0-7645-1652-3)

Fireworks 4 For Dummies
(0-7645-0804-0)

Illustrator 10 For Dummies
(0-7645-3636-2)

QuarkXPress 5 For Dummies
(0-7645-0643-9)

Visio 2000 For Dummies
(0-7645-0635-8)

Available wherever books are sold. Go to www.dummies.com or call 1-877-762-2974 to order direct.

FOR DUMMIES®

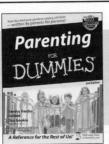

The advice and explanations you need to succeed

SELF-HELP, SPIRITUALITY & RELIGION

Sex For Dummies
0-7645-5302-X

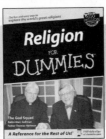

Parenting For Dummies
0-7645-5418-2

Religion For Dummies
0-7645-5264-3

Also available:

The Bible For Dummies
(0-7645-5296-1)

Buddhism For Dummies
(0-7645-5359-3)

Christian Prayer For Dummies
(0-7645-5500-6)

Dating For Dummies
(0-7645-5072-1)

Judaism For Dummies
(0-7645-5299-6)

Potty Training For Dummies
(0-7645-5417-4)

Pregnancy For Dummies
(0-7645-5074-8)

Rekindling Romance For Dummies
(0-7645-5303-8)

Spirituality For Dummies
(0-7645-5298-8)

Weddings For Dummies
(0-7645-5055-1)

PETS

Puppies For Dummies
0-7645-5255-4

Dog Training For Dummies
0-7645-5286-4

Cats For Dummies
0-7645-5275-9

Also available:

Labrador Retrievers For Dummies
(0-7645-5281-3)

Aquariums For Dummies
(0-7645-5156-6)

Birds For Dummies
(0-7645-5139-6)

Dogs For Dummies
(0-7645-5274-0)

Ferrets For Dummies
(0-7645-5259-7)

German Shepherds For Dummies
(0-7645-5280-5)

Golden Retrievers For Dummies
(0-7645-5267-8)

Horses For Dummies
(0-7645-5138-8)

Jack Russell Terriers For Dummies
(0-7645-5268-6)

Puppies Raising & Training Diary For Dummies
(0-7645-0876-8)

EDUCATION & TEST PREPARATION

Spanish For Dummies
0-7645-5194-9

Algebra For Dummies
0-7645-5325-9

The ACT For Dummies
0-7645-5210-4

Also available:

Chemistry For Dummies
(0-7645-5430-1)

English Grammar For Dummies
(0-7645-5322-4)

French For Dummies
(0-7645-5193-0)

The GMAT For Dummies
(0-7645-5251-1)

Inglés Para Dummies
(0-7645-5427-1)

Italian For Dummies
(0-7645-5196-5)

Research Papers For Dummies
(0-7645-5426-3)

The SAT I For Dummies
(0-7645-5472-7)

U.S. History For Dummies
(0-7645-5249-X)

World History For Dummies
(0-7645-5242-2)

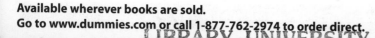